Pvt. Ltd.

Production Operation Management

Suchismita Satapathy

2018

Studium Press (India) Pvt. Ltd.

Production Operation Management

ISBN: 978-93-85046-28-5

Published by:

Studium Press (India) Pvt. Ltd.
4735/22, 2nd Floor, Prakash Deep Building
(Near Delhi Medical Association),
Ansari Road, Darya Ganj, New Delhi-110 002
Tel.: + 91-11-43240200-15 (15 lines); Fax: 91-11-43240215
E-mail: pubdir@studiumpress.in

Printed at India

About the Author

Dr Suchismita Satapathy is currently working as an Associate Professor in the School of Mechanical Sciences, Kalinga Institute of Industrial Technology (KIIT), University. She has published more than 55 articles, many national and international journals and conferences. She has more than 15 years of teaching and research experience. She has contributed 2 books, 5 book chapters. Her area of interest is Production Operation Management, Operation Research etc.

Acknowledgement

I would like to deeply thank my publisher to give me an opportunity to publish my content. He has also helped me a lot by taking out his precious time to help me carry out my experiments and encouraged me to complete my work accurately within the time, I was given to do so. They have been a guiding force with encouragement to perform my work. I would like to thank my husband to encourage me to complete my book project. My daughter Meghana also helped me alot by giving relaxation from some of her valuable family time. I would like to express my thanks to my father Dr R.B Satapathy and my mother B.P. Mishra, my in laws Dr S.N. Mishra and Dr B.M. MIshra, who have inspired me to work for this book. KIIT authority Prof (Dr) A samant is always an inspiration for me in achieving my goal. My college, friends of KIIT, my students all have equally encouraged me. At last i wouldlike to thank and owe my contribution before almighty God for invisible help.

Preface

Production and Operations Management deals with managing the transformation to create products or services. This is an important as it keeps the business fresh and allows for new products and services to be created. The operations manager is responsible for ensuring that the business remains effective by creating new products and services that will meet the customers' needs. Cost, quality and delivery are all needs that the customer will be interested in. The operations manager will have some responsibility in deciding what processes should be used to produce the product. This book will provide an insight to the students, faculties and researchers about the scheduling of tasks and jobs to ensure that the needed capacity is achieved. This will also help them to manage the inventory by deciding what to order, when to order it and how much to order. The movement of the products will also be important in this role. Not only Btech, Mtech, MBA, ICWA all students will be benifitted by reading the content of this book.

Table of Contents

1

Over-view of Production and Operation Management and Production Planning Control

1.1 INTRODUCTION

This chapter introduces the nature of production planing and control as it has evolved and is in use in many Organizations. Vertually every organizations small, medium, large or manufacturing, service, profit or non profit has main function the production of defined goal / objective or output from its processes to provide effective customer satisfaction. This chapter has given stress on Operations management. As it is a critical job oriented managerial function in all types of organizations – starting from private manufacturing sectors to public service sectors. Operation management (OM) is responsible in the process of producing a product or service. Scope of operations management has increased significantly in recent years due to the global competition, shorter product/service lifecycles, increasingly demanding consumers and momentous improvement of information and process technology. So business organizations are more serious about their operations function and trying their best to improve efficiency and productivity by varying their quality of products and services. Now a days OM is situated at the center of business but still under the governance of design, planing and control. Day by day OM is also required in multidisciplinary business functions.

Operation Management (OM) is the management process, in which Input like 3 M's material, machine, money with value added process and human labour converted to output like product or service. An operation is some step in the overall process of producing good or service. In a company the proction system mostly uses facilities, machines, equipment and operating methods to produce product or service to fulfill customers' demand. Fig. 1.1 operation mannagement process, shows the relation between input and output (*i.e.,* the transformation of raw material to finished product.)

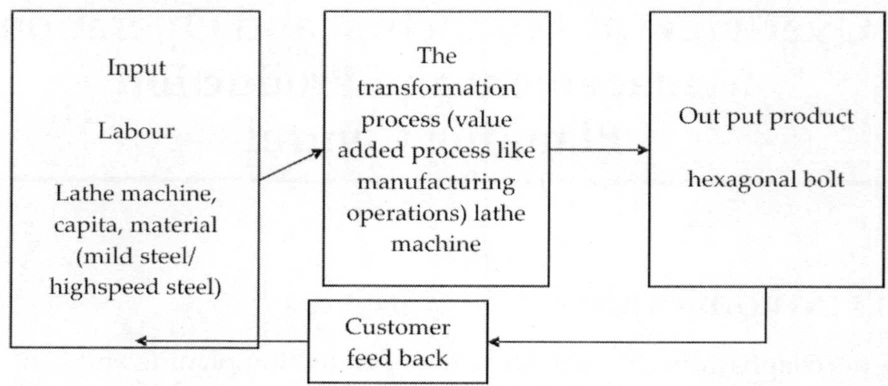

Fig. 1.1 Operation management process

Product is tangible where as service is intangible. Product carries inventory but service carries no inventory. For example pen, mobile, car, bus, television, etc. are example of products but medical facilities, internet facility, arranging food for parties, telephonic conversion are services. Some companies provide both product and service for *example*: food we used to take in resturant is product but comfort and catering provided to us in deliverying food is service. Similarly the oil filled is product but deliverying oil changed process is service. Table 1.1 shows the difference between product and service.

Table 1.1: Product verses service

Product	*Service*
Tangible	Intangible
Quality of output is same as good product with fixed dimensions as it is machine dependent.	Quality of output is variable. As service is not same type, for example in a resturant not only delicios food is served, good facilities are provied for comfort. So the service quality out put is varying in nature for customer satisfaction.
Inventory is found	No inventory

Quality of output is same as good product with fixed dimensions as it is machine dependent. Quality of output is variable. As service is not same type, for example in a resturant not only delicios food is served, good facilities are provied for comfort. So the service quality out put is varying in nature for customer satisfaction.

Any operating system converts inputs to outputs, using physical facilities to fulfill customer demand. These system of operations are organized into correct sequence to develop larger system of production. In Manufacturing oriented system the inputs are material, energy, labour, technology, machines, facilities and information system etc. but in service oriented system the inputs are dominated by service provider. So to manage productive system the first factors that plays important role is parameters involved in conversion and the second one is controling the conversion process. Every function in the organization operates together, whether marketing, finance and accounting, production, purchasing or human resources, adds importance to the customer. Table 1.2 example of production/operating system explains the details of systems and inputs with addition to transformation process final output.

Table 1.2: Example of production/operating system

System	*Inputs*	*Components*	*Transform function*	*Outputs*
Educational institutes	Students	Teachers, books, class-room, online videos, lectures, lab room	Imparting know-ledge and skill	Educated individuals
Restaurant	Hungry customers	Chef, waiter, hotel manager, infrasture for dining and ambience	Food, serving	Satishfied customer
Auto factory	Sheet steel, engine	Tools equipment, labourers	Assembly of cars	Cars
Hospitals	Patient	Doctors, nurses, MDs	Health care	Healthy individuals

1.2 OPERATIONS PERFORMANCE OBJECTIVES

Operations management has an impact on the five broad categories of stakeholders in any organization. Stakeholders is a broad term but is generally used to mean anybody who could have an interest in, or is affected by, the operation. The five groups are:

Customers – Customers are the most apparent stakeholders. The type and quality of product/good and service will be provided to them directly affecting them and their value affects business.

Suppliers – Operations and suppliers aim always colide with each other and operation has major impact on suppliers.If suppliers perfectly supply then only operation can be proper.

Shareholders – The process of operation is perfect means they can properly producing goods and services, the more likely the whole business will show a profit and shareholders will be one of the major beneficiaries of this.

Employees – If the organization will prospour then the profit will be high. The employ will get good salary, more and more recognisation. However operations responsibilities to employees go far beyond this. It includes the general working conditions which are resolute by the way the operation has been designed.

Society – Society may have no direct economic relation with the company, but individuals and groups in society in general can be impacted by the way the operation managers perform. The most obvious example is in the ecological responsibility/sustainbility exhibited by operations manager.

1.3 SCOPE OF OPERATION MANAGEMENT

The main objectives of operation management is to satisfy the needs of customers by producing product or providing service. The main objective of all organizations is to efficiently produce goods or services. Operations management is the policy used to attain this objective.

1.3.1 Production Management *verses* Operation Management

The study of set of activities comprising supervision, planning and designing of business operations in the field of manufacturing of goods and services is termed as operations management. The purpose of operations management is to make certain that the operations of a business are efficient and effective and result in minimum of wastage. Operations management tries to cut down resources involved in operations while at the same time making operations more effective and productive. In fact operations management is more concerned on processes than people or products. Operations management in a nutshell is using physical resources in an optimum manner, converting input into output, so as to supply to the market the desired and finished product.

Production management on the other hand focuses specifically on the production of goods and services and is concentrated upon churning output from input. It is a broad sum of activities that go into turning raw material into final, finished product. Production managem-ent is not a subset of operations management, but production manage-ment in itself is a broad subject that comprises production planning and control, inventory management and operations control. Production management includes all management activities spanning selection. Designing, operating, controlling and updating production system.

Operations management is focused upon administration, planning and execution of operations involved in production of goods and services and trying to minimize the resources at the same time increasing output, production management is more concerned with input/output and churning out products in the shape of desired finished product. Production and operations management are more similar than different: if manufacturing products is a prime concern then it is called production management, whereas management of services is somewhat broader in scope and called operations management.

1.3.2 Scopes of Supply Chain Management, Production Management and Operation Management

Supply chain management is primarily concerned with the efficient integration of suppliers, factories, warehouses and stores so that merchandise is produced and distributed in the right quantities, to the right locations and at the right time, and so as to minimize total system cost subject to satisfying customer service requirements.

Scopes of supply chain management

These issues span a large spectrum of a firm's activities, from the strategic through the tactical to the operational level:

- The strategic level deals with decisions that have a long-lasting effect on the firm. This includes decisions regarding product design, what to make internally and what to outsource, supplier selection, and strategic partnering as well as decisions on the number, location, and capacity of warehouses and manufacturing plants and the flow of material through the logistics network.
- The tactical level includes decisions that are typically updated anywhere between once every quarter and once every year. These include purchasing and production decisions, inventory policies, and transportation strategies, including the frequency with which customers are visited.
- The operational level refers to day-to-day decisions such as scheduling, lead time quotations, routing, and truck loading. Below we introduce and discuss some of the key issues, questions, and trade-offs associated with different decisions.

Distribution network configuration

Consider several plants producing products to serve a set of geographically dispersed retailers. The current set of warehouses is deemed inappropriate and management wants to reorganize or redesign the distribution network. This may be due, for example, to changing demand patterns or the termination of a leasing contract for a number of existing warehouses. In addition, changing demand patterns may require a change in plant production levels, a selection of new suppliers, and a new flow pattern of goods throughout the distribution network. To select a set of warehouse locations and capacities, determine production levels for each product at each plant, and set transportation flows between facilities, either from plant to warehouse or warehouse to retailer, in such a way as to minimize total production, inventory, and transportation costs and satisfy service level requirements. This is a complex optimization problem, and advanced technology and approaches are required to find a solution.

Inventory control

Consider a retailer that maintains an inventory of a particular product. Since customer demand changes over time, the retailer can use only historical data to predict demand. The retailer's objective is to decide at what point to reorder a new batch of the product and how much to order so as to minimize inventory ordering and holding costs. To fullfill uncertainty in customer demand, uncertainty in the supply process, inventory is kept in stock.

Production sourcing

In many industries, there is a need to carefully balance transportation and manufacturing costs. In particular, reducing production costs typically implies that each manufacturing facility is responsible for a small set of products so that large batches are produced, hence reducing production costs. Unfortunately, this may lead to higher transportation costs. Similarly, reducing transportation costs typically implies that each facility is flexible and has the ability to produce most or all products, but this leads to small batches and hence increases production costs. Finding the right balance between the two cost components is difficult but needs to be done monthly or quarterly.

Supply contracts

In traditional supply chain strategies, each party in the chain focuses on its own profit and hence makes decisions with little regard to their impact on other supply chain partners. Relationships between suppliers and buyers are established by means of supply contracts that specify pricing and volume discounts, delivery lead times, quality, returns and so forth. Particularly, the impact of volume discount and revenue-sharing contracts on supply chain performance and pricing strategies can be applied by suppliers to provide incentives for buyers to order more products by which the supplier profit increases.

Distribution strategies

An important challenge faced by many organizations is how much should they centralize (or decentralize) their distribution system. The impact of each strategy on inventory levels and transportation costs, the impact on service levels etc. are finally, decides how much products be transported by air from centralized locations to the various demand points. These concepts are not only important for a single firm determining its distribution strategy, but also very important for competing retailers that need to decide how much they can collaborate with each other.

Supply chain integration and strategic partnering

Designing and implementing a globally optimal supply chain is quite difficult because of its dynamics and the conflicting objectives employed by different facilities and partners. Nevertheless, Dell, Wal-Mart and Procter and Gamble success stories demonstrate not only that an integrated, globally optimal supply chain is possible, but that it can have a huge impact on the company's performance and market share.

Outsourcing and off shoring strategies

Rethinking the supply chain strategy not only involves coordinating the different activities in the supply chain, but also deciding what to make internally and what to buy from outside sources. How can a firm identify what manufacturing activities lie in its set of core competencies and thus should be completed internally and what product and components should be purchased from outside suppliers, because these manufacturing activities are not core competencies?

Product design

Effective design plays several vital roles in the supply chain. Most obviously, certain product designs may increase inventory holding or transportation costs relative to other designs, while other designs may facilitate a shorter manufacturing lead time. Unfortunately, product redesign is often expensive. When is it worthwhile to redesign products so as to reduce logistics costs or supply chain lead times.

Information technology and decision-support systems

Information technology is a critical enabler of effective supply chain management. Indeed, much of the current interest in supply chain management is motivated by the opportunities that appeared due to the abundance of data and the savings that can be achieved by sophisticated analysis of these data. The primary issue in supply chain management is not whether data can be received, but what data should be transferred.

Customer value

Customer value is the measure of a company's contribution to its customer, based on the entire range of products, services and intangibles that constitute the company's offerings. In these years this measure has superseded measures such as quality and customer satisfaction. Obviously, effective supply chain management is critical if a firm wishes to fulfill customer needs and provide value.

Smart pricing

Smart Pricing Revenue management strategies have been applied successfully in industries such as airlines, hotels and rental cars. In recent years, a number of manufactures, retailers and carriers have applied a variation of these techniques to improve supply chain performance. In this case, the firm integrates pricing and inventory (or available capacity) to influence market demand and improve the bottom line.

The scope of production management with various areas of business organisation as are follows: The basic functions of business organisation are finance, marketing, finance and production and industrial engineering.

Finance and production

Finance provided the necessary funds for the maintenance of production and marketing activities. Funds not only comes from the sale of goods and services but also acquired through loans – from banks and other financial institutions, sale of stock investment and income.

Marketing

The object of production activity is to provide inputs which include raw materials men, machine, operating supplies, semi finished products, water, power and place etc. the inputs are assembled and changed to finished goods thereby creating value. The finished products and services are available so that the marketing functions can be utilised to provide, sell and distribute them. Thus production and marketing are separate yet inter-dependent functions in business.

Personnel and production

The personnel function in any business organisation is mainly concerned with all matters related to manpower as an input system of business organisation. From the view point of the production manager following are the various areas of mutual interest. (i) Recruitment and selection (ii) Training and development of employees (iii) Labour relations (iv) Safety (v) Wage and salary administration including various incentive programmes. (vi) Motivating employees to give their best.

Production and industrial engineering

This department is responsible for translating the ideas developed in research and development, marketing research into realities. The main object is to search for the most efficient way of producing products under certain constraints such as material, manpower, machines, money etc.

1. ***Job production:*** In job production the whole product is looked as one job which is to be completed before going on to next. The most common examples are building a ship or a large civil engineering construction job. Job production is hot confined to large projects, it could be the making of a special piece of equipment or a tool.
2. ***Batch production:*** If qualities of more than one are being made, it is sometimes convenient to split the production into a series of manufacturing stages or operations. Each operation is completed as one of the single items being made, before the next operation is started. In this way a group of identical products or a batch are made, which move through the production process together.
3. ***Flow production:*** When there is a continuous demand for a product, it is sometimes worthwhile setting-up facilities to make that product and no other product. In these circumstances flow production may be the best way of operating. Here the manufacturing is broken down into operations, but each unit moves or flows, from one operation to the next individually and not as one of a batch example are motor manufacturing, fertiliser,

pharmaceutical and urea manufacturing. Since only one product is being made there are no problems about priorities, but it is necessary to balance the work load at all stages of manufacture. Examples are motor car manufacturing.

1.3.3 The Main Activities of Production Operation Management Are

Product selection and design

To design a new product first of all ideas must be properly analysed and then these ideas must be converted to reality. All most all business organizations have to plan, design, develop and introduce new products to servive among competitors and grow the organizational strategies. Developing the new products and introducing them in the market is the prime goal of all the organizations. The products should be designed in such a way that satisfy customer demand and fullfill customer's expectation value enginering or value analysis helps to eliminate the cost building or manufacturing with improving features and specification. Value engineering (VE) is concerned with new products. It is applied during product development. The focus is on reducing costs, improving function or both, by way of teamwork-based product evaluation and analysis. This takes place before any capital is invested in tooling, plant or equipment.

Value Analysis (VA) is concerned with existing products. It involves a current product being analysed and evaluated by a team, to reduce costs, improve product function or both. Value analysis exercises use a plan which step-by-step, methodically evaluates the product in a range of areas. These include costs, function, alternative components and design aspects such as ease of manufacture and assembly.

Process selection and planing

Selection of a process involves taking decisions to select technology, machines and equipment, lay out.

First of all a process is planned, then to optimise the output from the given process optimum automation and mechaninisation is done. The products should be designed in such a way that satisfy customer demand and fullfill customer's expectation.

Facility location

Location of production and operation process plays an important role. Any worng decision may be disastrous. Location must be in such a place that cut down production and distribution cost. Although there are many options available for facility location, still a proper evaluation is essential to find important and diverse factors for taking strong decision regarding facility location.

Facility layout and material handling

Plant layout deals with arrangement of machines and plant facilities. The machines should be arranged in such a manner that the work place provides the smooth production flow, no overlaping, no intruption.

The plant lay out may be three types, product layout, process layout and group technology layout.

In product layout machines are arranged in a sequence required for processing of a particular product where as in process layout machines performing similiar processes are grouped together. The combined of both product layout and process layout is called as group technology layout. The selection of particular flow patern and material handling equipment is dependent on the distance between the work station, intensity of flow or trafic, size shape and nature of materials to be handeled.

Capacity planning

Capacity means a level of out put of the conversion process over a period of time. Capacity planing is done for short term basis or long term basis. Full capacity indicates maximum level of out put. Process industries are long term planned industries, they usualy planned expansion, contranction of facilities. Tools help in capacity planing are marginal costing, learning curve, linear programming, decision trees etc. the operational level decisions are short term, usualy consists of planing and control of production activities.

The operational decisions are as follows.

Production planning

Production planning aims at setting the goals or targets and assigning the resources like men, machines, materials and plant services, among varied production operations. Planning is a pre operation activity, it may be prior planning or active planning. Prior planing means preproduction planning and active planning means actual production planing. It aims at anticipating the probable difficulties, so that they can be easily eliminated before action. Modules of prior planing are product development and design, forecasting, aggregate planning, master scheduling, orderwriting, material requirement planning etc. and modules of active planing are process planning, scheduling, routing etc.

Production control

Control is a management process which aims to see that activities are carried on in live with predetermined standards. Production control has two phases. Progress reporting and corrective action. In progress reporting the data of the job complition like material rejection, process variation, equipment failures are collected and compared with present performance. In corrective action the provisions are made for unexpected events. For example creating schedule flexibility, make or buy decision, capacity modification etc.

Inventory control

Inventory control deals with the control over raw materials, work in progress, finished products, store supplies, tools etc. The raw material should be purchased at right time at right quantity from right source at right price. Storekeeping is also an important aspect of inventory control.

Quality control

The quality control is maintained by testing actual production and by ascertaining whether they conform to set standards. The raw materials, work in progress, finished products are inspected at various stages of production.

Method study

Unnecessary movements should be eliminated and suitable positioning of workers should be developed and continuous monitoring by time study and method study must be done for repetative actions.

Maintainance and replacement

By effective maintainance capacity can be properly utilized and operations systems more productive. Maintainances are catagorized to break down maintainance, corective/preventive maintainance and predictive or periodic maintainance.

Cost reduction and control

Cost reduction ultimately improves productivity, the industries become competative. Value engineering, budget control, cost control are the tools help to reduce cost. Fig. 1.2 shows functions of operation management and strategies of operation management.

1.4 FACTORS AFFECTING OPERATION MANAGEMENT

Global Competition

The services or products provided by companies if allowed to serve to international customers. It is called global competition. Global competition has increased profits and flattens the playing field in business.

For example: Competition for eating chocolates is open to all without discriminating gender, age, income and nationality can be called as global competition.

Quality, Customer Service and Cost Challenges

The customer service is the main differentiator between good, bad companies. Good quality customer service, cost of the product keeps customers coming back to the company.

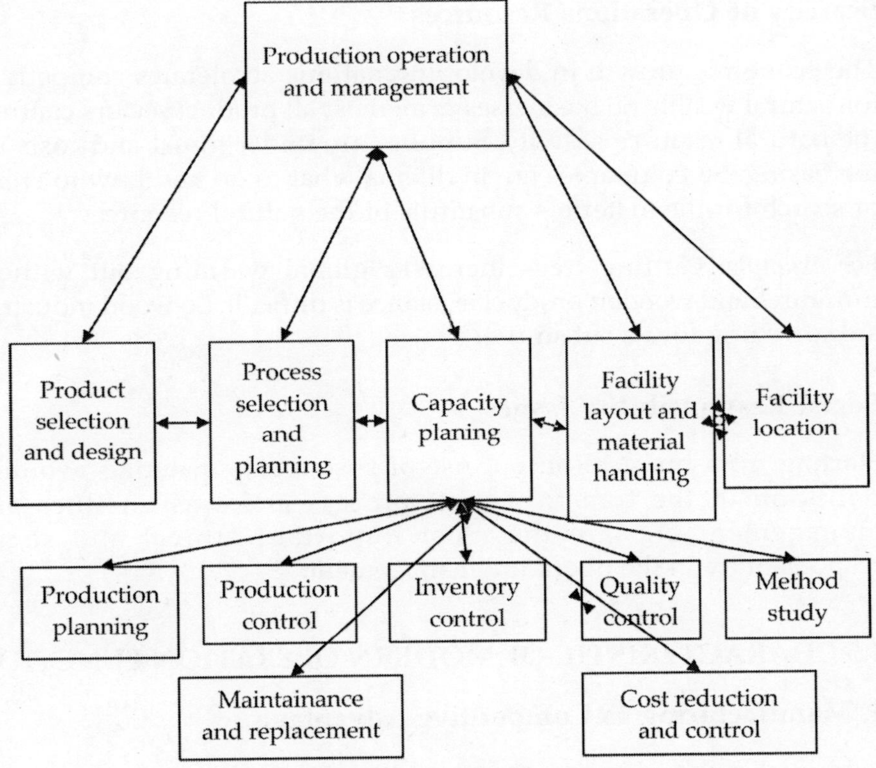

Fig. 1.2 Functions of operation management

Rapid Expansion of Advanced Technologies

As the technology is advanceing day by day, it has changed the way the world operates.

For example: Mobile technology, internet facilities etc. have given the opportunity to communicate from opposite ends of the globe.

Continued Growth of the Service Sector

As the informtion technology, globalization concept is changing the need and preference of customers are also more advanced day by day. So service sectors are more in demand. Service operation management system are also continuosly nourishing them selves to fulfill market demand and customer demand as well.

Scarcity of Operations Resources

The economic growth in developing nations accelerates competition for natural wealth. So businesses in all most all product sectors confront the natural resource scarcity. Supplies are under threat and costs are increasing. So companies are in dilema what to do and how to create or search for the materials substitute of the natural resources.

For example: Cutting trees increases global warming but without furnitures and wooden product existance is difficult. So wood industries are searching for its substitute.

Social-Responsibility Issues

Starting from input to output use of sustainable materials avoiding pollution in the transformation process and waste reduce and management etc. are the most important ethical and social responsibility in the operation management.

1.5 CHARACTERISTIC OF MODERN OPERATION FUNCTION

1. Manufacturing as Competitive Advantage

Advanced manufacturing focuses on products that are intrinsically difficult. But standard manufacturing approaches and low cost labour is not the proper solution for this era. Now a days demand was high and production capacities were excess. Competition is rising and firms are searching the way to gain competitive advantage to survive and succeed. So to gain a competitive edge and plants are determined to take advantage of the potential. Some tools like Total Quality Management (TQM), time-based competition, Business Process Reengineering (BPRE), Just in Time (JIT), focused factory (revised), Flexible Manufacturing Systems (FMS), Computer Integrated Manufacturing (CIM) and the virtual corporation are applied by companies to gain competitive advantage.

2. Services Orientation

The service sectors GDP is increasing more and more compared to manufacturing sectors. As service sectors are gaining greater importance these days. The production system has to try their best to be in competition and to get the better position in market, needs to be organized and perform well, to fulfill the requirements of the service component. The service sector deals with-

(a) Intangible and perishable (service capacity cannot be stored, saved, returned, or resold once rendered to a customer) nature of the services,
(b) Regular interaction with clients or customers,
(c) Small volumes of production to serve local markets and,
(d) Need to locate facilities to serve local markets.

There is increased presence of professionals on the production side, instead of technicians and engineers. Educational institutions, hospitals, Banking services are catagorised as high contact services. Electricity and water utlity, Its firms are example of medium contact services manufacturing firms producing home made appliances, electronics goods manufacturer are example of low contact services.

3. Disappearance of Smokestacks

Smokestacks (the term used by Alvin Toffler in his book Power Shift) represented industrial establishments which ejected thick smoke, polluting the environment around. Smokestacks not only disgorged reek, they produced nauseating smell, generated dust, created sound and in general, were similar to ghosts. It represents the pollution caused by the smoke coming from chimneys of industries that apears and disappears like an extinct ghost.

Ref- Powershift

Knowledge, Wealth and Violence at the Edge of the 21st century is the third book in a trilogy written by the futurist Alvin Toffler, following on from Future Shock and The Third Wave. The hardcover first edition was published October 1, 1990. ISBN 0-553-05776-6.

4. Small has Become Beautiful

Small scale industries or manufacturing units are emerging at a very first rate that not only helps in increasing standardization, customization and flexible manufacturing system etc. but also increases the economic systems. It was explained by an economist that smaller industries with group ownership, at regional work places utilizing local labours, local resources gives more profit and increases the mass production capacity by increasing economic of scale.

1.6. RECENT TRENDS IN PRODUCTION / OPERATIONS MANAGEMENT

Global Market Place

Globalization of business have increases the economic advantage, increased the level of competition, among manufacturing firms throughout the world. So companies/industries are trying their best to impliment advance technology in their opertion system to produce best product to survive in the competative market.

Production/Operations Strategy

The approach, dependable with organization strategy that is used to guide the operations function for overall success of business and the necessity for relating it to their overall business strategy (*i.e.*, quality management and service/manufacturing strategy).

Total Quality Management

The regular practised approach, which has been adopted by firms/ industries/companies to accomplish customer satisfaction for improving the quality of goods and services.

Flexibility

The capability to adjust quickly to changes like volume of demand, in the product mix demanded and in product design or in delivery schedules, has become a major competitive advantage to the firms.

Time Reduction

Minimizing manufacturing cycle time, avoiding idle time and speed in a product provides competitive frame to the firm over other firms. When companies can provide products at the same price and quality, quicker delivery (short lead times), it will attract more and more customers and increase the productivity of the company. So there will be zero losses, no bottleneck situation and organizational performance will also increase.

Technology

Advanced technologies like automation, computerization, information and communication technologies have modified the companies operating system. New technologies like CAD/CIM, CAPP, GT and FMS have changed the manufacturing of the products and processes and generated great impact on competitiveness and quality.

Worker Involvement

Assigning responsibility to all the employees starting from lower level to upper level for decision making and problem solving, this is known as employee involvement and empowerment. For example quality circles and quality improvement teams etc.

Re-engineering

To improve the performance of a firm/company, that involves in redesigning the business processes without hampering environmental condition.

Environmental Issues

By implimenting waste management techniques like reducing waste, recycling waste, reusing waste, using less-toxic chemicals and using biodegradable materials for packaging and by encorporating pollution free sustainable practices in the Organization environmental issues can be resolved.

Corporate Downsizing (Right Sizing)

Due to high competition in the market, to pay dividend, to avoid low productivity and to survive in the market the company incorporate downsizing. To enhance the economic value of organisation rightsizing is done.

Supply Chain Management

Management of supply chain, from suppliers to final customers reduces the cost of transportation, warehousing and distribution throughout the supply chain.

Lean Production

It is the systematic method of eliminating waste as implemented by Toyota production system of reducing wastes. To minimise resources and to produce high volume high quality and different variety goods lean production is useful. These systems use flexible manufacturing systems and multi-skilled work force to have advantages of both mass production and job production (or craft production).

1.7. DECISION MAKING IN PRODUCTION OPERATION FUNCTION

Operations managers are required to make a series of decisions in the production function. They plan, organize, staff, direct and control all the activities in the process of converting all the inputs into finished products. At each level, operating managers are expected to make decisions and implement them too. The decisions made by operations managers about the activities of production systems tend to fall into three general categories as follows:

1. Strategic

Decisions relating to products, processes and manufacturing facilities. These decisions are major ones, having strategic importance and long-term significance for the organization.

2. Operating

Decisions relating to planning production to meet demand. These decisions are necessary in order to ensure that, the ongoing production of goods and services meets the market demand and provides reasonable profits for the organization.

3. Control

Decisions relating to planning and controlling operations. These decisions concern the day to day activities of workers, quality of products and services, production and overhead costs and maintenance of machines. Table 1.3 shows three types of decisions strategic, operating and control in production operation function

Table 1.3: Decision making in production operation function

	Strategic	*Operating*	*Control*
Area of involvement	Production processes	Production planning systems	Productivity and employees
	Production technology	Independent demand Inventory demand	Total quality control
	Facility layout	Resource requirements planning systems	Project planning and control techniques
	Allocating resources	Shop floor planning and control Materials management	Maintenance management and reliability
Nature of activities	Planning for the optimal distribution of	Aggregate planning and master production scheduling inventories.	Planning for the effective and efficient
	Including process design selecting and managing production	Planning and controlling finished goods	Use of human resources in operations
	Planning the arrangement of facilities	Planning materials and capacity requirements	Planning and controlling the quality of products and services
	Developing long range production plans and technology	Short range decisions about what to produce and when to	Planning and controlling projects
	Scare resources among product lines or business units	Produce at each work centre. Managing all facts of materials system	Planning for maintaining the machines and facilities of production
Example	Planning products, processes and facilities	Planning production to meet demand	Planning and controlling operations

1.8 PRODUCTION AND OPERATIONS STRATEGY – ELEMENTS OF OPERATION STRATEGY

Operations Strategy Comprises Six Components

1. Positioning the production system

Selecting the type of product design, type of production processing system and the type of finished goods inventory policy for each major product line in the business plan involves positioning the product line.

A. *Product focused*: The groups of machine, tools and workers arranged according to their respective tasks in order to place together a product.

   Example: Mass production system.

B. *Process focused*: The system which is highly flexible and can easily be modified to support other product design. It is designed to support production departments that perform a single task like painting or packing.

2. Focus of factories and service facilities

Production facility organized about a definite, hardly-limited set of resources, to provide a narrow range of operations or services in manufacture of a few products at low-cost and high-throughput. Most mass production facilities are designed as focused factories. See also flexible factory.

3. Product/Service design and development

The product /service design involves, converting customers' wants and needs, refine existing products and services, develop new products and services, formulate quality goals, formulate cost targets, construct and test prototypes, document specifications and translate products and service specification into process specifications. The process of design has certain steps that comprise motivation, ideas for improvement, organizational capabilities and forecasting.

Product design combines ergonomics (Study of capabilities and limitations of mental and physical work in different settings) with product and business knowledge to generate ideas and concepts and convert them into physical and usable objects or servicee.

4. Technology selection and process development

All the process of production is planned in detail. The technology to be used in the production process is selected from range of options.

5. Allocation of resources to strategic alternatives

As these resource like capital, machine and materials inputs are essential to production activities, their shortages can control production performance significantly. Hence the operation manger have to plan the optimal use of resources, both in terms of minimizing wastage, and in terms of their allocation to the best strategic use.

6. Facility planning

- The location of the production facilities is one of the key decisions an operation manager has to make since it is critical to the competitiveness of the organization.
- Setting up production facilities with adequate capacity involves massive initial investment.
- Strategically right options should be carefully weighed against all available alternatives. These decisions also influence the future decisions on probable capacity expansions plans.
- Operation managers also make decisions, *i.e.,* decision on internal arrangement of workers and department within the facility

1.8.1 Operations Competitive Priorities

1. Product and service design
2. Cost
3. Location
4. Quality
5. Quick response
6. Flexibility
7. Inventory management

8. Supply chain management
9. Service

1.9. TYPES OF PRODUCTION SYSTEM

The operations/production system can be equated with the flow of materials - flow into, flow through and flow out of the conversion process. Depending on the flow characteristics, there are four classes of the production system.

1. Mass production or flow line production system/flow shop
2. Batch production system
3. Job shop
4. Projects (unit manufacture)
5. Mass Production system or flowshop

In these systems, the same sequence of operation is undergone using specialized equipments. Maintenance must be very good to prevent the breakdown of the whole system. Fig. 1.3 shows example of mass production system.

Example: Auto assembly, assembly assembly of television set

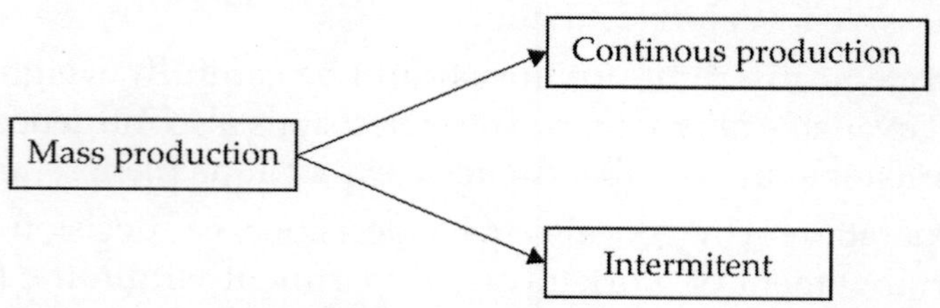

Fig. 1.3: Mass production

Continuos production system produces same type of output like cigaretes, fertilizers, cement etc. Intermitent production, the process is intrupted for specification variations, like Bottling company, textile, television set up etc.

Batch Production System

In this system, intermedate product with intermittent volume is produced. Machines are general purpose. Pharmaceutical companies make medicinal formulations by batch production system. Production problems are complex here.

Job Shop

In this system different types of products follow different sequence. Job shop results more set up time, more in process inventory, complex scheduling, varying quality etc. job shop is technically speaking a queuing problem. Simulation techniques do help in analyzing it.

Example. Paint shop, machine tool shop.

Projects

A project refers to the process of creating a complex one of a kind product or service with a set of well defined tasks. Consider the manufacturing of a ship, starting of new industry, fabricating boilers, dam construction. Such products are never made in large numbers. Manpower, facilities and other resources center around such products. PERT/CPM or network analysis is a useful technique to plan and control such projects.

1.10 IMPORTANT QUESTIONS WITH ANSWER

The POM department is headed by a senior vice president of operations who organizes the department with the assist of plant manager as well as staff heads, who are reporting to him.

Duties and Responsibilities of Production Managers in Manufacturing

- Location planning of company/factory
- Purchasing equipments essential for production
- Layout of equipments within the factory
- Production processes and equipments designing
- Product design
- Designing production work and establishing work standards
- Capacity planning

- Production planning and scheduling
- Production control
- Inventory management
- Supply chain management
- Quality control
- Production equipment maintenance and repair
- Measurement and monitoring of productivity
- Industrial relations
- Health and safety
- Staff selection and liaisoning.
- Budgeting and capacity planning
- Planing for information system
- Updating records and videos
- Organising inspections

Emerging Role of the Production and Operations Manager

- Contribute in strategic decision making of the company. (Decision taken in machining shops)
- Participate in the implementation and use of Enterprise Resource Planning in the company.
- Mechanized the processes as per the necessities of the company.
- Increase the research and development effort to update with modern technology in increasing self-reliant new technologies.
- Decrease delay in implementation of projects [new products/ services launching; expansion of facilities] due to increased competition.
- Follow the environment policies by implementing environment and pollution norms established by the government from time to time.
- Participate in concurrent engineering teams for new product design and old product development.
- Build up long-term strategic relationship with supplies by acting as supply chain managers.

- Pay more attention to technology management, in view of joint ventures of multinational companies with domestic companies.
- Act as an internal quality auditor in quality inspection and certification programming like ISO 9000 series and ISO 14000.

1.11. ROLE OF OPERATIONS IN STRATEGIC MANAGEMENT

The responsibility of the operations function means something away from its observable responsibilities and tasks. The three roles for operations management are:

- The implementer of business strategy
- The supporter of business strategy
- The driver of business strategy

Judging the Operations Contribution

It is a theoretical model that allows organizations to think about how good their operations are. It is not an accurate tool for measuring operations excellence.

Operations Performance Objectives

Operations management has a force on the five types of stakeholders in any organization. The five groups of stakeholders are:

- *Customers* – These are the most obvious people who will be affected by any business. What the chapter goes on to call the five operations performance objectives apply primarily to this group of people.
- *Suppliers* – Operations can have a major impact on suppliers, both on how they prosper themselves and on how effective they are at supplying the operation.
- *Shareholders* – Clearly, the better an operation is at producing goods and services, the more likely the whole business is to prosper and shareholders will be one of the major beneficiaries of this.
- *Employees* – Similarly, employees will be generally better off if the company is prosperous; if only because they are more likely

to be employed in the future. However operations responsibilities to employees go far beyond this. It includes the general working conditions which are determined by the way the operation has been designed.

- *Society* – Although often having no direct economic connection with the company, individuals and groups in society at large can be impacted by the way its operations managers behave. The most obvious example is in the environmental responsibility exhibited by operations managers.

There are also six performance objectives like quality, speed, dependability, flexibility, Reliability and cost etc.

Quality

Quality is the first among all performance objectives and quality is discussed largely in terms of it meaning conformance. Quality is that a product or service means, it conforms to its specifications.

There are two important points to remember when reading the section on quality as a performance objective.

- The external influence of good quality in operations is that the customers having no complain about. And if they have nothing to complain about they will enjoy their product/service.
- Inside the operation quality has a different affect. If conformance quality is high in all the operations processes means less activities with mistakes. This usually means that cost is saved, dependability increases.

Flexibility

Flexibility means operation in some way. There are different types of flexibility (product/service flexibility, mix flexibility, volume flexibility and delivery flexibility). Externally the different types of flexibility allow an operation to fit its products and services to its customers in some way. Mix flexibility allows an operation to produce a wide variety of products and services for its customers to choose from. Product/ service flexibility allows it develop new products and services incorporating new ideas which customers may find attractive. Volume and delivery flexibility allow the operation to adjust its output levels and its delivery procedures in order to cope with unexpected changes in how many products and services customers want, or when they want them, or where they want them. There are also some internal affects related to performance objective. Thre are three most important internal effects, namely flexibility speeds up response, flexibility.

Speed

Speed means time between an external or internal customer requesting a product or service.

- Externally speed is important because it helps to respond quickly to customers. Again, this is usually viewed positively by customers who will be more likely to return with more business. Sometimes also it is possible to charge higher prices when service is fast. The postal service in most countries and most transportation and delivery services charge more for faster delivery, for example.
- The internal affects of speed have much to do with cost reduction. The chapter identifies two areas where speed reduces cost (reducing inventories and reducing risks). The examples used are from manufacturing but the same thing applies to service operations.

Dependability

Dependability means customers get their products or services on time. It has also external and internal affects. Dependability is a particularly important criterion used to determine whether suppliers have their contracts renewed. So, again, the external affects of this performance objective are to increase the chances of customers returning with more business.

Reliability

Reliability refers to the time until a product breaks down and has to be repaired, but not replaced. This feature is very important for products that have expensive maintenance.

Reliability may also describe the ability to function at a specified moment or interval of time (Availability). Reliability means probability of failure as the frequency of failures; or in terms of availability, as a probability derived from reliability, testability and maintainability. Testability, maintainability and maintenance are often defined as a part of "reliability engineering" in reliability programs. Reliability plays a key role in the cost-effectiveness of system.

Cost

The cost structure of different organisations can vary greatly. If, high quality, high speed, high dependability and high flexibility product is produced in a factory definitely it also save the operation cost.

Key Notes

1. Value Analysis (VA) is concerned with existing products. It involves a current product being analysed and evaluated by a team, to reduce costs, improve product function or both.
2. Operating system converts inputs to outputs, using physical facilities to fulfill customer demand.
3. Operation Management (OM) is the management process, in which Input like 3M's material, machine,Money with value added process and human labour converted to output like product or service.

EXERCISE 1.1

1. Explain Operations Strategy, with Example

Ans. An operations strategy consists of a sequence of decisions that, over time, enables a business unit to achieve a desired operations structure, infrastructure and set of specific capabilities in support of the competitive priorities. Operations strategy is the collective concrete actions chosen, mandated, or stimulated by corporate strategy. It is, of course, implemented within the operations function. This operations strategy binds the various operations decisions and actions into a cohesive consistent response to competitive forces by linking firm policies, programs, systems and actions into a systematic response to the competitive priorities chosen and communicated by the corporate or business strategy. In simpler terms, the operations strategy specifies how the firm will employ its operations capabilities to support the business strategy.

Operations strategy has a long-term concern for how to best determine and develop the firm's major operations resources so that there is a high degree of compatibility between these resources and the business strategy. Very broad questions are addressed regarding how major resources should be configured in order to achieve the firm's corporate objectives. Some of the issues of relevance include long-term decisions regarding capacity, location, processes, technology and timing.

Example: Wal-Mart is one of the most successful and largest retailers in U.S. history. It's operations strategy is to use low inventory levels and prices to generate faster sales based on low prices and value. Keeping inventory low allows the company to keep prices low for their customers, as well as replace products with new items once inventory is gone. This also increase demand. High demand combined with low prices leads to increased sales for the company.

Online

Online merchants typically have very different operations strategies than brick-and-mortar retailers. For example, the operations strategy for an online merchant likely involves creating and maintaining a website that is easy to use and reliable, so when customers come to the site, they can easily navigate through it to make a purchase. An online merchant's operations strategy puts a lot of emphasis on the design and usability of the site, which includes product photos and descriptions that entice visitors to make a purchase. The checkout process also must be easy and fast.

2. With Examples Explain Types of Production System

Ans. The first choice typically faced in process management is that of process choice. Manufacturing and service operations can be characterized as one of the following:

1. Project
2. Job shop
3. Batch flow
4. Line flow
5. Continuous flow

The nature of these processes are discussed below and summarized in the manufacturing product-process matrix on page 8.

Project process

Examples of a project process are building a shopping center, planning a major event, running a political campaign, putting together a comprehensive training program, constructing a new hospital, doing management consulting work, or developing a new technology or product. A project process is characterized by a high degree of job customization, the large scope of each project and the release of substantial resources, once a project is completed. A project process lies at the high-customization, low-volume end of the process-choice continuum. The sequence of operations and the process involved in each one are unique to each project, creating one-of-a-kind products or services made specifically to customer order. Although some projects may look similar, each is unique. Firms with project processes sell themselves on the basis of their capabilities rather than on specific products or services. Projects tend to be complex, take a long time and be large. Many interrelated tasks must be completed, requiring close coordination. Resources needed for a project are assembled and then released for further use after the project is finished. Projects typically make heavy use of certain skills and resources at particular stages and then have little use for them the rest of the time. A project process is based on a flexible flow strategy, with work flows redefined with each new project.

Job shop process

Next in the continuum of process choices is the job shop process. Examples are custom metal processing shop, hospital emergency rooms, custom plastic injection molding shop, or making customized cabinets. A job shop process creates the flexibility needed to produce a variety of products or services in significant quantities. Customization is relatively high and volume for any one product or service is low. However, volumes aren't as low as for a project process, which by definition doesn't produce in quantity. The work force and equipment are flexible and handle various tasks. As with a project process, companies choosing a job process often bid for work. Typically, they make products to order and don't produce them ahead of time. The specific needs of the next customer are unknown and the timing of repeat orders from the same customer is unpredictable. Each new order is handled as a single unit - as a job. A job shop process primarily involves the use flexible flow strategy, with resources organized around the process. Most jobs have a different sequence of processing steps.

Batch flow process

Examples of a batch flow process are scheduling air travel, manufacturing garments, furniture manufacturing, making components that feed an assembly line, processing mortgage loans and manufacturing heavy equipment. A batch flow process differs from the job process with respect to volume, variety and quantity. The primary difference is that volumes are higher because the same or similar products or services are provided repeatedly. Another difference is that a narrower range of products or services is provided. Variety is achieved more through an assemble-to-order strategy than the job shop's make-to-order strategy. Some of the components for the final product or service may be produced in advance. A third difference is that production lots or customer groups are handled larger quantities (or batches) than they are with job shop processes. A batch of one product or customer group is processed and then production is switched to the next one. Eventually, the first product or service is produced again batch flow processes have average or moderate volumes, but variety is still too great to warrant dedicating substantial resources to each product or service. The flow pattern is jumbled, with no standard sequence of operations throughout the facility. However, more dominant paths emerge than at a job shop and some segments of the process have a linear flow.

Line flow process

Products created by a line process include automobiles, appliances, personal computers and toys. Services based on a line process are fast-food restaurants and cafeterias. A line flow process lies between the batch and continuous processes, volumes are high and products or services are standardized, which allows resources to be organized around a product or service. Materials move linearly from one operation to the next according to a fixed sequence, with little inventory held between operations. Each operation performs the same process over and over with little variability in the products or services provided. Production orders aren't directly linked to customer orders, as is the case with project and job processes. Manufacturers with line flow processes often follow a make-to-stock strategy, with standard products held in inventory so that they are ready when a customer places an order. This use of a line flow process is sometimes called mass production. However the assemble-to-order strategy and mass customization are other possibilities with line flow processes. Product variety is possible by careful control of the addition of standard options to the main product or service. The pacing of production may be either machine-paced or worker-paced.

Continuous flow process

Examples are petroleum refineries, chemical plants and plants making beer, steel and processed food items. Firms with such facilities are also referred to as the process industry. An electric generation plant represents one of the few continuous processes found in the service sector. A continuous process is the extreme end of high-volume, standardized production with rigid line flows and tightly linked process segments. Its name derives from how materials move through the process. Usually one primary material, such as a liquid, gas, wood fibers, or powder, moves without stopping through the facility. The process often is capital intensive and operated round the clock to maximize utilization and to avoid expensive shutdowns are start-ups.

3. Describe the Scopes and Functions of Operation Management

Ans. Production and operations management concern with the conversion of inputs into outputs, using physical resources, so as to provide the desired utilities to the customer while meeting the other organizational objectives of effectiveness, efficiency and adoptability. It distinguishes itself from other functions such as personnel, marketing, finance etc. by its primary concern for 'conversion by using physical resources'. Following are the activities which are listed under production and operations management functions:

1. Location of facilities
2. Plant layouts and material handling
3. Product design
4. Process design
5. Production and planning control
6. Quality control
7. Materials management
8. Maintenance management

Location of facilities

Location of facilities for operations is a long-term capacity decision which involves a long term commitment about the geographically static factors that affect a business organization. It is an important strategic level decision-making for an organization. It deals with the questions such as 'where our main operations should be based?'

The selection of location is a key-decision as large investment is made in building plant and machinery. An improper location of plant may lead to waste of all the investments made in plant and machinery equipments. Hence, location of plant should be based on the company's expansion plan and policy, diversification plan for the products, changing sources of raw materials and many other factors. The purpose of the location study is to find the optimal location that will results in the greatest advantage to the organization.

Plant layout and material handling

Plant layout refers to the physical arrangement of facilities. It is the configuration of departments, work centres and equipment in the conversion process. The overall objective of the plant layout is to design a physical arrangement that meets the required output quality and quantity most economically.

According to *James Moore, "Plant layout is a plan of an optimum arrangement of facilities including personnel, operating equipment, storage space, material handling equipments and all other supporting services along with the design of best structure to contain all these facilities".*

'Material Handling' refers to the 'moving of materials from the store room to the machine and from one machine to the next during the process of manufacture'. It is also defined as the 'art and science of moving, packing and storing of products in any form'. It is a specialised activity for a modern manufacturing concern, with 50 to 75% of the cost of production. This cost can be reduced by proper section, operation and maintenance of material handling devices. Material handling devices increases the output, improves quality, speeds up the deliveries and decreases the cost of production. Hence, material handling is a prime consideration in the designing new plant and several existing plants.

Product design

Product design deals with conversion of ideas into reality. Every business organization have to design, develop and introduce new products as a survival and growth strategy. Developing the new products and launching them in the market is the biggest challenge faced by the organizations. The entire process of need identification to physical manufactures of product involves three functions: marketing, product development, manufacturing. Product development translates the needs of customers given by marketing into technical specifications and designing the various features into the product to these specifications. Manufacturing has the responsibility of selecting the processes by which the product can be manufactured. Product design and development provides link between marketing, customer needs and expectations and the activities required to manufacture the product.

Process design

Process design is a macroscopic decision-making of an overall process route for converting the raw material into finished goods. These decisions encompass the selection of a process, choice of technology, process flow analysis and layout of the facilities. Hence, the important decisions in process design are to analyse the workflow for converting raw material into finished product and to select the workstation for each included in the workflow.

Production planning and control

Production planning and control can be defined as the process of planning the production in advance, setting the exact route of each item, fixing the starting and finishing dates for each item, to give production orders to shops and to follow up the progress of products according to orders.

The principle of production planning and control lies in the statement 'First Plan Your Work and then Work on Your Plan'. Main functions of production planning and control includes planning, routing, scheduling, dispatching and follow-up.

Planning is deciding in advance what to do, how to do it, when to do it and who is to do it. Planning bridges the gap from where we are, to where we want to go. It makes it possible for things to occur which would not otherwise happen.

Routing may be defined as the selection of path which each part of the product will follow, which being transformed from raw material to finished products. Routing determines the most advantageous path to be followed from department to department and machine to machine till raw material gets its final shape.

Scheduling determines the programme for the operations. Scheduling may be defined as 'the fixation of time and date for each operation' as well as it determines the sequence of operations to be followed.

Dispatching is concerned with the starting the processes. It gives necessary authority so as to start a particular work, which has already been planned under 'Routing' and 'Scheduling'. Therefore, dispatching is 'release of orders and instruction for the starting of production for any item in acceptance with the route sheet and schedule charts'.

The function of **follow-up** is to report daily the progress of work in each shop in a prescribed proforma and to investigate the causes of deviations from the planned performance.

Quality control

Quality control (QC) may be defined as 'a system that is used to maintain a desired level of quality in a product or service'. It is a systematic control of various factors that affect the quality of the product. Quality control aims at prevention of defects at the source, relies on effective feed back system and corrective action procedure.

Quality control can also be defined as 'that industrial management technique by means of which product of uniform acceptable quality is manufactured'. It is the entire collection of activities which ensures that the operation will produce the optimum quality products at minimum cost.

The main objectives of quality control are:

- To improve the companies income by making the production more acceptable to the customers *i.e.,* by providing long life, greater usefulness, maintainability etc.
- To reduce companies cost through reduction of losses due to defects.
- To achieve interchangeability of manufacture in large scale production.
- To produce optimal quality at reduced price.
- To ensure satisfaction of customers with productions or services or high quality level, to build customer goodwill, confidence and reputation of manufacturer.
- To make inspection prompt to ensure quality control.
- To check the variation during manufacturing.

Materials management

Materials management is that aspect of management function which is primarily concerned with the acquisition, control and use of materials needed and flow of goods and services connected with the production process having some predetermined objectives in view.

The main objectives of materials management are:

- To minimize material cost.
- To purchase, receive, transport and store materials efficiently and to reduce the related cost.
- To cut down costs through simplification, standardisation, value analysis, import substitution, etc.
- To trace new sources of supply and to develop cordial relations with them in order to ensure continuous supply at reasonable rates.
- To reduce investment tied in the inventories for use in other productive purposes and to develop high inventory turnover ratios.

4. Differentiate Between Product and Service

Ans. A product is a good. Traditionally, this has meant a physical good, but it can also apply to informational goods, so that a "product" can be software or subscriptions. "Fair use" laws can apply to a product. When selling a product, you are usually selling its features, mainly how they meet a customer's needs. Products can sometimes be rented.

A service is an act, and its receipt of sale is a contract. When selling a service, you are often selling expertise or transfer of labor. For example, in selling software-as-a-service (SAAS), you are selling a reduction in IT support and uptime SLAs, as well as selling features that address a customer's pain points. Services are less transferrable than products and, unless a one-time service, often involve recurring costs.

Products and services can be sold bundled. For example, cruises involve both products (lodging, food) and services (housekeeping, babysitting) etc.

5. With Example explain the role of decision making in production operation function.

Ans. Present in chapter 1.7

6. Explain the scopes of supply chain management and operation management.

Ans. Present in chapter 1.3.2.

1.1 OPERATIONS MANAGEMENT

1. Which of the following functions is not a core function of an organization

   a. The accounting and finance function
   b. The marketing (including sale) function
   c. The operation function
   d. The product or service development function

2. Most operation produce a mixture of both products and services which of the following business is closest to producing 'pure' services?

   a. IT company
   b. Counselor /therapist
   c. Steel company
   d. A restaurant

3. Operations can be classified according to their volume and variety of production as well as the degree of variation and visibility. Which of the following operations would be classified as high volume, low variety?

   a. A front office bank
   b. A family doctor
   c. A carpenter
   d. A fast food restaurant

4. Which of the following activities is not a direct responsibility of operations management?

   a. Developing an operations strategy for the operation
   b. Planning and controlling the operations
   c. Determining the exact mix of products and services that customers will want
   d. Designing the operations products, services and process

5. **Operations can be classified according to the degree of variations in demand and visibility of the operations as well as their volume and variety of production which of the following operations would be classified as high variation and high visibility?**
   a. A front office staff
   b. A family doctor
   c. A carpenter
   d. A fast food restaurant
6. **Which of the following would not be normally be considered a general characteristics of a service?**
   a. Production and consumption are simultaneous
   b. Low contact service can often be made more efficient than high contract
   c. Production and consumption can always be spatially separated
   d. Many services involve both tangible and intangible outputs
   e. Production and sales cannot easily be separated functionally
7. **Which of the following would not be normally considered as a key feature of operations management?**
   a. Most new technology is implemented
   b. World class operations can give an organization competitive advantage
   c. Operations researches mathematical techniques for optimizing process
   d. Operations is the part of an organization which creates wealth through the management of the transformation process
   e. Operations is the area of a business where most people
8. **Which of the following is the least likely decision to be made by operations managers?**
   a. Selecting the locations and layout of a facility
   b. Designing and improving the jobs of the workspace
   c. How to use quality techniques to reduce waste
   d. Deciding which market areas to manufacture products for
   e. How much capacity is required to balance demand

9. Operations management is applicable

a. Mostly to the service sector
b. To services exclusively
c. Mostly to the manufacturing sector
d. To the manufacturing and service sectors
e. To the manufacturing sector exclusively

10. The field of operations management is shaped by advances in which of the following fields?

a. Chemistry and physics
b. Industrial engineering and management science
c. Biology and anatomy
d. Information science
e. All of the above

11. The five element in the management process are

a. Plan, direct, update, lead and surprise
b. Accounting /finance, marketing, operations and management
c. Organize, plan, control, staff and manage
d. Plan, organize, staff, lead and control
e. Plan, lead, organize, manage and control

12. The responsibilities of the operations manager include

a. Planning, organizing, staffing, procuring and reviewing
b. Forecasting, designing, planning, organizing and controlling
c. Forecasting, designing, operating, procuring and reviewing
d. Planning, organizing, staffing, leading and controlling
e. Designing and operating

13. Which of the following is not an element of management process

a. Pricing
b. Staffing
c. Planning
d. Controlling
e. Leading

14. Which of the following illustrate an activity that does not add value?

a. Training employees

b. Ordering parts from a supplier

c. Making a part

d. Accumulating parts in front of the next work centre

15. Which of the following statements regarding a pull system is true?

a. Large lots are pulled from upstream stations

b. Work is pulled to the downstream work stations before it is actually needed

c. Manufacturing cycle time is increased

d. Problems become more obvious

Answers

1. a; **2.** b; **3.** d; **4.** c; **5.** b; **6.** c; **7.** d; **8.** d; **9.** c; **10.** b; **11.** c; **12.** D; **13.** a; **14.** d; **15.** d

2

Operations Planning

2.1 DEMAND FORECASTING

Defination

Forecasting defined

Forecasting means predicting for future. Forecasting is a technique of anticipating future problems and estimating events for products and services and the resources necessary to produce these outputs.

2.1.1 Demand Forecasting Is Needed For

- New facility planning
- Production planning
- Scheduling of activities for optimum utilization of plant capacity
- To prepare material requirement planning
- Forcasting is going to provide a future trend for product design and development
- Work force scheduling
- Financial planning

2.1.2 Types of Forecasts

Technological forecasts

Technology forecast deals with certain characteristics like technical performance, rate of technological advances. It is a prediction of the future characteristics of useful machines, products, process, procedures or techniques. TIFAC (Technology Information, Forecasting and Assessment Council) which promotes action oriented studies and forecasting in seleced areas.

Economic forecasts

Govt. organizations and other agencies are predicting future estimates on the general business. For example: predicting future tax revenues, business growth, level of employment etc.

Demand forecasts

Predicting level of demand for products and service in a business environment is caled as demand forecast.

2.1.3 Objectives of Demand Forecasting

- Short range objectives of demand forecasting
- Formulation of production strategy and policy
- Formulation of pricing policy
- Planning and control of sales
- Financial planning
- Medium or long-range objectives
- Long-range planning for production capacity
- Labour requirements (Employment levels)
- Restructuring the capital structure

2.1.4 Steps in the Forecasting Process

The seven basic steps

- Determine the purpose (objectives) of the forecast
- Select the items for which forecasts are needed
- Determine the time horizon for the forecast
- Select the forecasting model (method or technique)
- Gather and analyse the data needed for the forecast

- Prepare the forecast
- Monitor the forecast

2.1.5 Forecasting Techniques

Qualitative methods consist mainly of subjective inputs, often of non-numerical description.

Jury of administrative opinion method involves taking judgment of a small group of high-level managers and results in a group estimate of demand.

Sales force composite method is based on estimate of expected sales by sales persons.

Market research method or consumer survey method determines consumer interest in a product or service by means of a consumer survey.

Delphi method is a procedure for acquiring informed judgments and opinions from knowledgeable individuals using a series of questionnaires to develop a consensus forecast about what will occur in the future. It is a judge mental method which uses a group process that allows experts to make forecasts. It was developed at the Rand Corporation shortly after world war II to forecast the impact of a hypothetical nuclear attack on the United States. Although the delphi method has been used for a variety of applications, forecasting has been one of its primary uses. It has been especially useful for forecasting technological change and advances. Quantitative methods IT involve either projection of historical data or the development of association models which attempt to use causal variables to arrive at the forecasts. Fig. 2.1 shows forcasting qualitative and quantitative method, where delphi method, market survey are the mostly used practices by many industries. In Fig. 2.1 some common quantitative methods are explained *i.e.,* hand fitting, time series, least square and time series model.

Time series models

Use a series of past data to make a forecast for the future. Time series is a time-ordered sequence of observations taken at regular intervals over a period of time.

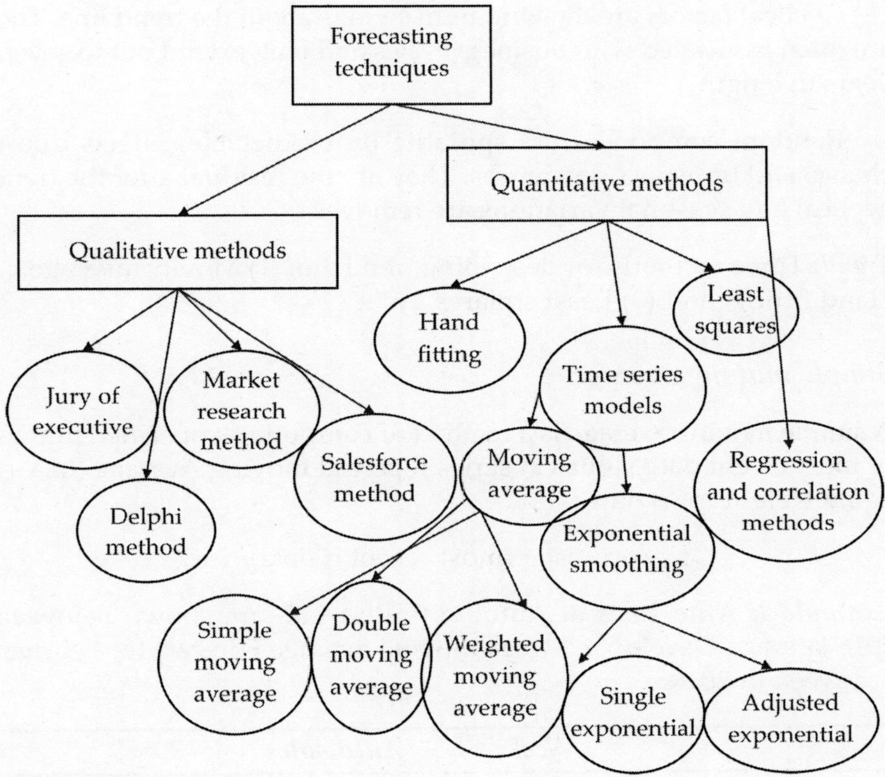

Fig. 2.1: Forcasting technique (Source Google)

Yc = T. S. C. R multiplicative model

Yc = T + S + C + R additive model

Where T is Trend, S is Seasonal, C is Cyclical and R is Random components of a series.

Trend is a gradual long-term directional movement in the data (growth or decline).

Seasonal effects are similar variations occurring during corresponding periods, *e.g.*, December retail sales. Seasonal can be quarterly, monthly, weekly, daily, or even hourly indexes.

Cyclical factors are the long-term swings about the trend line. They are often associated with business cycles and may extend out to several years in length.

Random component are sporadic (unpredictable) effects due to chance and unusual occurrences. They are the residual after the trend, cyclical and seasonal variations are removed.

Trend: Three methods for describing trend are: (1) Moving average, (2) Hand fitting, and (3) Least squares.

Simple moving average

A simple moving average is a method of computing a specified number of most recent data values in series.n period moving Average (MA-n): equal weight for n data

Forecast = (most recent n data)/n

Example 1: Auto sales at Autolite (India) Ltd. are shown below for 2016 January. Develop a 3-week moving average Forecast for February 3rd week in 2016.

Week	*Auto sales*
Jan 1	8
2	10
3	9
4	11
Feb 1	10
2	13
3	–

Answer: Moving average $= \dfrac{\sum \text{demand in previous n periods}}{\text{n}}$

Week	*Auto sales*	*Three-week average*	*Moving*	*Forecast (Ft)*
Jan 1	8			
2	10			
3	9			
4	11	(8 + 9 + 10) / 3 = 9		
Feb 1	10	(10 + 9 + 11) / 3 = 10		9
2	13	(9 + 11 + 10) / 3 = 10		10
3	-	(11 + 10 + 13) / 3 = 11	1/3	10 (Ans)

Weighted moving average

n Period weighted moving average (WMA-n):
flexible weight assignment

Forecast = (weight * most recent n data) / (weight)

Example 2: Autolite (India) Ltd's decides to forecast auto sales by weighting the three weeks the example.1.

Weights applied	*Period*
3	Last week
2	Two weeks ago
1	Three weeks ago
6	Total

Autolite (India)

$$\text{Weighted moving average} = \frac{\sum \text{(weight for period n)(demand in period n)}}{\sum \text{weights}}$$

Week	*Auto sales*	*Three-week moving average*	*Forecast (Ft)*
Jan 1	8		
2	10		
3	9		
4	11	[(3*9) + (2*10) + (1*8)] / 6 = 55/6	
Feb 1	10	[(3*11) + (2*9) + (1*10)] / 6 = 61/6	55/6
2	13	[(3*10) + (2*11) + (1*9)] / 6 = 61/6	61/6
3	-	[(3*13) + (2*10) + (1*11)] / 6 = 70/3	61/6(Ans)

Exponential smoothing

Exponential smoothening is a moving-average forecasting technique that weighting of past actual data points in an exponential manner.

Forecast = a (Previous actual sales) + (1–a) Previous forecast

$$\text{Forecast} = \alpha A_{t-1} + \alpha(1-\alpha)\ A_{t-2} + \alpha(1-\alpha)\text{^}2\ A_{tt-3} + \alpha(1-\alpha)\text{^}3\ A_{t-4} + \text{——}$$

The forecast is a weighted average of the actual sales from the previous period and the forecast from the previous period. It is the weight applied to the actual sales for the previous period. (1–a) is the weight applied to the forecast for the previous period. Valid values for a range from 0 to 1, and usually fall between 0.1 and 0.4. The sum of the weights is 1.00. a+ (1–a) = 1

You should assign a value for the smoothing constant, a. If you do not assign values for the smoothing constant, the system calculates an assumed value based upon the number of periods of sales history specified in the processing option 11a.

Forecast specifications

a = The smoothing constant used in calculating the smoothed average for the general level or magnitude of sales. Valid values for a range from 0 to 1.

n = The range of sales history data to include in the calculations. Generally one year of sales history data is sufficient to estimate the general level of sales. For this example, a small value for n (n = 3) was chosen in order to reduce the manual calculations required to verify the results. Exponential smoothing can generate a forecast based on as little as one historical data point, so that most recent data carry more weight in the moving average. With simple Exponential smoothening, the forecast F_t is made up of the last period forecast F_{t-1} plus a portion, α, of the difference between the last periods actual demand D_{t-1} and last period forecast F_{t-1}.

$$F_t = F_{t-1} + \alpha\ (D_{t-1} - F_{t-1})$$

α varies from 0.1 to 0.3.

Example 3: A firm uses simple exponential smoothing with $\alpha = 0.2$ to forecast demand. The forecast for the week of January 1 was 400 units whereas the actual demand turned out to be 450 units. Calculate the demand forecast for the February 3rd week, when subsequent demands are 460,465 434,420,498 and 462 units respectively.

Ans. $F_t = F_{t-1} + \alpha\ (D_{t-1} - F_{t-1})$

Fjan 2 = 400 + 0.2(450 – 400) = 410 units

Week	*Dt*	*Ft*
Jan 1	450	Fjan2 = 400 + 0.2(450–400) = 410 units
2	460	Fjan3 = 410 + 0.2(460–400) = 420 units
3	465	429
4	434	430
Feb 1	420	428
2	498	442
3	462	446 Ans.

Adjusted exponential smoothing

Adjusted exponential smoothing models have all the features of simple exponential smoothing models, plus they project into the future (for example, to time period t + 1) by adding a trend correction increment, T_t, to the present period smoothed average, $F_t(F_t + 1) = (F_t + T_t)$

The components of a trend-adjusted forecast that utilizes a second smoothing coefficient β. The β value determines the extent to which the trend adjustment relies on the latest difference in forecast amounts $(F_t - F_{t-1})$ *versus* the previous trend T_{t-1}.

$$F_t = \alpha\, D_{t-1} + (1-\alpha)(F_{t-1} + T_{t-1})$$

$$T_t = \beta\,(F_t - F_{t-1}) + (1-\beta)\,T_{t-1}$$

Example 4: Compute the adjusted exponental forcast for the first week of March for a firm with the following data. Assume the forcast for the first week of January F0=600. $T_0 = 0$. $\alpha = 0.1$, $\beta = 0.2$

	January				*February*			
Week	1	2	3	4	1	2	3	4
Demand	650	600	550	650	625	675	700	710

Ans. $F_t = \alpha\, D_{t-1} + (1-\alpha)\,(F_{t-1} + T_{t-1}) = 0.1 * 650 + (1-0.1)\,(600+0) = 605$ (this is F_{t-1} for Jan 2 week).

$$Tt = \beta\,(F_t - F_{t-1}) + (1-\beta)\,T_{t-1} = 0.2\,(605-600) + 0.8{*}0 = 1.00$$

$$F_{t+1} = F_t + T_t = 605 + 1 = 606$$

Week	F_{t-1}	D_{t-1}	F_t	T_t	F_{t+1}
Jan 1	600	650	605	1	606
2	605	600	605.40	0.880	606.38
3	605.40	550	600.65	-0.246	600.40
4	600.65	650	605.36	0.742	606.10
Feb 1	605.36	625	607.99	1.120	609.1
2	607.99	675	615.70	2.440	618.14
3	615.70	700	626.33	4.080	630.41
4	626.33	710	738.37	5.670	644.04 Ans.

Simple regression expresses the relationship between a dependent variable Y and a independent variable X in terms of the slope and intercept of the line of best fit relating the two variables. **Fig. 2.2** shows Linear Regression model where trend line $y = a + bx$ to fit the past data the best. (minimizing mean squared errors) $Y_i = a + bX_i$

Y = Dependent variable X = Independent variable

a = Y-intercept of the line b = Slope of the line

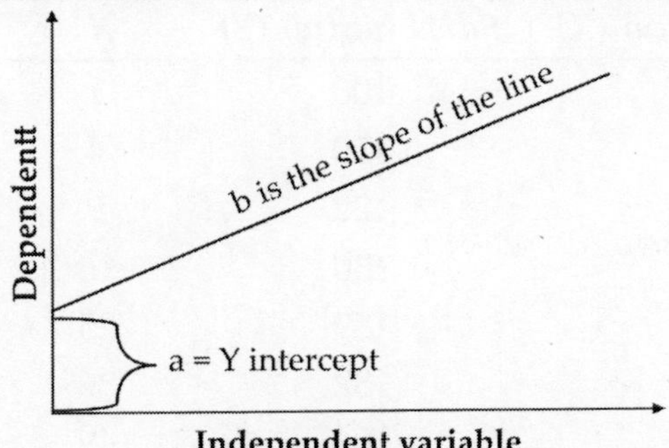

Fig. 2.2 Linear regresion model

$$\text{best slope: } b = \frac{\sum xy - n\overline{x}\overline{y}}{\sum x^2 - n\overline{x}^2}$$

$$\text{best intercept: } a = \overline{y} - b\overline{x}$$

where $\overline{x}$ and $\overline{y}$ are averages of x's and y's

***Example 5*:** Use the sales data given below to determine: (a) The least squares trend line, and (b) The predicted value for 2018 sales.

Year	*Sales (units)*
2011	100
2012	110
2013	122
2014	130
2015	139
2016	152
2017	164

Ans. To minimize computations, transform the value of x (time) to simpler numbers. In this case, designate year 2011 as year 1, 2012 as year 2, etc.

Year	*Time period (X)*	*Sales (units) (Y)*	X^2	*XY*
2011	1	100	1	100
2012	2	110	4	220
2013	3	122	9	366
2014	4	130	16	520
2015	5	139	25	695
2016	6	152	36	912
2017	7	164	49	1148
	S X = 28	S Y =917	S X^2=140	S XY = 3961

$$\bar{x} = \frac{\sum x}{n} = \frac{28}{7} = 4$$

$$\bar{y} = \frac{\sum y}{n} = \frac{917}{7} = 131$$

$$b = \frac{\sum xy - n\bar{x}\bar{y}}{\sum x^2 - n\bar{x}^2} = \frac{3961-(7)(4)(131)}{140-(7)(4^2)} = \frac{293}{28} = 10.46$$

$$a = \bar{y} - b\bar{x} = 131 - (10.46 \times 4) = 89.16$$

Therefore, the least squares trend equation is:

$= a + bx = 89.16 + 10.46x$

To project demand in 2018, we denote the year 2018 as $x = 8$ and:

Sales in 2018 = 89.16 + 10.46 * 8 = 172.84 *Ans.*

Fig. 2.3 shows positive,negative and zero correlation by plotting graph, where height is taken in *y* axis and weight is taken on *x* axis. Simple correlation expresses the degree or closeness of the relationship between two variables in terms of a correlation coefficient that provides an indirect measure of the variability of points from the line of best fit. Neither regression nor correlation gives proof of a cause-effect relationship.

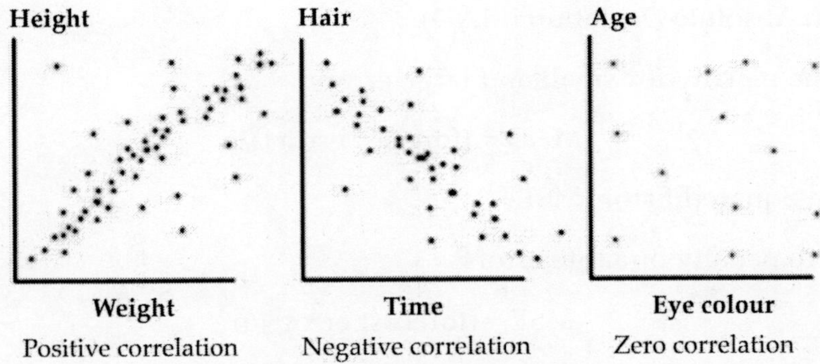

Fig. 2.3: Positive, negative and zero correlation

Qualitative method and quantitative method both are practised in industry.

2.1.5.1 Diference between qualitative and quantitative forecasting

Qualitative technique	*Quantitative techniques*
This technique is usefull when situation is fuzzy	It is used in steady situations
For small data also it can be resolved	Large no of past data is necesary
Prediction can be done for new products	Prediction can be done for existing products
Theoretical methods required.	Involves mathematical techniques
Example: forecasting newly introduced	*Example:* Sales of color TVs online sales

2.1.6 Choosing a Forecasting Method

All criteria are a function of the forecast error

$$\text{Forecast error} = \text{Actual realization (Y)} - \text{forecast (F)}$$

Bias – measures the direction of forecast

$$\text{Bias} = (\Sigma\text{forecast error})/n$$

Mean Absolute Deviation (MAD)

– same penalty for small and large errors

MAD = (forecast error I)/n

Mean Squared Error (MSE)

– more penalty on large errors

$$MSE = (\text{forecast error}^2)/n$$

Mean Absolute Percent Error (MAPE)

– relative error, scale independent

MAPE = (forecast error I/Actual Data)/n

2.1 PRACTICE QUESTIONS

Example 6: A company records indicate that monthly sales for a seven-month period are as follows:

Month	*Sales (000, unit)*
Feb	19
Mar	18
Apr	15
May	20
Jun	18
July	22
Aug	20

(a) Plot the monthly data as can be seen in the table above.

(b) Forecast the monthly sales using linear trend equation,

(c) A five-month moving average and exponential smoothing technique? Assume that smoothing constant and March forecast value are 0.20 and 19 respectively.

(d) The naive approach

(e) A weight average method conducting 0.60 for August, 0.30 for July, and 0.10 for June.

(f) Which method seems least appropriate? Why?

Ans.

(b) 19

(c) 19.26

(d) It may be around 20 (19.26)

(e) WA = 0.60 (20) + 0.30 (22) + 0.10 (18) = 20.4

(f) Probably trend method because the data appear to vary around Y = 16.86 + 0.50(4) =18.86.

The instant paper clip office supply company sells and delivers office supplies to companies, schools and agencies within a 50-mile radius of its warehouse. The office supply business is competitive, and the ability to deliver orders promptly is a big factor in getting new customers and maintaining old ones. (office typically order not when they run low on supplies, but when they completely run out. As a result, they need their orders immediately). The manager of the company wants to be certain that enough drivers and vehicles are available to deliver orders promptly and that they have adequate inventory in stock. Therefore, the manager wants to be able to forecast the demand for deliveries during the next month. From the records of previous orders, management has accumulated the following data for the past 10 months:

Month	Jan.	Feb.	Mar.	Apr.	May	Jun.	Jul.	Aug.	Sep.	Oct.
Orders	120	90	100	75	110	50	75	130	110	90

a. Compute the monthly demand forecast for February through November using the naive method.

b. Compute the monthly demand forecast for April through November using a 3-month moving average.

c. Compute the monthly demand forecast for June through November using a 5-month moving average.

d. Compute the monthly demand forecast for April through November using a 3-month weighted moving average. Use weights of 0.5, 0.33, and 0.17, with the heavier weights on the more recent months.

e. Compute the mean absolute deviation for June through October for each of the methods used. Which method would you use to forecast demand for November?

Solution

a. The naive method simply uses the demand for the current month as the forecast for the next month: $F_{t+1} = D_t$. So for February we would have $F_{Feb.} = D_{Jan.} = 120$. Similarly, $F_{Nov.} = D_{Oct.} = 90$. See the table below for the other months.

b. For a simple 3-month moving average, we take the average of the previous three months' demand as our forecast for next month:

$$F_{t+1} = \frac{{}^{D}t + {}^{D}t+1 + {}^{D}t+2}{3}$$

Since we need at least three months to compute the average, and we only have data beginning in January, April is the earliest month for which we can compute the forecast:

$$F_{Apr} = \frac{{}^{D}Mar. + {}^{D}Feb. + {}^{D}Jan.}{3} = \frac{100+90+120}{3} = 103.3$$

The forecasts for the other months are reported in the table below.

c. The 5-month moving average is similar to the 3-month moving average, except now we take the average of the previous five months' demand. We start with the forecast for June (since we need at least five months' worth of previous demand):

$$F_{Jun.} = \frac{{}^{D}May + {}^{D}Apr. + {}^{D}Mar. + {}^{D}Feb. + {}^{D}Jan.}{5}$$

$$= \frac{110+75+100+90+120}{5} = 99.0$$

The forecasts for the remaining months are computed similarly, 5 and the values are reported in the table below.

d. Simple moving averages (like parts b and c above) place an equal weight on all of previous months. A weighted moving average allows us to put more weight on the more recent data. For a weighted 3-month moving average we have $F_{t+1} = w_1D_t + w_2D_{t-1} + w_3D_{t-2}$ (Note that the weights should add up to 1). Using the weights specified in the question, the forecast for April is computed as $F_{Apr.} = 0.5(D_{Mar.}) + 0.33(D_{Feb.}) + 0.17(D_{Jan.}) = 0.5(100) + 0.33(90) + 0.17(120) = 100.1$. Forecasts for May through November are reported in the table below.

		Forecast			
Month	*Orders*	*Naive method*	*3-Month moving avg.*	*5-Month moving avg.*	*3-Month weighted avg.*
Jan.	120	—	—	—	—
Feb.	90	120	—	—	—
Mar.	100	90	—	—	—
Apr.	75	100	103.3	—	100.1
May	110	75	88.3	—	85.8
Jun.	50	110	95.0	99.0	96.8
Jul.	75	50	78.3	85.0	74.1
Aug.	130	75	78.3	82.0	72.7
Sep.	110	130	85.0	88.0	98.3
Oct.	90	110	105.0	95.0	110.7
Nov.	?	90	110.0	91.0	103.4

e. Mean absolute deviation is one measure of how close the forecast is to the actual demand. Recall that forecast error is simply $E_t = D_t - F_t$, and that the absolute deviation is simply the absolute value of error: $|E_t|$. For example, the error for the Naive Method for June is $E_{Jun.} = D_{Jun.} - F_{Jun.} = 50 - 110 = -60$. To compute the mean absolute deviation, take the absolute value of each error term, add them up, and divide by the number of terms: MAD = $|Et|$ (Note: You must take the absolute value of n each error term before adding them up!). In this case, we compute the mean over five months. The error and MAD for the months June through October are reported below. In general, the forecast accuracy increases as more information is incorporated into the forecast.

		Error ($E_t = D_t - F_t$)			
Month	*Orders*	*Naive method*	*3-Month moving avg.*	*5-Month moving avg.*	*3-Month weighted avg.*
Jun.	50	–60	–45.0	–49.0	–46.8
Jul.	75	25	–3.3	–10.0	0.9
Aug.	130	55	51.7	48.0	57.3
Sep.	110	–20	25.0	22.0	11.8
Oct.	90	–20	–15.0	–5.0	–20.7
	MAD	36.0	28.0	26.8	27.5

f. PM Computer Services assembles customized personal computers from generic parts. Formed and operated by part-time umass lowell students Paulette Tyler and Maureen Becker, the company has had steady growth since it started. The company assembles computers mostly at night, using part-time students. Paulette and Maureen purchase generic computer parts in volume at a discount from a variety of sources whenever they see a good deal. Thus, they need a good forecast of demand for their computers so that they will know how many parts to purchase and stock. They have compiled demand data for the last 12 months as reported below.

Period	*Month*	*Demand*	*Period*	*Month*	*Demand*
1	January	37	7	July	43
2	February	40	8	August	47
3	March	41	9	September	56
4	April	37	10	October	52
5	May	45	11	November	55
6	June	50	12	December	54

2

a. Use exponential smoothing with smoothing parameter $\alpha = 0.3$ to compute the demand forecast for January (Period 13).

b. Use exponential smoothing with smoothing parameter $\alpha = 0.5$ to compute the demand forecast for January (Period 13).

c. Paulette believes that there is an upward trend in the demand. Use trend-adjusted exponential smoothing with smoothing parameter $\alpha = 0.5$ and trend parameter $\beta = 0.3$ to compute the demand forecast for January (Period 13).

d. Compute the mean squared error for each of the methods used.

Solution

a. The formula for exponential smoothing is: $F_{t+1} = F_t + \alpha(D_t - F_t)$. To determine the forecast for January, F_{13}, we need to know the forecast for December, F_{12}. This, in turn, requires us to know the forecast for November, F_{11}. So we need to go all the way back to the beginning and compute the forecast for each month. For period 2, we have $F_2 = F_1 + \alpha(D_1 - F_1)$. But how do we get the forecast for period 1? There are several ways to approach this, but we'll just use the demand for period 1 as both demand and forecast for period 1. Now we can write $F_2 = F_1 + \alpha(D_1 - F_1) = 37 + 0.3(37 - 37) = 37$. For period 3 we have $F_3 = F_2 + \alpha(D_2 - F_2) = 37 + 0.3(40 - 37) = 37.9$. The forecasts for the other months are show in the table below. For period 13 we have $F_{13} = F_{12} + \alpha(D_{12} - F_{12}) = 50.85 + 0.3(54 - 50.85) = 51.79$.

b. For $\alpha = 0.5$ we follow the same exact procedure as we did in part a. See the table below for the forecast values.

c. Incorporating a trend simply requires us to include a bit more information. The formula is: $F_{t+1} = A_t + T_t$ where $A_t = \alpha D_t + (1 - \alpha)(A_{t-1} + T_{t-1})$ and $T_t = \beta(A_t - A_{t-1}) + (1 - b)T_{t-1}$. Once again we need to go back to the beginning in order to find the necessary values to plug into the formula and once again we need to make some assumptions about our initial values. For period 2, we have $F_2 = A_1 + T_1$, so to get the process started, let $A_0 = 37$ and $T_0 = 0$. We can now compute A_1 and T_1 as follows: $A_1 = \alpha D_1 + (1 - \alpha)(A_0 + T_0) = 0.5(37) + (1 - 0.5)(37 + 0) = 37$, and $T_1 = \beta(A_1 - A_0) + (1 - b)T_0 = 0.3(37 - 37) + (1 - 0.3)(0) = 0$. Therefore, the forecast for period 2 is $F_2 = A_1 + T_1 = 37 + 0 = 37$. For period 3, we first compute A_2 and T_2 as follows: $A_2 = \alpha D_2 + (1 - \alpha)(A_1 + T_1) = 0.5(40) + (1 - 0.5)(37 + 0) = 38.5$, and $T_2 = \beta(A_2 - A_1) + (1 - \beta)T_1 = 0.3(38.5 - 37) + (1 - 0.3)(0) = 0.45$. The forecast for period 3 is $F_3 = A_2 + T_2 = 38.5 + 0.45 = 38.95$. The forecasts for the remaining months are reported in the table below.

Period	Month	Demand	Expon. smooth. α = 0.3	Expon. smooth. α = 0.5	Trend- smooth. A_t	adjusted (α = 0.5, β = 0.3) T_t	Expon. F_t
1	Jan.	37	37.00	37.00	37.00	0.00	37.00
2	Feb.	40	37.00	37.00	38.50	0.45	37.00
3	Mar.	41	37.90	38.50	39.98	0.76	38.95
4	Apr.	37	38.83	39.75	38.87	0.20	40.73
5	May	45	38.28	38.38	42.03	1.09	39.06
6	Jun.	50	40.30	41.69	46.56	2.12	43.12
7	Jul.	43	43.21	45.84	45.84	1.27	48.68
8	Aug.	47	43.15	44.42	47.05	1.25	47.11
9	Sep.	56	44.30	45.71	52.15	2.41	48.31
10	Oct.	52	47.81	50.86	53.28	2.02	54.56
11	Nov.	55	49.07	51.43	55.15	1.98	55.30
12	Dec.	54	50.85	53.21	55.56	1.51	57.13
13	Jan.	?	51.79	53.61	57.07		

3

d. To compute the mean square error, first compute the error for each period: $E_t = D_t - F_t$. Take that E^2 number and square it, then take the average over all periods: MSE = ᵗ (Note: you must square

Month	Demand	Expon. E_t	Smooth. α = 0.3 E_t^2	Expon. E_t	Smooth. α = 0.5 E_t^2	Trend- α = 0.5, E_t	Adj. β = 0.3 E_t^2
Jan.	37	0.00	0.00	0.00	0.00	0.00	0.00
Feb.	40	3.00	9.00	3.00	9.00	3.00	9.00
Mar.	41	3.10	9.61	2.50	6.25	2.05	4.20
Apr.	37	–1.83	3.35	–2.75	7.56	–3.73	13.93
May	45	6.72	45.14	6.63	43.89	5.94	35.24
Jun.	50	9.70	94.15	8.31	69.10	6.88	47.33
Jul.	43	–0.21	0.04	–2.84	8.09	–5.68	32.26
Aug.	47	3.85	14.86	2.58	6.65	–0.11	0.01
Sep.	56	11.70	136.85	10.29	105.86	7.69	59.20
Oct.	52	4.19	17.55	1.14	1.31	–2.56	6.55
Nov.	55	5.93	35.19	3.57	12.76	–0.30	0.09
Dec.	54	3.15	9.94	0.79	0.62	–3.13	9.78
		MSE	31.31		22.59		18.13

n the error terms before adding them up!). Take the exponential smoothing method with a = 0.3, for example. In the month of April, the error is $E_{Apr.} = D_{Apr.} - F_{Apr.} = 37 - 38.83 = -1.83$. We square this value, add it to the other squared error terms and divide by 12 to get the mean. The error, squared error and MSE for each of the methods are reported below. The trend-adjusted forecast, which incorporates the most information, has the highest accuracy (lowest MSE).

Forecasting formulas

Simple moving average	Weighted moving average
$F_{t+1} = \frac{D_t + D_{t+1} + D_{t+2} + \dots + D_{t-n+1}}{n}$	$F_{t+1} = w_1 D_t + w_2 D_{t-1} + \dots + w_n D_{t-n+1}$
Exponential smoothing	**Trend-adjusted exponential smoothing**
$F_{t+1} = \alpha D_t + (1 - \alpha) F_t$ $= F_t + \alpha (D_t - F_t)$	$F_{t+1} = A_t + T_t$ where $A_t = \alpha D_t + (1 - \alpha)(A_{t-1} + T_{t-1})$ and $T_t = \beta (A_t - A_{t-1}) + (1 - b) T_{t-1}$

Error	Mean squared error	Mean absolute deviation
$E_t = D_t - F_t$	$MSE = \frac{E_t^2}{n}$	$MAD = \frac{\lvert E_t \rvert}{n}$

2.1.7. What is Time Series Analysis Forecasting

Ans. A time series is a collection of data recorded over a period of time—weekly, monthly, quarterly, or yearly. There are four components to a time series: the trend, the cyclical variation, the seasonal variation and the irregular variation.

Secular Trend: The long-term trends of sales, employment, stock prices and other business and economic series follow various patterns. Some move steadily upward, others decline and still others stay the same over time.

Cyclical Variation: The second component of a time series is cyclical variation. A typical business cycle consists of a period of prosperity followed by periods of recession, depression and then recovery with no fixed duration of the cycle. There are sizable fluctuations unfolding over more than one year in time above and below the secular trend. In a recession, for example, employment, production, the SandP/TSX composite index and many other business and economic series are below the long-term trend lines. Conversely, in periods of prosperity they are above their long-term trend lines.

Seasonal Variation: The third component of a time series is the seasonal component. Many sales, production and other series fluctuate with the seasons. The unit of time reported is either quarterly or monthly. Almost all businesses tend to have recurring seasonal patterns. Men's and boys' clothing, for example, have extremely high sales just prior to christmas and relatively low sales just after christmas and during the summer. Toy sales is another example with an extreme seasonal pattern.

Irregular Variation: Many analysts prefer to subdivide the irregular variation into episodic and residual variations. Episodic fluctuations are unpredictable, but they can be identified. The initial impact on the economy of a major strike or a war can be identified, but a strike or war cannot be predicted. After the episodic fluctuations have been

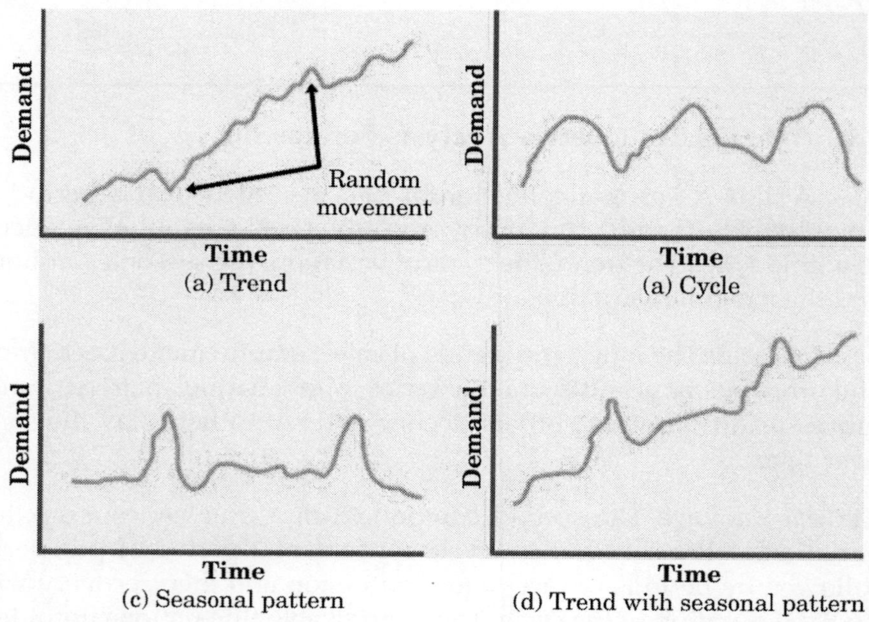

Fig. 2.4: Trends in forcasting

removed, the remaining variation is called the residual variation. The residual fluctuations, often called chance fluctuations, are unpredictable and they cannot be identified. Of course, neither episodic nor residual variation can be projected into the future. Fig. 2.4 shows trends in forcasting. 2.4 a shows graph between demand and time trend. Fig. 2.4 a, b, c, d shows cyclic, seasonal pattern with and without trend.

2.2 MATERIAL MANAGEMENT

2.2.1. Why Materials Management?

- Materials is one of the five M's (Men, Material, Money, Machine and Methods) of an industrial organization.
- Materials offer considerable scope for improving profit.
- Materials form an important form of current assets in any organization.
- Value addition is the margin between the raw material value and finished goods value.
- Suppliers and materials management account for more than 50 percent of total value.
- Quality of the finished product depends on quality of materials used.
- Conservation of materials and their availability for posterity is one of the planks of social responsibility of business.
- Exploring new sources of supply is a challenge for material management executives.

2.2.2 Materials Management

- Material management involves organizing and coordinating all management functions that are responsible for every aspect of materials, storage and transformation.
- Buying, storage and movement of material are the three basic objectives of materials management.
- Optimum investment in inventory is the prime objective of materials management.

- Development of personnel is very important for long-term growth of a firm.
- Engineering groups are primarily responsible for standards of specifications.

2.2.3 Importance of Materials Management

- Lower prices for materials and equipment
- Faster inventory turnover
- Continuity of supply
- Reduced lead time
- Reduced transportation costs
- Less duplication of efforts
- Elimination of buck-passing
- Reduced materials obsolescence
- Improved supplier relationships and better records and information
- Better interdepartmental cooperation
- Personnel development

2.2.4 Functions of Materials Management

- Materials planning and programming
- Raw material purchase
- Receiving, store keeping and warehousing
- Issuing of material
- Inventory control
- Value engineering
- Transportation of materials
- Vendor development
- Vendor rating
- Disposal of scrap and surpluses

2.2.5 Objectives

- Primary Objectives

- Buying the best item at the lowest cost
- Reduction in inventory cost and high inventory turnover
- Maintaining the flow of production
- Maintaining the consistency of quality
- Optimization of acquisition and possession, resulting in lower cost
- Cordial relationship with suppliers
- Maintaining good records
- Contribution towards competitiveness
- Personnel development
- Secondary objectives
- Promotion of standardization with suppliers
- Development of reciprocal relations with customers
- Committees to decide on economic make–or- buy decisions
- Development of inter departmental relationships

2.2.6 Material Planning and Control

Material planning is a scientific technique of determining in advance the requirements of raw materials, ancillary parts and components, spares etc. as directed by the production programme. It is a subsystem in the overall planning activity. There are many factors, which influence the activity of material planning. These factors can be classified as macro and micro systems.

Macro factors: Some of the micro factors which affect material planning, are price trends, business cycles govt. import policy etc.

Micro factors: Some of the micro factors that affect material planning are plant capacity utilization, rejection rates, lead times, inventory levels, working capital, delegation of powers and communication.

2.2.7 Inventory Control

Inventory control: Is the supervision of supply, storage and accessibility of items in order to ensure an adequate supply without excessive oversupply.

It can also be referred as internal control - an accounting procedure or system designed to promote efficiency or assure the implementation of a policy or safeguard assets or avoid fraud and error etc.

2.2.8 Objectives of Inventory Control

- To ensure adequate supply of products to customer and avoid shortages as far as possible.
- To make sure that the financial investment in inventories is minimum (*i.e.,* to see that the working capital is blocked to the minimum possible extent).
- Efficient purchasing, storing, consumption and accounting for materials is an important objective.
- To maintain timely record of inventories of all the items and to maintain the stock within the desired limits.
- To ensure timely action for replenishment.
- To provide a reserve stock for variations in lead times of delivery of materials.
- To provide a scientific base for both short-term and long-term planning of materials.

2.2.9 Inventory Costs

Inventory costs includes ordering cost plus carrying costs.

Ordering cost

Cost of procurement and inbound logistics costs form a part of ordering cost. Ordering cost is dependant and varies based on two factors - The cost of ordering excess and the cost of ordering too less.

Both these factors move in opposite directions to each other. Ordering excess quantity will result in carrying cost of inventory. Where as ordering less will result in increase of replenishment cost and ordering costs.

These two above costs together are called total stocking cost. If you plot the order quantity *vs* the TSC, you will see the graph declining gradually until a certain point after which with every increase in quantity the TSC will proportionately show an increase.

This functional analysis and cost implications form the basis of determining the inventory procurement decision by answering the two basic fundamental questions - how much to order and when to order.

How much to order is determined by arriving at the economic order quantity or EOQ.

Carrying cost

Inventory storage and maintenance involves various types of costs namely:

- Inventory storage cost
- Cost of capital
- Inventory carrying involves inventory storage and management either using in house facilities or external warehouses owned and managed by third party vendors. In both cases, inventory management and process involves extensive use of building.

Purchase costs

This is what is paid to the supplier/seller by the buyer in exchange of the product.

Inventory is usually a large investment for many firms. It is normally the second largest item in the balance sheet among the assets after fixed assets. Thus, inventory should only be held if the benefits (service to customers) exceeds the inventory costs. Also in inventory modeling, purchase costs is a relevant factor to inventory policy due to availability of quantity discounts.

Thus, for inventories,

(Total Cost) TC = Purchase costs + Holding costs + Ordering costs + Shortage costs

The objective of any inventory management systems or models is to minimize these total costs.

Software applications and hardware equipments coupled managed by operations and management staff resources.

Inventory storage cost

Inventory storage costs typically include cost of building rental and facility maintenance and related costs. Cost of material handling equipments, IT hardware and applications, including cost of purchase, depreciation or rental or lease as the case may be. Further costs include operational costs, consumables, communication costs and utilities, besides the cost of human resources employed in operations as well as management.

Cost of capital

Includes the costs of investments, interest on working capital, taxes on inventory paid, insurance costs and other costs associate with legal liabilities.

The inventory storage costs as well as cost of capital is dependant upon and varies with the decision of the management to manage inventory in house or through outsourced vendors and third party service providers.

2.2.10 Inventory Models

There are generally two types of inventory management models:

- Deterministic and Stochastic

Brief comparison is given below:

Differences between deterministic and probalistic models

Deterministic	*Stochastic (probabilistic)*
i) Certainly model; Factors known with certainty and usually constant	i) Models to cope with uncertainty; Factors are uncertain and are usually variable.
ii) Simple model	ii) More complex model
iii) Not very realistic	iii) Reflect reality better than deterministic model

2.2.11 Basic Economic Order Quantity (EOQ) Model

Characteristics of the model

1. Durable (not perishable) product model.
2. Merchandizing (not manufacturing) firm.
3. Single product (not multiple product) model.

Assumptions of Basic EOQ Model

Demand is constant and known with certainty.

Lead-time is constant and known with certainty

There are no shortages - hence no shortage cost (no stock-outs). This is implied by assumptions 1 and 2.

All items for a given order arrive in one batch or at the same time. *i.e.,* simultaneous or instantaneous arrival. In particular they do not arrive gradually.

Purchase cost is constant *i.e.,* no discounts, hence for the basic EOQ model, purchase cost is irrelevant since total purchase cost is the same regardless of the quantity ordered.

Holding cost per unit p.a. is constant. This implies that total holding cost is an increasing linear function of quantity of stock in the year.

Ordering cost per order is constant irrespective of size of order.

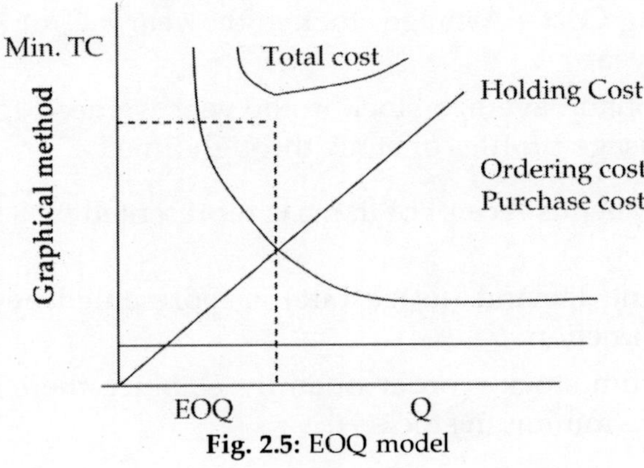

Fig. 2.5: EOQ model

TC function shape is not influenced by the purchase cost *i.e,.* it is irrelevant for EOQ determination where there are no discounts. Fig. 2.5 shows EOQ Model which is plotted by taking cost on y axis and order size on x -axis.The dotted line explains Total cost is minimum where holding cost = Ordering cost.

Thus we need formula for both holding and ordering cost. We shall utilize the following variables:

Definition of the variables

Let Q - Order quantity per order (the unknown / a decision variable)

D – Annual demand
C_o - Ordering cost per order placed
C_h - Holding cost per unit per year
C_p - Unit purchase cost
i - Holding cost expressed as a percentage of unit cost of item.

Note: $C_h = C_p \times i$
e.g., Supposing C_h=Sh. 20 and C_p =100 then it follows that i=20%

The cost formula are as follows;

i. Ordering Cost = Annual no. of orders × C_o

$$1. = \frac{D}{Q} x\, Co$$

ii. Holding Cost = Average stock in the year × C_h or Average stock in the year × C_p × i

Thus to obtain average stock in the year we need to examine the receipt and usage profiles of stock through time.

1. Instantaneous receipt of items is represented by a 90^0 or vertical line
2. Constant demand (usage rate) is represented by a decreasing linear function.
3. Maximum stock = order quantity Q, since there are no stock-outs *i.e.,* minimum stock = 0

Average stock = (Max. stock + Min. stock)/2 = (Q +0)/2 = Q/2

Thus Holding cost = $\frac{Q}{2} C_h = \frac{Q}{2} C_{pi}$

At min.TC $\frac{Q}{2} C_h = \frac{D}{Q} C_o$

To obtain the EOQ we make Q the subject as follows;

$$\text{EOQ} = \sqrt{\frac{2DCo}{Cpi}} \quad \text{Or} \quad \text{EOQ} = \sqrt{\frac{2DCo}{Ch}}$$

Calculus approach

TC = Purchase Cost + Holding Cost + Ordering Cost (recall there are no shortage costs)

In symbolic form: $TC = DC_p + \frac{QCh}{2} + \frac{D}{Q} C_o$

The objective now is to find Q which minimizes TC. We apply first order and second order conditions as follows:

$$\text{FOC: } \frac{dTC}{dQ} = \frac{C_h}{2} - DC_o Q^{-2} = 0$$

$$\frac{Ch}{2} - DCo / Q^2 = 0$$

$$C_h/2 = DC_o/Q^2$$

Re-arranging: $Q^2 = 2DC_o/C_h$

Hence $Q = \sqrt{\frac{2DCo}{C_h}}$

To confirm the turning point is a minimum, we apply SOC as follows;

SOC: $d^2TC/dQ^2 = 2DC_oQ^{-3} = 2DC_0/Q^3 > 0$ *i.e,* +ve, since D, Q, C_o are all positive values. Hence turning point is minimum.

For example 8: Star logistics Ltd. has established that annual quantity for a given item is 4000 units. The cost of placing an order is Rs 5000 and the price per unit is Rs 200. Inventory holding cost percentage is 20% of purchase cost.

Required: Formulate the best (optimal) entry policy for this item *i.e.*

Quantity to order (EOQ)

Frequency for ordering and when to order

Re-order level/point; For ROP take lead-time to be 15 days while one year has 300 working days

Total cost associated with the policy.

Suppose it actually turns out that

Ordering cost per order = Rs 6000 and

Inventory hold cost percentage I = 15% and yet the policy formulated in (a) above is implemented for a year determine the cost of predition error.

Solution:

a) **From the illustration we can see that**; annual demand, D=4000 units; cost of ordering, Co = Rs. 5000; carrying cost percentage, i =20% of unit cost; unit purchase cost, Cp=Rs 200. Then;

$$EOQ = \sqrt{\frac{DCo}{C_{pi}}} = \sqrt{\frac{2\times 4000\times 5000}{200\times 0.2}} = 1000 \text{ units}$$

Frequency of ordering

This is related to the annual number of orders, N which is given as ; $N = \frac{D}{Q} = \frac{4000}{1000} = 4$ orders

Given that one year is 12 months, therefore make an order after every, 12/4 = 3 months or quarterly.

2.2.12 *Basic EOQ Model with Discounts*

Presence of discount has certain advantage and disadvantages as follows;

Advantages

Generally discounts result in lowering certain inventory costs such as;

i) Purchase cost

ii) Shortage cost – since bulk purchases will generally mean higher stock levels on average.

iii) Ordering cost – since bulk purchases results in fewer orders.

Disadvantages of discounts

Generally since taking of discounts mean bulk purchases holding costs will increase due to raised average stock levels.

Types of discounts: there are generally two types;

1. ***Single discount offer*** *e.g.,* unit selling prices is Rs.10 but purchases of 100 units and above will get a discount of 3%.
2. ***Multiple discount offers*** – also called price-breaks, here the supplier provides a list of price /quantity ranges such as the following;

Quantity range	*Unit selling price (Rs.)*
1 – 100	10
101 – 200	9.70
201 – 400	9.50
Above 400	9.00

Principles of inventory policy optimization with discounts

I. Irrespective of the nature of discount, always work with total cost (including purchase cost) since purchase cost will differ among alternative inventory policies when there are discounts.

II. In order to minimize inventory costs, purchase the least quantity to just qualify for discounts in order to take maximum advantage of discount. This is because as the size of order increases holding cost will increase much faster than the savings made from decrease in ordering cost and purchase costs as depicted below;

Observation

As: Q tends to infinity *i.e*, becomes increasingly large, ordering cost tends to zero so that TC tends to holding cost.

Importance

At higher order quantities holding cost is dominant in the inventory total cost function, whereas ordering cost becomes increasingly insignificant. Hence at higher order quantities management of inventory costs is essentially the management of holding cost.

Example 9: PACL ltd buys 400 units of an item at a purchase cost Rs 5000 per unit and ordering cost of Rs 2,000 per order placed. The carrying cost is estimated at 24% of cost of an item p.a. The Co. has received a 2% discount offer for purchases of 100 or more units.

Required:

a) Determine the best inventory policy for this item.
b) Determine the discount level at which the firm will be indifferent between taking and not taking the discount offer.

Solution

Steps

1. Calculate the EOQ with no discount and find the resulting TC
2. Find TC when discount is taken. The EOQ will be lowest quantity to just qualify for discount

3. Compare TC in 1 and 2 and hence make the decision

a) 1) No discount = $EOQ = \sqrt{\frac{2DCo}{Cpi}} = \sqrt{\frac{2 \times 400 \times 2000}{5000 \times 0.24}}$ = 37 units

$$\text{TC} = \text{DCp} + {}^{Q}\!/_{2}\, Cpi + \frac{D}{Q} \times C_o$$

$$= 400 \times 5000 + \frac{37}{2} \times 5000 \times 0.24 + \frac{400}{37} x2000 = \text{Rs } 2{,}043{,}822$$

2) Taking discount offer

EOQ with discount = 100 units, since this is the least quantity to just qualify for discount.

Cp with discount = 5000 × (1– 0.02) = 49,000

$$\text{TC} = 400 \times 4900 + 100/2 \times 4900 \times 0.24 + \frac{400}{100} x2000$$

= Rs 2,026,800

3) *Decision*

Take the discount offer since it is less costly than NOT taking it.

Therefore, EOQ = 100 units

Timing of orders

Annual No. of orders, $\text{N} = \frac{D}{Q} = \frac{400}{100}$ = 4 orders

Therefore make an order every 12/4 = 3 months or quarterly

b) Let x represent discount level for cost indifference point. At this point the following conditions will hold:

TC (with discount) = TC (no discount)

$$400 \times 5000(1 - \chi) + \left(\frac{100}{2} \times 5000(1 - \chi) x0.24 \right) + \frac{400}{100} \times 2000$$

= 2043822

$$2000000(1-\chi)+250000(1-\chi)\times 0.24+8000=2043822$$
$$2000000-2000000\chi+60000-60000\chi+8000=2043822$$
$$2068000-2060000\chi=2043822$$
$$2068000-2043822=2060000\chi$$
$$\chi=0.0117$$
$$\chi=1.17\%=1.2\%\ (1\ \text{dp})$$

Multiple discount offers (price breaks)

This is an extension of the single discount offer in the sense that a price / quantity schedule is available or provided instead of a single offer.

The solution approach can be broken down into the following steps:

1. Calculate EOQ for each price/quantity range.
2. The EOQ calculated in 1 will fall in one of 3 categories which will be differently treated as follows:
   a. ***Below range*** – Ignore the calculated EOQ but calculate TC for the least quantity in the range.
   b. *Within range* – Evaluate total cost for the EOQ calculated.
   c. *Above range* – Ignore the range since there would be another range which will yield lower total cost.

Example 10: A company buys 30,000 units for an item per year at an ordering cost of Rs 2500 per order and holding cost chards are 20% of the cost of average inventory per annum.

The following price quality schedule is available from the supplier.

Quantity (unit)	***Unit price (Rs)***
1 3000	21:00
300 5000	19:00
5000 7000	17:00
7001 9000	15:50
9001 and above	13:50

Required

Recommend the best inventory policy for this item.

Solution

Quantity range (units)	***Unit cost (Rs)***	$EOQ=\sqrt{\frac{2x30000x2500}{Cpx0.2}}$	***Remark***
1–3000	21.00	5976	Above=Ignore
3001–5000	19.00	6283	Above=Ignore
5001–7000	17.00	6642	Within=evaluate Q=6642
7001–9000	15.50	6956	Below=evaluate Q=7001
9001 and above	13.50	7454	Below=evaluate Q=9001

Total cost calculations

$$Q = 6642$$

$$Tc = (30{,}000x17)+\left(\frac{6642}{2}x17x0.2\right)+\frac{30{,}000}{6642}x2{,}500 = \text{Rs } 532583$$

$$Q = 7001$$

$$Tc = (30{,}000x15.5)+\frac{7001}{2}x15x0.2+\frac{30{,}000}{7001}x2500 = \text{Rs } 486564$$

$$Q = 9001$$

$$Tc = (30{,}000x13.5)+\left(\frac{9001}{2}x13.5x0.21\right)+\frac{30{,}000}{9001}x2{,}500=425{,}484$$

Best inventory policy

$$EOQ = 9001 \text{ units}$$

Timing of orders = $N = D/Q$ = 3 orders

Make an order every $^{12}/_{3}$ = 4 months

Example 11: JAV Plastics buys raw plastic resin in 1,000-pound cartons. The company uses approximately 3,125 cartons per year. The cost of placing an order is Rs 20 per order. Storage and handling costs are Rs 50 per carton. Assume 250 working days a year.

a. What is the most economical order size?
b. Determine the average number of cartons on hand.
c. How many orders will be placed per year?
d. What is the ordering interval?
e. What is the total cost of ordering and holding the rawplastic?

Solution

D = 3,125 cartons, C_o = Rs 20, H = Rs 50

a. $EOQ = \sqrt{2DC_o/H} = \sqrt{2(3,125)(20)/50} = 50$ cartons

b. Q/2 = 50/2 = 25 cartons

c. D/Q = 3,125/50 = 62.5 (*i.e.,* order 62 times one year and 63 times the other year assuming all the parameters remain constant)

d. Q/D = 50/3,125 = 0.016 year = 0.016x250 days = 4 days

e. TC = (Q/2)H + (D/Q)C_0
= (50/2)(50) + (3,125/50)20 = 1,250 + 1,250 = 2,500

2.2.13 Reorder Point (ROP) Model

It is not enough to know how much to order; it is also important to know at what point to order. The ROP model determines when to order. When the quantity on hand drops to a predetermined amount, it is time to reorder. This amount includes expected demand during lead time and usually some safety stock to reduce the probability of a stock-out. Fig. 2.6 explains Rol and SS. To avoid stock out situation SS acts as a cushion and ROl is the level where the demand is ordered and recieved.

Suppose the daily demand (d) is 20 units and the lead time (LT) is 3 days. This basically means if we order now, our order will arrive after 3 days. Hence, we must order 3 days in advance. Since the daily demand is 20, the demand or consumption during these 3 days will be:

$$20 \times 3 = 60$$

$$(d)\ (LT) = dLT$$

Hence, we should place our order 3 days in advance or as soon as our inventory level drops to 60. This is the reorder point. Therefore,

$$ROP = 20 \times 3 = 60$$

$$ROP = dLT$$

We must have 60 units in stock to meet the demand during the lead time of 3 days. Hence, we can call 60(dLT) the lead-time demand. We must at least have enough inventory to cover the lead-time demand. Since the lead-time demand may vary, it is advisable to carry some extra inventories (safety stock) on top of the lead-time demand.

The amount of safety stock depends on σ which is the standard deviation of the lead-time demand. The safety stock is a multiple of σ or zσ where z is the multiple determined from the standard normal table. For example, if the objective is to meet the demand during 90% of the lead-time cycles, the z value would be approximately 1.28σ and

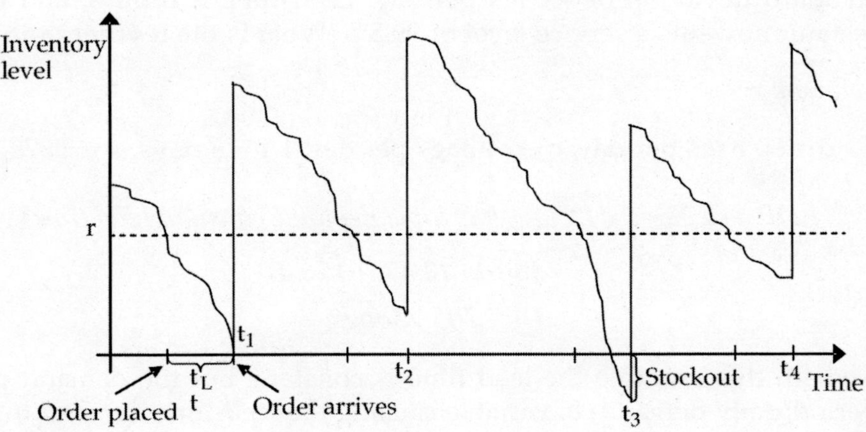

Fig. 2.6: ROL and SS

the safety stock would be 1.28σ; 90% here is called the service level. Hence, ROP is established above the average lead-time demand (dLT) by incorporating safety stocks. Actually, the complete ROP equation becomes

$$ROP = dLT + z\sigma$$

Example 12: The demand during the lead time of six weeks is 150. The standard deviation of the demand during the lead time is 5, and the desired service level is 98.9%. What is the reorder point?

Solution: dLT = 150, σ = 5, z = 2.29

$$ROP = dLT + z\sigma = 150 + 2.29(5) = 161.45 \text{ units}$$

Note: Here, the lead-time demand is variable as there is a standard deviation associated with it. This variability may either be due to the variability of the demand per period (units/day, units/week, etc.) or the variability of the lead time (days, weeks, etc.) or both. In this example we do not know whether the demand or the lead time is variable or both are variable, therefore, we use the general case formula of ROP = dLT + zσ, where dLT = average demand during the lead time and σ = standard deviation of the demand during the lead time.

Example 13: A fast food restaurant uses an average rate of 30 ten-pound bags of frozen french fries per day. Daily demand is normal and has a standard deviation of 4 bags per day. Lead time is 6 days, and the restaurant wants a service level of 99.5%. What is the reorder point?

Solution:

d = 30 bags per day, σ_d = 4 bags per day, LT = 6 days, z = 2.575

$$ROP = dLT + z\sqrt{LT}\ \sigma_d \text{ (variable demand, constant lead time)}$$
$$= 30(6) + (2.575)\sqrt{6}\ (4)$$
$$= 205.23 \text{bags}$$

Note: In this example the lead time is constant, but the demand per period(daily demand) is variable causing the lead-time demand to be variable. We can also use the general case formula,

Example 14: Everything is the same as in the previous example, except now daily demand is constant and the lead time is variable with a standard deviation of 2 days. Determine the ROP.

Solution:

$$d = 30 \text{ bags/day, } LT = 6 \text{ days, } \sigma_{LT} = 2 \text{ days, } z = 2.575$$

$$ROP = dLT + z_d\sigma_{LT} \text{ (constant demand, variable lead time case)}$$

$$= 30(6) + 2.575\ (30)(2) = 334.5 \text{ bags}$$

In this example, the demand per period (daily demand), d, is constant, but the demand during the lead time, σ is variable due to the variability of the lead time. We can also use the general case formula, $ROP = dLT + z\sigma$ by computing $\sigma = d\sigma LT$ and substituting it into the general case ROP formula.

2.2.14 P (Periodic) Type and Q (Perpectual/continuous) Type Inventory

In a periodic system the account Inventory will:

Have a constant balance (the ending balance from the previous period) not include the cost of purchases (they are recorded in a purchases account) be adjusted at the end of the accounting period (so the balance reports the costs actually in inventory).

Require a physical inventory at least once per year (and estimates within the year)

Require a cost flow assumption (FIFO, LIFO, average)

Require a calculation of the cost of goods sold (to be used on the income statement).

Beginning Balance of Inventory + Cost of Inventory Purchases - Cost of Ending Inventory = Cost of Goods Sold.

In a office supply store and trying to count and record every ball point pen in stock. Now multiply that for an office supply chain. For these reasons, many companies perform a physical count only once a quarter or even once a year. For companies under a periodic system, this means that the inventory account and cost of goods sold figures are not necessarily very fresh or accurate.

In a *perpetual system* the account Inventory will:

Be debited when there is a purchase of goods (there is no Purchases account) be credited for the cost of the items sold (and the account cost of goods sold will be debited) have its balance continuously or perpetually changing because of the above entries require a physical inventory to correct any errors in the inventory account require a cost flow assumption (FIFO, LIFO, average).

For example, at a grocery store using the perpetual inventory system, when products with barcodes are swiped and paid for, the system automatically updates inventory levels in a database.

It is possible that a company will use the periodic system in its general ledger and use a different computer system outside of its general ledger to track the flow of goods in and out of inventory.

2.2.14 ABC Analysis

Inventory ABC Classification (as known as ABC analysis) is a term used to define an inventory categorization technique often used in materials management.

The ABC Classification provides a mechanism for identifying items that will have a significant impact on overall inventory cost, while also providing a mechanism for identifying different categories of stock that will require different policy settings and inventory control.

The ABC analysis is done to manage different stocked items (or SKU's) that are not all equal in value or order frequency. A best practice is for an organization to group their inventory into three categories (A, B, and C) Fig. 2.7

'A Classification' items are very important for an organization. Because of the high demand of these 'A' items, frequent value analysis is required. These are your fast moving and typically lower value items that drive the largest percentage of your target service levels and customer satisfaction rates.10% of material consume 70% of source.

'B Classification' items are important, but of course less important than 'A' items and more important than 'C' items. These are typically mid range in inventory value and order frequency. 20% of material conume 20% of source.

'C Classification' items are marginally important. Typically, very low order frequency and high inventory value. These items are usually stocked with very low quantities or not at all due to the high carrying costs associated with the stock levels.170% of material consumes 10% of source.

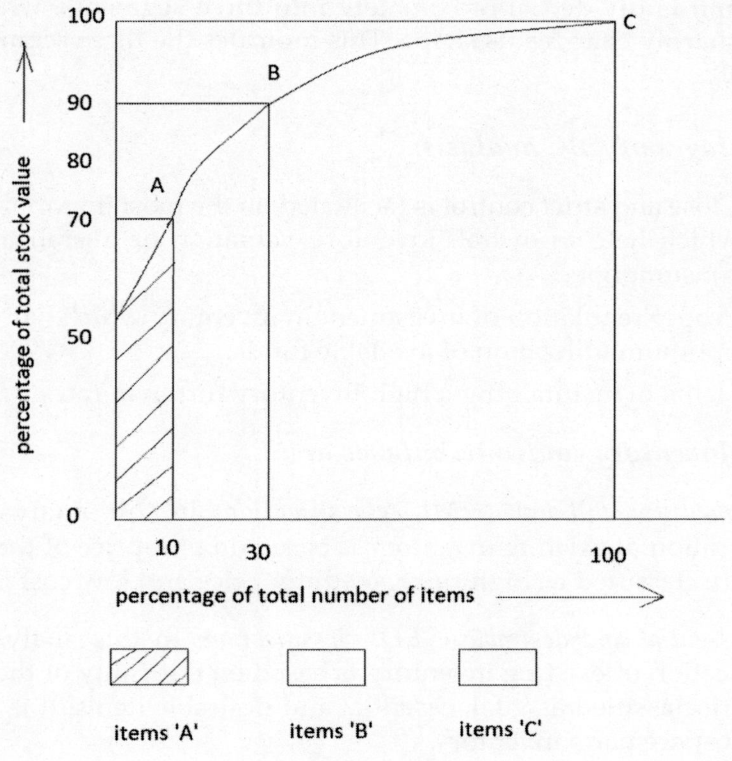

Fig. 2.7: ABC Analysis

Steps

STEP 1: Compute the annual usage value for every item in the sample by multiplying the annual requirements by the cost per unit.

STEP 2: Arrange the items in descending order of the usage value calculated above.

STEP 3: Make a cumulative total of the number of items and the usage value.

STEP 4: Convert the cumulative total of number of items and usage values into a percentage of their grand totals.

STEP 5: Draw a graph connecting cumulative % items and cumulative % usage value. The Fig. 2.7 shows ABC graph which is drwan by taking percentage of totalnumber of items and percentage of total stock.where the graph is divided approximately into three segments, where the curve sharply changes its shape. This indicates the three segments A, B and C.

Advantages of ABC analysis:

1. Close and strict control is facilitated on the most important items which help in overall inventory valuation or overall material consumption.
2. Proper regulation of investment in inventory which will ensure optimum utilization of available funds.
3. Helps in maintaining a high inventory turnover rates.

Other Inventory contro techniques are:

High, medium and low (HML) classification: In this analysis, the classification of existing inventory is based on unit price of the items. They are classified as high price, medium price and low cost items.

Vital, essential and desirable (VED) classification: In this analysis, the classification of existing inventory is based on criticality of the items. They are classified as vital, essential and desirable items. It is mainly used in spare parts inventory.

Scarce, difficult and easy to obtain (SDE): In this analysis, the classification of existing inventory is based on the items.

GOLF analysis: In this analysis, the classification of existing inventory is based sources of the items. They are classified as Government supply, ordinarily available, local availability and foreign source of supply items.

SOS analysis: In this analysis, the classification of existing inventory is based nature of supply of items. They are classified as seasonal and off-seasonal items.

Fast moving, slow moving and non-moving (FSN).

Example 15:

Item no.	101	102	103	104	105	106	107	108	109	110
Unit cost	5	11	15	8	7	16	20	4	9	12
Annual demand	48000	2000	300	800	4800	1200	18000	300	5000	500

Ans.

Item number	*Unit cost*	*Annual demand*	*Total cost per year*
101	5	48,000	240,000
102	11	2,000	22,000
103	15	300	4,500
104	8	800	6,400
105	7	4,800	33,600
106	16	1,200	19,200
107	20	18,000	360,000
108	4	300	1,200
109	9	5,000	45,000
110	12	500	6,000

	Unit cost	*Annual demand*	*Total cost per year*	*Usage as a % of total usage*
101	5	48,000	240,000	32,5%
102	11	2,000	22,000	3%
103	15	300	4,500	0,6%
104	8	800	6,400	0,9%
105	7	4,800	33,600	4,6%
106	16	1,200	19,200	2,6%
107	20	18,000	360,000	48,8%
108	4	300	1,200	0,2%
109	9	5,000	45,000	6,1%
110	12	500	6,000	0,8%
Total usage			737,900	100%

Item number	*Cumulative % of items*	*Unit cost*	*Annual demand*	*Total cost per year*	*Usage as a % of total usage*	*Cumulative % of total*
107	10%	20	18,000	360,000	48,8%	48.8%
101	20%	5	48,000	240,000	32,5%	81.3%
109	30%	9	5,000	45,000	6,1%	87.4%
105	40%	7	4,800	33,600	4,6%	92%
102	50%	11	2,000	22,000	3,0%	94.9%
106	60%	16	1,200	19,200	2,6%	97.5%
104	70%	8	800	6,400	0,9%	98.4%
110	80%	12	500	6,000	0,8%	99.2%
103	90%	15	300	4,500	0,6%	99.8%
108	100%	4	300	1,200	0,2%	100%
Total usage				737,900	100%	

Category	*Items*	*Percentage of items*	*Percentage usage (%)*	*Action*
Class A	107, 101	20%	81,6%	Close control
Class B	109, 105, 102, 106	40%	16,2%	Regular review
Class C	104, 110, 103, 108	40%	2,5%	Infrequent review

2.3.1 Capacity Planning Definition

Capacity planning is the procedure to determinee the production capacity required by an organization to meet varying demands for its products.

Output achieveed for a specific period of time is called as capacity of the system design capacity is the maximum output possible as indicated by equipment manufacturer under ideal working condition. Production capacity is the maximum output possible from equipment under normal working condition or day. Sustainable capacity is the maximum production level achievable in realistic work condition and considering normal machine breakdown, maintenance, etc.

$$\text{Efficiency} = \frac{\text{Actual output}}{\text{Effective capacity}}$$

$$\text{Utilisation} = \frac{\text{Actual output}}{\text{Design capacity}}$$

Capacity planning consists of activities like

- Assessing existing capacity
- Forecasting future capacity needs
- Identifying alternative ways to modify capacity
- Evaluating financial, economical and technological capacity alternatives understand the application of some decision-making processes involved in capacity planning

The long range planning generally considers planning horizons of one year or longer. A time period of one year or longer is needed to provide sufficient time to build a new facility, to expand the existing facility or to move to a new facility due to forecasted changes in demand.

We determine long-term capacity needs by forecasting demand over a time horizon and then converting those forecasts into capacity requirements.

Long-term considerations relate to overall level of capacity, such as facility size (affected by trends and cycles). Long range capacity planning: T>1 year.

Decisions

1. Planning for capacity that requires a long time to acquire. e.g., Plant/building/equipment/high cost facility.
2. Intermediate range capacity planning: T(6-18 months). Decisions: planning for capacity requirement (month or quarterly). e.g., work force size/new tools/inventory.
3. Short range capacity planning: T (1-6moth). Decisions: weekly (or daily) capacity planning. e.g., overtime use/personnel transfer/ alternative routings.

Ways of changing long range capacity

Expand capacity

- Subcontract with other companies to become suppliers of the expanding firm's components or entire products

- Acquire other companies, facilities, or resources
- Develop sites, buildings, buy equipment
- Expand, update, or modify existing facilities
- Reactivate facilities on standby status

Reduce capacity

Sell existing facilities, sell inventories and layoff or transfer employees

Mothball facilities and place on standby status to avoid high operating costs and reactivate facilities when demand increases- better to include, sell inventories and layoff of transfer employees

Develop and phase in new products as other products decline

Capacity planning methods vary according by industry or service yet many of the principles are similar.

- *A long-term view* may cover months to years. An operations strategy/policy is needed covering overall organizational capacity (production sites, hotels, hospital wings (rooms and beds), warehouses, production lines/machinery, computer up-grades and investment in new facilities, etc. Long range capacity of an organization is dependent on various other capacities like design capacity, production capacity, sustainable capacity and effective capacity
- *Medium-term*: The strategic capacity planning undertaken by organization for 2 to 3 years of a time frame is referred to as medium term capacity planning.forecasting demand then scheduling available capacity to best meet or balance that demand. This typically involves manufacturing or requirements planning, machine scheduling, staffing rotas and materials requirements planning. These plans reflect different levels of aggregation.
- *Short-term day-to-day adjustments*: The strategic planning undertaken by organization for a daily weekly or quarterly time frame is referred to as short term capacity planning. Our aggregate plans help in assigning production/service capacity to accommodate the demand but many details are only revealed

in operation. Unforeseen contingencies occur by the hour, day or week. Figure 2.8 explains Rough cut planning Local staffs need the expertise, discretion and some "slack" for flexibility to make locally identified adjustments - without upsetting the objectives of the aggregate plans.

2.3.2 Rough Cut Plan

It is the process of converting the master production schedule(MPS) into necessities for key resources such as direct labor and machine time. Rough cut capacity planning involves validating the works orders produced by the Material Requirement Planing.(MRP) system. This is achieved through calculating the capacity required to complete the works order and comparing this against the available capacity. Fig 2.8

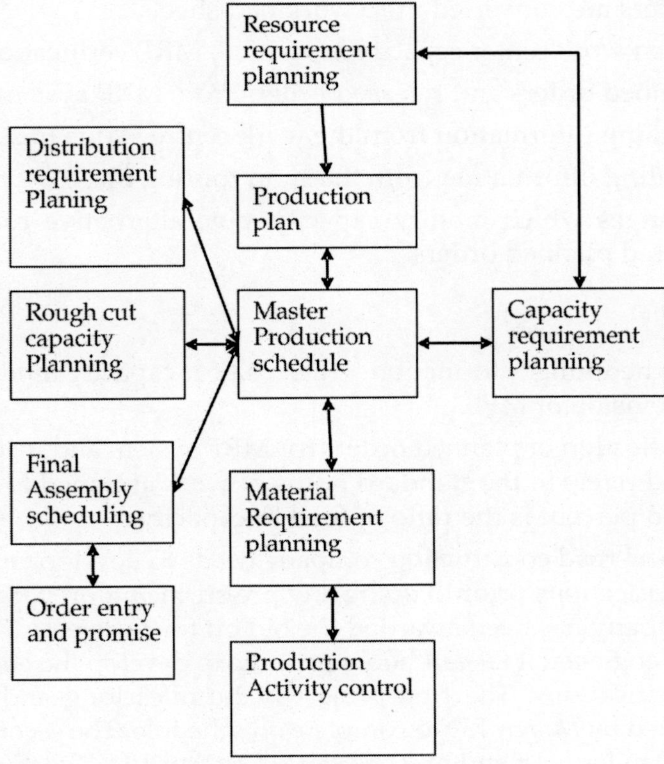

Fig. 2.8: Rough cut planning

shows the links of roughcut capacity planning,which is connected to distribution network,final assembly scheduling,order entryand promise. The available capacity be greater than the required capacity, then the plan is valid, otherwise the MRP system will have to recalculate the works orders to attain a valid capacity plan. Normally the analysis is based around key resources or bottlenecks - if there is sufficient capacity available at these resources then it is assumed that there is sufficient capacity available throughout the rest of the system.

2.3.3 Capacity Requirements Planning (CRP)

The process of determining the number of labour personnel and equipment capacities are required to meet the production objectives in MPS and MRP, is known as capacity requirement planning (CRP).

- Orders are converted in to workload sheets
- When work center capacity is verified, MRP verification is done
- Planned orders and released orders from MRP system.
- Loading information from the work centre status file.
- Routing information from the shop routing file.
- Changes which modify capacity, give alternative routings or altered planned orders.

For example:

- Rescheduling information which call for capacity modifications or revision of MPS.
- Verification of planned orders for MRP system and load reports. Load refers to the standard hours of work assigned to a facility. Load percent is the ratio of load to capacity.
- A local road construction company needs to develop engineering specifications prior to doing any pre-surfacing preparation. The company has been awarded the bid on four projects. They have one engineer. It takes 4 hours per mile to develop the engineering specifications. The first project is 30 miles long and must be started by March 15th to complete on schedule. The second project is 20 miles long and must be started by April 1st. The third project is 5 miles long and must be started by May 1st. The fourth project

is 15 miles long and must be started by May 23rd. It is now February 15th the engineer works a 40 hours week and is very experienced so he operates at 100% efficiency. Assume one project can not be started until the previous project is completed. Does the engineer have enough time to accomplish the specifications on time.

Numbers of hours = 40

Shifts = 1

Efficiency = 100%

Utilization = 4/5 = 80%

Capacity = 40 × 1 × 0.8 × 1.00 = 32 hours

Project 1 capacity = 4 (weeks) × 32 = 128

Project 2 capacity = 2 (weeks) × 32 = 64

Project 3 capacity = 4 (weeks) × 32 = 128

Project 4 capacity = 3 (weeks) × 32 = 96

- To operate at maximum capacity, companies must use the resources available. If resources under underutilized, the profit margin will not be maximum.
- Using capacity requirements planning helps a company identify potential problems, such as eliminating the possibility of overworking the current staff, overloading machines, losing customers because the work could not be completed as scheduled, paying penalties for late delivery.

$$\text{Utiliaation} = \frac{\text{Actual hours charged}}{\text{Scheduled available hours}}$$

$$\text{Efficiency} = \frac{\text{Standard hours earned}}{\text{Actual hours charged}}$$

2.3.4 Aggregate Planning

Aggregate planning involves planning the best quality to produce in the intermediate-range horizon (3 months to one year).

Aggregate production planning is the process of determining output levels of product groups over the next 6 to 18 months period.

Objectives of Aggregate Planning

The overall objective is to balance conflicting objectives involving customer service, work force stability, cost and profit.

- To establish company-wide strategic plan for allocating resources.
- To develop an economic strategy to meet customer demand.
- Aggregate planning or aggregate capacity planning

It facilitates fully loaded facilities and minimizes overloading and underloading and keeps production costs low.

Adequate production capacity is provided to meet expected aggregate demand.

Orderly and systematic transition of production capacity to meet the peaks and valleys of expected customer demand is facilitated.

Steps in aggregate capacity planning

Fig. 2.9: Shows steps of agrregate planing.

Determine the demand (i.e., sales forecast) for each product for each time period (i.e., weeks or months or quarters) over the planning horizon (6 to 12 months).

Determine the aggregate demand by summing up the demand for individual products.

Transform the aggregate demand for each time period into workers, materials, machines required to satisfy aggregate demand.

Identify company policies that are pertinent (e.g., policy regarding safety stock maintenance, maintaining stable workforce etc.).

Determine unit costs for regular time, overtime, subcontracting, holding inventories, back orders, layoffs etc.

Develop alternative resource plans for providing necessary production capacity to support the cumulative aggregate demand and compute the cost of each alternative plan.

Select the resource plan from among the alternatives considered that satisfies aggregate demand and best meets the objectives of the firm.

For example:

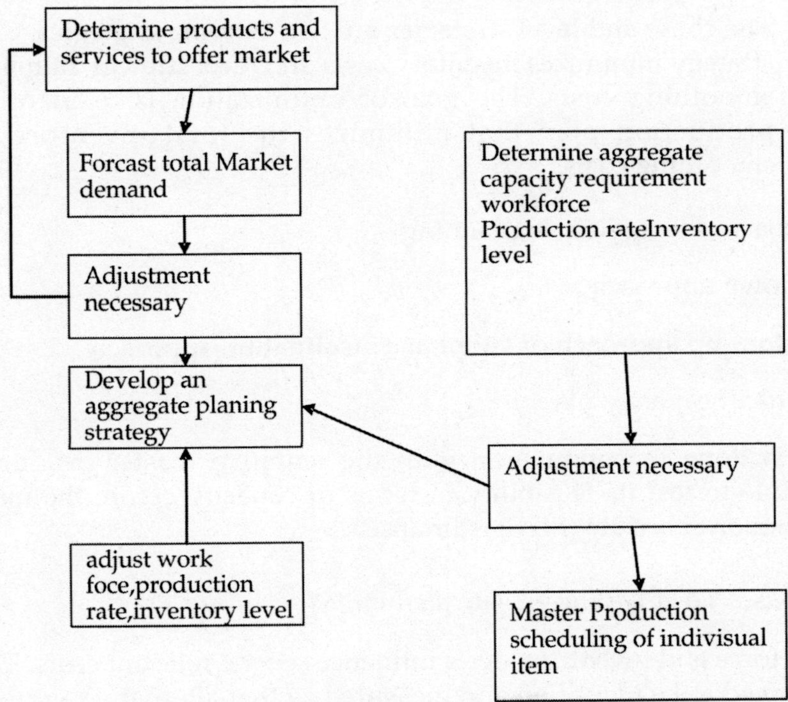

Fig. 2.9: Agrregate planing

Examples

- Chase strategy
- Level strategy
- Optimization
- Chase strategy
- Produce as much as needed
- Zero inventory, no holding cost, no shortages
- Zero inventory is difficult to achieve because work hours may not be flexible

- Low inventory costs, high smoothing costs
- Level strategy
- Produce a constant amount each period
- Stable workforce, no hiring/firing, no overtime, no subcontract
- Low smoothing costs, high inventory costs
- The chase and level strategies are two extreme strategies. Chase strategy minimizes inventory costs and level strategy minimizes smoothing costs. The goal of optimization is to identify a production plan that minimizes the total inventory and smoothing costs.

Approaches to aggregate planning

Top down approach

A bottom-up approach or subplan consolidation approach

Rough-cut capacity planning

This is done in conjunction with the tentative master production schedule to test its feasibility in terms of capacity before the master production schedule (MPS) is finalised.

Costs associated with aggregate planning:

Work force and inventory levels influence several relevant costs. These costs need to be identified and measured so that alternative aggregate plans can be evaluated on a toal cost criterion.

Those costs are

- Pay roll costs
- Costs of overtime, second shifts and sub-contracting
- Costs of hiring and laying off workers
- Costs of excess inventory and backlog
- Costs of production rate changes

Example16: Beta corporation has developed a forcast for group of items that has the following demand pattern.

Quarter	*Demand forcast*	*Cummulative demand*
1	270	270
2	220	490
3	470	960
4	670	1630
5	450	2080
6	270	2350
7	200	2550
8	370	2920

a. Supose that the firm estimates that it costs Rs 150 per unit to increase the production rate, Rs 200 per unit to decrease the production rate, Rs 50 per unit per quarter to carry the items on inventory and Rs 100 per unit if subcontracted. Compare the cost incurred if pure strategies are followed.

b. Given these costs, evaluate the following mixed strategy. The company decides to maintain a constant production rate of 250 units per quarter and permits 20% overtime when the demand exceeds the production rate. The incremental cost of overtime is Rs 25 per hour. It plans to meet the excess demand by hiring and firing of workers.

Ans. Varying the work force size to met demand.

Quarter	*Demand forcast*	*Cost of increasing production level Rs.*	*Cost of decreasing production level Rs*	*Total cost of plan.Rs.*
1	270			
2	220		10,000	10,000
3	470	37,500		37,500
4	670	30,000		30,000
5	450		44,000	44,000
6	270		36,000	36,000
7	200		14,000	14,000
8	370	25,500		25,500

Changing inventory levels

Quarter	*Demand forcast*	*Cummulative demand*	*Production level*	*Cumulative Production level*	*Inventory*	*Adujusted inventory with 255*	*Cost of holding inventory Rs*
1	270	270	365	365	95=365-270	95+255=350	17,500
2	220	490	365	730	240=730-490	495	24,750
3	470	960	365	1095	135	390	19,500
4	670	1630	365	1460	-170	85	4,250
5	450	2080	365	1825	-255	0	0
6	270	2350	365	2190	-160	95	4,750
7	200	2550	365	2555	5	260	13,000
8	370	2920	365	2920	0	255	12,750

Cost calculation for subcontracting

Quarter	*Demand forecast*	*Production units*	*Sub contracting units*	*Incremental cost at Rs 100/unit*
1	270	200	270-200=70	70*100=7000
2	220	200	20	2000
3	470	200	270	27,000
4	670	200	470	47,000
5	450	200	250	25,000
6	270	200	70	7000
7	200	200	0	0
8	370	200	170	17,000

Among these three plans plan 2 (changing inventory level) has the least cost.

Example 17: Previous problem solved by mixed strategy, it has the following components.

Maintain a constant production rate of Rs 250 per quarter.

Permit 20% overtime when the demand exceeds production rate. The incremental cost of overtime is Rs 25 per unit.

To meet any further demand it choses to hire and fire workers.

Quarter	*Demand forcast*	*Regular production unit*	*Additional units needed*	*Overtime production*	*Aditional-units needed after regular time-overtime production*	*Cost of Inventory*	*Cost of over time*	*Cost of changing workforce*	*Total cost*
1	270	250	20	50	-30*-30	1500	1250	0	2750
2	220	250	-30	0	-30*-60	3000	0	0	3000
3	470	250	220	50	170*119	0	1250	16,500	17,750
4	670	250	420	50	370*370	0	1250	39,000	40,250
5	450	250	200	50	150*150	0	1250	44,000	45.250
6	270	250	20	50	-30*-30	1500	1250	30,000	32,750
7	200	250	-50	0	-50*-80	4000	0	0	4000
8	370	250	120	50	70*-10	500	1250	0	1750
							Total	1,47,500	

Relationship to master production scheduling

Objectives of master production scheduling

To schedule end items to be completed promptly and when promised to customers.

To avoid overloading or underloading the production facility so that production capacity is efficiently utilized and low production costs result.

Functions of MPS:

- Translating aggregate plans
- Evaluating alternative master schedules
- Generating material and capacity requirements
- Facilitating information processing
- Maintaining priorities
- Utilizing the capacity effectively.

2.3.5 Material Requirements Planning (MRP)

Material Requirements Planning (MRP) is a Production System that is Specifically Designed to Handle Dependent Demand Inventory Items.

A Computerized Inventory Control Production Planning System Schedules Component and Items When they are Needed – no Earlier and no Later.

MR Master Schedule

Master schedule: One of three primary inputs in MRP; states which end items are to be produced, when these are needed, and in what quantities.

Cumulative lead time: The sum of the lead times that sequential phases of a process require, from ordering of parts or raw materials to completion of final assembly.

Time fences: Series of time intervals during which order changes are allowed or restricted.

Bill-of-Materials (BOM)

Bill of materials: One of the three primary inputs of MRP; a listing of all of the raw materials, parts, subassemblies, and assemblies needed to produce one unit of a product.

Product structure tree: Visual depiction of the requirements in a bill of materials, where all components are listed by levels.

MRP Processing

Fig. 2.10 Shows inputs of bills of material.

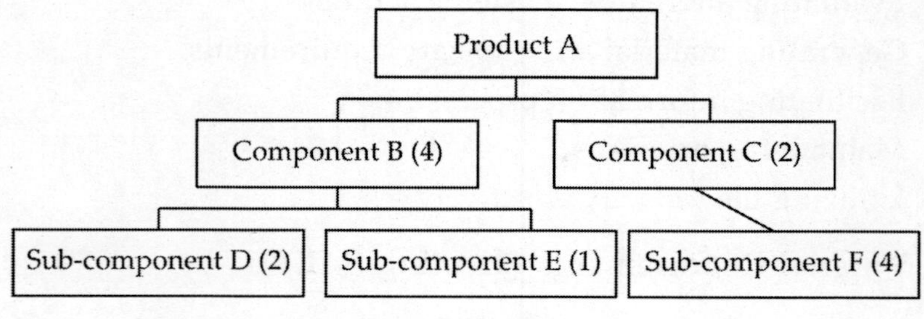

Fig. 2.10: Bill of material

Inputs bill of material includes MPS, MRP and planned order release. Let the total product is A and it has two subassemblies B (4) nos and C (2nos), Further B contains D (2nos) and E (1), and C contains F (4nos).

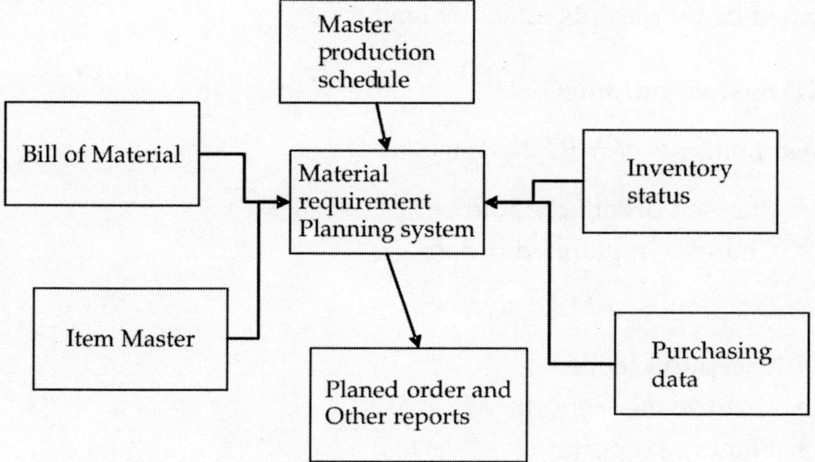

Fig. 2.11: Material requirement planning

Which includes input and output of MRP

- Gross requirements
- Scheduled receipts
- Projected on hand
- Net requirements
- Planned-order receipts
- Planned-order releases

Gross requirements: Total expected demand for an end item or raw material in a time period

Scheduled receipts: Open orders scheduled to arrive from vendors or elsewhere in the pipeline

Projected on hand: Expected amount of inventory that will be on hand at the beginning of each period

Net requirements: The actual amount needed in each time period

Planned order receipts: Quantity expected to be received by the beginning of the period in which it is shown

Planned order releases: Planned amount to order in each time period - planned order receipts offset by lead time

MRP System outputs

Primary outputs of MRP systems:

- Planned order schedule
- Changes in planned orders

Secondary inputs of MRP system:

- Exception reports
- Performance reports
- Planning reports

Example 18: To manufacture one fire extinguisher, the details of bill of material along with economic order quantity and stock on hand for the final product and sub assemblies shown below in MPS. complete the material requirement plan for fire extinguisher and cylinder.

Week	1	2	3	4	5	6	7	8
Demand	100		150	140	200	140		300

Details of Bill of material

Parts required	*Order quantity*	*No of units*	*Leadtime*	*Stock on hand*
Fire extinguisher	300	1	1	150
Cylinder	450	1	2	350

Ans. MRP calculation for fire extinguisher, EOQ = 300, LT = 1

Period	0	1	2	3	4	5	6	7	8
Projected requirement		100		150	140	200	140		300
Receipts				300		300			300
Stock on hand	150	50	50	200	60	160	20	20	20
Planned order release			300		300			300	

MRP calculation for cylinder EoQ=450,Lt=2weks

Period	0	1	2	3	4	5	6	7	8
Projected requirement			300		300			300	
Receipts					450			450	
Stock on hand	350	350	50	50	200	200	200	350	350
Planned order release			450			450			

P Outputs (Primary Reports)

Planned orders - schedule indicating the amount and timing of future orders.

Order releases - Authorization for the execution of planned orders.

Changes - Revisions of due dates or order quantities, or cancellations of orders.

- Safety stock
- Lot sizingLot-for-lot ordering
- Economic order quantity
- Fixed-period ordering
- Part-period model
- Requirements of MRP

- Computer and necessary software
- Accurate and up-to-date
- Master schedules
- Bills of materials
- Inventory records
- Integrity of data

2.3.5.1. MRP II (Manufacturing Resources Planning)

It is an integrated method of operational and financial planning for manufacturing companies. MRP II serves as an extension of MRP (closed loop manufacturing resource planning, also abbreviated as CLMRP).

The typical MRP II system employs a modular organizational structure. Modules keep track of and regulate, specific characteristics and functions of the entire organization. Examples include, but are not limited to, the following:

- Product design
- Product specifications
- QC (quality control)
- QA (quality assurance)
- Shop floor control
- Order management
- Purchasing
- Inventory
- Cost calculation
- Cost reporting
- General accounting
- Cash flow
- Tax calculation
- Tax payments

The MRP II process is carried out by a synergistic combination of computer and human resources. The MRP II differs fundamentally from point contact planning, in which individual characteristics and functions have their own dedicated systems.

Expanded MRP with and emphasis placed on integration business systems in the manufacturing industry have evolved in functionality over the years. The early systems were called MRP (Material Requirements Planning) systems because there was an innovative module called MRP within it, which calculated purchase and works order requirements based on predicted or actual demand for products. MRP II (Manufacturing Resource Planning) was the next generation of integrated manufacturing systems which used more sophisticated, iterative planning cycles to take account of factory capacity as well as the materials requirements.

MRP II systems were eventually replaced with ERP (Enterprise Resource Planning) systems which added more applications and catered for industries beyond manufacturing. Today all integrated business solutions including those for the manufacturing sector are described as ERP systems.

Material requirements planning (MRP) and manufacturing resource planning (MRPII) are both incremental information integration business process strategies that are implemented using hardware and modular software applications linked to a central database that stores and delivers business data and information.

MRP is concerned primarily with manufacturing materials while MRP II is concerned with the coordination of the entire manufacturing production, including materials, finance and human relations. The goal of MRP II is to provide consistent data to all members in the manufacturing process as the product moves through the production line.

Paper-based information systems and non-integrated computer systems that provide paper or disk outputs result in many information errors, including missing data, redundant data, numerical errors that result from being incorrectly keyed into the system, incorrect calculations based on numerical errors and bad decisions based on incorrect or old data. In addition, some data is unreliable in non-integrated systems because the same data is categorized differently in the individual databases used by different functional areas.

MRP II systems begin with MRP, material requirements planning. MRP allows for the input of sales forecasts from sales and marketing. These forecasts determine the raw materials demand. MRP and MRP II systems draw on a master production schedule, the breakdown of specific plans for each product on a line. While MRP allows for the coordination of raw materials purchasing, MRP II facilitates the development of a detailed production schedule that accounts for machine and labor capacity, scheduling the production runs according to the arrival of materials. An MRP II output is a final labor and machine schedule. Data about the cost of production, including machine time, labor time and materials used, as well as final production numbers, is provided from the MRP II system to accounting and finance.

- Financial planning
- Marketing
- Engineering
- Purchasing
- Manufacturing

Example 19: A company manufactures iron box the mps of the final assembly is given below. The initial stock on hand 150 units. Solve it by MRP method, if EOQ = 3592 units

Month	1	2	3	4	5	6	7	8
Projected requirement	-	3500	3000	4500	-	1000	4000	5500

Ans.

Month	1	2	3	4	5	6	7	8
Projected requirement	-	3500	3000	4500	-	1000	4000	5500
Receipt		3592	3592	3592		3592	3592	3592
Stock on hand (1150)	1150	1242	1834	926	926	3518	3110	1202
POR	3592	3592	3592		3592	3592	3592	

Lot- sizing rules

1. *Fixed order quantity (FOQ)*: A rule that maintain the same order quantity each time an order is issued

   Formula:

   (Projected on-hand inventory balance at end of week t) =

   (Inventory on hand at end of week t-1) + (Scheduled (or) planned receipts in week t) – Gross requirement in week t)
2. *Periodic order quantity (POQ)*: A rule that allows a different order quantity for each order issued but tends to issue the order at predetermined time intervals.

   Formula:

   (POQ lot size to arrive in week t) =

   (Total gross requirements for P weeks, including week t) – (Projected on-hand inventory balance at end of week t-1)
3. *Lot for lot (L4L):* A rule under which the lot size ordered covers the gross requirement of a single week.

   Formula:

   (L4L lot size) =

   (Gross requirement in week t) – (Projected on-hand inventory balance at the end of week t-1)

2.3.6 Facility Location

The selection of a place for locating a plant is one of the problems, perhaps the most important, which is faced by an entrepreneur while launching a new enterprise.

It is of 2 types:

1. Localization /centralization-means concentration of similar type of industries at some particular place. e.g., textile in Mumbai.
2. Delocalization /Decentralization-means spreading of similar type of industries at different places. e.g., banking industries

2.3.7 Factors Affecting Location and Site Decisions

Availability of raw material

Nearness to the potential market

Near to the source of operating requirements like electricity, disposal of waste, drainage facilities.

- Supply of labor
- Transport and communication facilities
- Integration with other group of companies
- Suitability of land and climate
- Availability of housing, other amenities and services
- Local building and planning regulations
- Safety requirements
- Others like low interest on loans, special grants, living standards

2.3.8 Steps of Selecting Plant Location

To be systematic in choosing a plant location, the entrepreneur would do well to proceed step by step, the steps being

- Deciding on domestic or international location
- Selection of region
- Availability of raw material
- Nearness to the market
- Availability of power
- Transport facilities
- Suitability of climate
- Government policy
- Competition between states
- Selection of community availability of labour

4. Civic amenities worker
    - Existence of complementary and competing industries - finance and research facilities.
    - Availability of water and fire-fighting facilities - local taxes and restrictions

- Momentum of a early start
- Personal factors
- Selection of the site
- Soil, size and topography
- Disposal of waste

2.4 LOCATION MODELS

- Factor rating method
- Point rating method
- Break – even analysis
- Quantitative factor analysis
- Factor rating method
- Popular because a wide variety of factors can be included in the analysis
- Six steps in the method
- Develop a list of relevant factors called critical success factors
- Assign a weight to each factor
- Develop a scale for each factor
- Score each location for each factor
- Multiply score by weights for each factor for each location
- Recommend the location with the highest point score

Example 20:

Relevent factors	*Assigned weight*	*Scores for locationA*	*Scores for locationV*	*Scores for locationC*	*Scores for locationD*
Production cost	0.35	50	40	60	30
Raw material supply	o.25	70	80	80	60
Labour availability	0.20	60	70	60	50
Cost of living	0.05	80	70	40	80
Environnnment	0.05	50	60	70	90
Markets	0.10	70	90	80	50
Total	1.00				

Ans.

Relevent factors	*Scores for locationA*	*Scores for locationV*	*Scores for locationC*	*Scores for locationD*
Production cost	0.35*50=17.5	14	21	10.5
Raw material supply	17.5	20	20	15
Labour availability	12	14	12	10
Cost of living	4.0	3.5	2.0	4.0
Environnnment	2.5	3.0	3.5	4.5
Markets	7.0	9.0	8.0	5.0
Total	60.5	63.5	66.5	49.0

2. Point rating method

In selecting a site or location, companies have several objectives, but not all are of equal importance. The relative weight a company assigns to each objective or to each location factor may be represented by the number of points a perfect site would receive in each category. Each potential site is then evaluated with respect to every factor a company is looking for and points are assigned for each factor. The site with the highest total number of points is considered superior to other sites.

3. Break even analysis

Method of cost-volume analysis used for industrial locations. Three steps in the method:

- Determine fixed and variable costs for each location
- Plot the cost for each location
- Select location with lowest total cost for expected production volume

***Example 21*:** Potential location A,B,C have the cost structure as shown below for manufacturing a product expected to sell for Rs 2700 per unit, find the most economical location for an expected volume of 2000 units per year.

Location	*Fixed cost/year*	*Variable cost/unit*
A	60 lakh	1500
B	70 lakh	500
C	50 lakh	4,000

Ans.

TC for A = Fixed cost + Variable cost * Volume = 60 lakh + 1500 * 2000 = 90 lakh

TC for B = 70 lakh + 500 * 2000 = 80 lakh (minimum)

TC for C = 50 lakh + 4000 * 2000 = 130 lakh

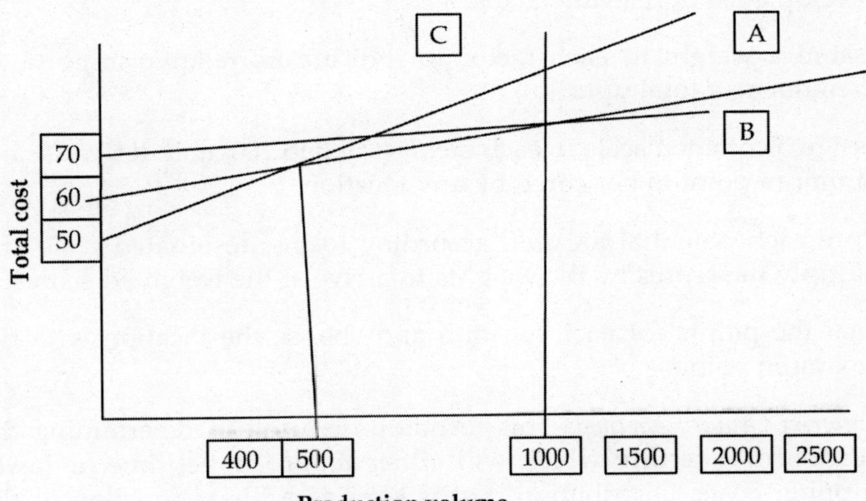

From the above calculation it is found that the cost of B is minimum hence selected for the lant location.

Let Q be the volume at which we switch from C to A

TC of site C = Total cost of site A

50 lakh + 4000 Q = 60 lakh + 1500 Q

Q = 400 units

TC of site A = Total cost of site B

60 lakh + 1500 Q = 70 lakh + 500 Q

Q = 1000 units

4. *Qualitative factor analysis method*

If economic criteria are not sufficiently influential to decide the location alternative, a system of weighting the criteria might be useful in making a plant location decision. This approach is referred to as qualitative factor analysis.

Steps:

Develop a list of relevant factos.

Assign a weight to each factor to indicate its relative importance (Weights may total upto 1.0)

Assign a common scale to each factor (say 0 to 100) and designate any minimum point to be scored by any location.

Score each potential location according to the designated scale and multiply the scores by the weights to arrive at the weighted scores.

Total the points for each location and choose the location with the maximum points

Center-of-Gravity Method: This technique is used in determining the location of a facility which will either reduce travel time or lower shipping costs. Distribution cost is seen as a linear function of the distance and quantity shipped. The Center of Gravity Method involves the use of a visual map and a coordinate system; the coordinate points being treated as the set of numerical values when calculating averages. If the quantities shipped to each location are equal, the center of gravity is found by taking the averages of the x and y coordinates; if the quantities shipped to each location are different, a weighted average must be applied (the weights being the quantities shipped).

Calculate X and Y coordinates for = center of gravity

Assumes cost is directly proportional to distance and volume shipped

where d_{ix} = x-coordinate of location i

d_{iy} = y-coordinate of location i

Q_i = Quantity of goods moved to or from location i

$$x \text{ coordinate} = \Sigma\, dixQi/\Sigma\, Qi$$

$$y \text{ coordinate} = \Sigma\, diyQi/\Sigma\, Qi$$

***Example* 22:** An auto mobile air conditioner manufacturer currently manufactures its RB-300 line at three locations plant A, plant B and plant C respectively. Using centre of gravity method find a new best location.

Plant	*Compressors required*	*Plant location matrix*
A	6,000	150,75
B	8,200	100,300
C	7,000	275,380

x = 150*6000 + 100*8200 + 275*7000/6000 + 8200 + 7200 = 172

y = 75*6000 + 300*8200 + 380*7000/6000 + 8200 + 7200 = 262.7

The location for plant is (172.273)

2.4.1 Facility Layout

A facility or plant layout is the placing of the right items coupled with the right place and the right method, to permit the flow of production process through the shortest possible distance in the shortest possible time.

Definition: Plant layout refers to the arrangement of physical facilities such as machines, equipment, tools, furniture etc. in such a manner so as to have quickest flow of material at the lowest cost and with the least amount of handling in processing the product from the receipt of raw material to the delivery of the final product.

2.4.2 Objectives of Good Plant Layout

A well designed plant layout is one that can be beneficial in achieving the following objectives:

- Proper and efficient utilization of available floor space
- Transportation of work from one point to another point without any delay
- Proper utilization of production capacity
- Reduce material handling costs
- Utilize labour efficiently
- Reduce accidents
- Provide for volume and product flexibility
- Provide ease of supervision and control
- Provide for employee safety and health
- Allow easy maintenance of machines and plant
- Improve productivity

2.4.3 Criteria For Good Layout

- Flexibility
- Maximum coordination
- Maximum visibility
- Maximum accessibility
- Minimum distance
- Minimum handling
- Minimum discomfort - proper light, ventilation etc.
- Inherent safety
- Efficient process flow
- Provision of space to workers

The Principles of Plant Layout

Integration of all factors - The plant should integrate all the essential resources of men, machines and materials in order to give an optimum level of production.

Minimum Movement - The less the movement of men, machines and materials, the less will be the cost of production. Thus, minimum movement of these resources will provide cost

Efficiency

Unidirectional flow - All materials should progressively move towards the same direction i.e., towards the stage of completion. Any back-tracking should be avoided here.

Efficient space handling - The space used up during the plant work also costs money as more the space required, more will be the floor rent. The materials should be organized in stacks in a proper and recognizable order to maintain space efficiency.

Maximum observation capacity - The layout of the plant should such that all of its resources and workforce can be observed and evaluated at all points in time. This helps in better supervision of work and helps in increasing both effectiveness and safety.

Maximum accessibility - The layout of the plant should ensure that all essential resources are accessible to the labour and machines without any delay. The aisles should be free from obstacles. The materials should be placed as close, to the machines concerned, as possible.

Minimum handling - The ineffective handling of materials leads to a rise in cost. Materials should be handled in stacks and transferred in one go. Handling of a material twice in the same direction must be avoided.

Maximum protection - The layout should ensure the protection of the materials and machines while they are in the working or the storage stage. The security system should be efficient without making too many doors or barriers.

Maximum flexibility - The plant layout should not be rigid and permanent. If the need arises, the plant layout should be able to change itself without being expensive.

Inherent safety - The environment of the plant should be safe for the workers as well as the machines. There should be fire extinguishers and fire exits placed strategically. There should be minimum contact of the labour to toxic chemicals and environment.

2.5 TYPES OF LAYOUT

There are mainly four types of plant layout:

- Product or line layout
- Process or functional layout
- Fixed position or location layout
- Combined or group layout

Product or line layout

Fig. 2.12 shows product layout where the machines and equipments are arranged in one line depending upon the sequence of operations required for the product. It is also called as line layout. The material moves to another machine sequentially without any backtracking or deviation i.e., the output of one machine becomes input of the next machine. It requires a very little material handling.

It is used for mass production of standardized products.

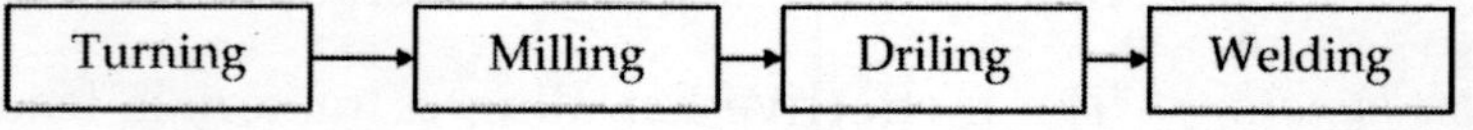

Fig. 2.12: Product layout

Advantages of product layout:

- Low cost of material handling, due to straight and short route and absence of backtracking
- Smooth and continuous operations
- Continuous flow of work
- Lesser inventory and work in progress
- Optimum use of floor space
- Simple and effective inspection of work and simplified production control
- Lower manufacturing cost per unit

Disadvantages of product layout:

- Higher initial capital investment in special purpose machine (SPM)
- High overhead charges
- Breakdown of one machine will disturb the production process.
- Lesser flexibility of physical resources.

Process layout:

Fig. 2.13 Explains process layout where the machines of a similar type are arranged together at one place. This type of layout is used for batch production. It is preferred when the product is not standardized and the quantity produced is very small.

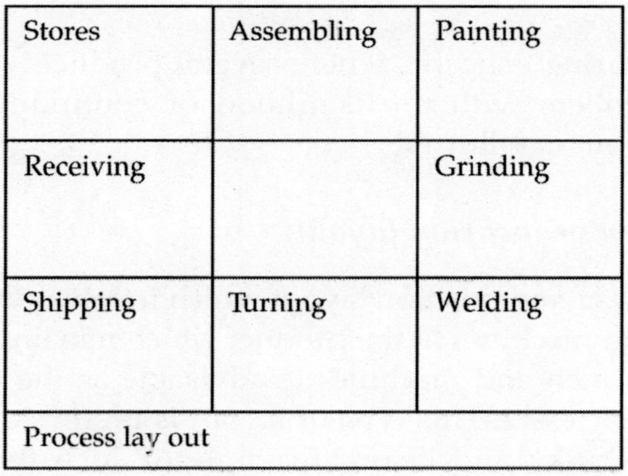

Stores	Assembling	Painting
Receiving		Grinding
Shipping	Turning	Welding
Process lay out		

Fig. 2.13: Process layout

Advantages of process layout:

- Lower initial capital investment is required
- There is high degree of machine utilization, as a machine is not blocked for a single product
- The overhead costs are relatively low
- Breakdown of one machine does not disturb the production process

- Supervision can be more effective and specialized
- Greater flexibility of resources

Disadvantages of process layout:

- Material handling costs are high due to backtracking
- More skilled labour is mandatory so cost is very high
- Work in progress inventory is high which demands greater storage space
- Frequent inspection is needed more which consequences in costly supervision

COMBINED LAYOUT

A combination of process and product layout is known as combined layout

Manufacturing concerns where several products are produced in repeated numbers with no likelihood of continuous production, combined layout is followed

Fixed position or location layout:

Fig. 2.14 Shows fixed position layout which involves the movement of manpower and machines to the product which remains stationary. The movement of men and machines is advisable as the cost of moving them would be lesser. This type of layout is preferred where the size of the job is bulky and heavy. Example of such type of layout is locomotives, ships, boilers, generators, wagon building, aircraft manufacturing, etc.

Advantages of fixed position layout:

- The investment on layout is very small.
- The layout is flexible as change in job design and operation sequence can be easily incorporated.
- Adjustments can be made to meet shortage of materials or absence of workers by changing the sequence of operations.

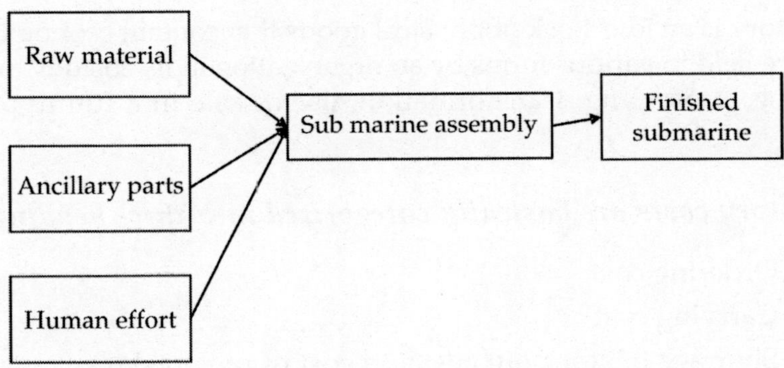

Fig. 2.14: Fixed position layout

Disadvantages of fixed position layout:

- As the production period being very long so the capital investment is very high.
- Very large space is required for storage of material and equipment near the product.
- As several operations are often carried out simultaneously so there is possibility of confusion and conflicts among different workgroups.

KEY NOTES

Time series: To get an idea about the variable that one wishes to forecast, it is most sensible to begin with a graphical plot of historic data, ordered by time points. Such data is called a time series.

Trend: A trend is a monotonic (increasing or decreasing) function of time. The simplest such function is a linear trend $\tau_t = a + bt$. Other popular trend models are quadratic $a + bt + ct^2$, exponential $a + be^{ct}$, or logarithmic $a + b\ln(ct)$. If $\tau_t = a$, independently of time then we say that there is no trend in the time series.

Inventory management requires constant and careful evaluation of external and internal factors and control through planning and review. Most of the organizations have a separate department or job function called inventory planners who continuously monitor, control and review inventory and interface with production, procurement and finance departments.

Inventory is an idle stock of physical goods that contain economic value and are held in various forms by an organization in its custody awaiting packing, processing, transformation, use or sale in a future point of time.

Inventory costs are basically categorized into three headings:

- Ordering cost
- Carrying cost
- Shortage or stock out cost and cost of replenishment
- Cost of loss, pilferage, shrinkage and obsolescence etc.
- Cost of logistics
- Sales discounts, volume discounts and other related costs.
- ABC Classification

Inventory in any organization can run in thousands of part numbers or classifications and millions of part numbers in quantity. Therefore inventory is required to be classified with some logic to be able to manage the same.

In most of the organizations inventory is categorized according to ABC classification method, which is based on pareto principle. Here the inventory is classified based on the value of the units. The principle applied here is based on 80/20 principles. Accordingly the classification can be as under:

A. Category Items Comprise 20% of SKU and Contribute to 80% of spend.
B. Category Items Comprise 30% of SKU and Contribute to 15% of spend.
C. Category Items Comprise 50% of SKU and Contribute to 5% of spend.

PROBABLE QUESTIONS AND ANSWERS

1. What is the delphi method? Describe its main advantages and limitations.

In the delphi method, experts are individually posed questions relating to an underlying forecasting problem. Then, an independent party seeks to form a consensus forecast by providing feedback to the various experts in a manner that prevents identification of individual positions. The method can be useful in providing consensus forecasts that are unaffected by the persuasive ability of individual expert participants. Needless to say, the effectiveness of this method is sensitive to the expertise of the independent party chosen.

2. Describe the main advantages and limitations of survey data.

Survey data can be highly useful in short-term forecasting when carefully used to elicit consumer perceptions and attitudes. However, survey data are "soft" when they don't relate to actual market transactions and can be unreliable when consumers have incentives to misreport information.

3. What is trend projection, and why is this method often employed in economic forecasting?

Trend projection involves a simple extrapolation of historical patterns of economic activity. A primary advantage is that many economic series involve a substantial trend element due to the effects of population and economic growth and can be readily forecast using trend projection methods. For example, when past use, personal selling or advertising creates a high degree of customer loyalty, a strong trend element in product sales data will emerge. Similarly, when repeat business is high, there is a large trend element in firm sales data. As a result, trend projection methods are often employed to forecast the long-term secular increase or decrease in economic data.

EXERCISE 2.1

Q 1. The instant paper clip office supply company sells and delivers office supplies to companies, schools and agencies within a 50-mile radius of its warehouse. The office supply business is competitive, and the ability to deliver orders promptly is a big factor in getting new customers and maintaining old ones. (Offices typically order not when they run low on supplies, but when they completely run out. As a result, they need their orders immediately.) The manager of the company wants to be certain that enough drivers and vehicles are available to deliver orders promptly and that they have adequate inventory in stock. Therefore, the manager wants to be able to forecast the demand for deliveries during the next month. From the records of previous orders, management has accumulated the following data for the past 10 months:

Month	Jan.	Feb.	Mar.	Apr.	May	Jun.	Jul.	Aug.	Sep.	Oct.
Orders	120	90	100	75	110	50	75	130	110	90

a. Compute the monthly demand forecast for February through November using the naive method.
b. Compute the monthly demand forecast for April through November using a 3-month moving average.
c. Compute the monthly demand forecast for June through November using a 5-month moving average.
d. Compute the monthly demand forecast for April through November using a 3-month weighted moving average. Use weights of 0.5, 0.33, and 0.17, with the heavier weights on the more recent months.
e. Compute the mean absolute deviation for June through October for each of the methods used. Which method would you use to forecast demand for November?

Ans. a. $F_{Feb.} = D_{Jan.} = 120$. Similarly, $F_{Nov.} = D_{Oct.} = 90$; b. 103.3; c. 9.0; d. 100.1; e. –60

Q 2. The polish general's pizza parlor is a small restaurant catering to patrons with a taste of European pizza. One of its specialties is polish prize pizza. Tammy Dough, manager of polish general, must forecast weekly demand for these special pizzas so that she can order the correct amount of pizza shells weekly. Recently, the demand has been as follows:

Week	*Number of polish prize pizzas sold*
September 1	50
September 8	65
September 15	52
September 22	60
September 29	70
October 6	60

Forecast the demand for polish prize pizza for September 22 – October 6, using the 3 period moving average method. Note: Round up all the forecast.

Forecast the demand for September 22 – October 6, using weights of 0.5, 0.3, 0.2 for the most recent, next recent and most distant data, respectively.

Assume that the forecast for September 1 to be 55. Forecast the demand for September 8-October 6 using the exponential smoothing method with a = 0.3.

Now, forecast the demand for September 8-October 6 using the exponential smoothing method with a = 0.6. How do they compare to that in part (c)?

Q 3. A firm believes that its annual profit depends on its expediture for research. The information for preceding six years is given below. Estimate the profit when expenditure is 6 units for 1996.

Ans. y = 18.32 + 2.379x, y = 37.352

Year	1990	1991	1992	1993	1994	1995	1996
Expenditure of research	2	3	5	4	11	5	6
Anual profit	20	25	34	30	40	31	-?-

Q 4. Compute the adjusted exponential forecast for the first week of June for a firm with the following data. Assume the forecast for the first week of April (F0) as 700 and corresponding initial trend (T0) as 0. Let $\alpha = 0.15$ and $\beta = 0.25$.

Ans. 662.18

MONTH

	APRIL				MAY			
WEEK	1	2	3	4	1	2	3	4
DEMAND	675	625	575	675	650	650	725	740

Q 5. The XYZ paint shop has recorded the demand for a particular colour during the past 6 months as shown below

Month	*Demand in litre*
January	19
February	17
March	22
April	27
May	29
June	33

Calculate a 3-month moving average for the data to forecast the demand for the next month.

Calculate a weighted average forecast for the data, using a weight of 0.6 for the most recent data and weights of 0.3 and 0.1 for successive older. (ans key-19.33,22,26) and (20.2,24.5,27.7)

Q 6. What is MRP II.

Q 7. Explain the basic inputs of MRP.

Q 8. A firm producing hand trolley has the following master production schedule.

Week	1	2	3	4	5	6	7	8
Demand	200	-	-	240	-	240	-	220

Each hand trolley has a bin, two wheel assemblies, two handle bars and a mounting base. Each wheel assembly has a wheel and two bearings. Order quantities, lead times and inventories on hand at the beginning of the period 1 are as shown below

Part	*Order Quantity*	*Lead Time*	*Inventory on hand*
Hand Trolley	350	1	220
Bin	400	2	250
Wheel assemblies	800	2	120

Complete the material requirement plan for the bin.

Q 9. What is material requirement planning, explain.

Q 10. Write the advantage,disadvantages of product, process and fixed layout.

Q 11. The Tarsmashis Corporation makes two versions of the same basic file cabinet, the TOL (Top-of-the-line) five drawer file cabinet and the HQ (High-quality) five drawer filing cabinet.

The TOL and HQ use the same cabinet frame and locking mechanism. The drawer assemblies are different although both use the same drawer frame assembly. The drawer assemblies for the TOL cabinet use a sliding assembly that requires four bearings per side whereas the HQ sliding assembly requires only two bearings per side. (These bearings are identical for both cabinet types.) 100 TOL and 300 HQ file cabinets need to be assembled in week #10. No current stock exists.

Develop a material structure tree for the TOL and the HQ file cabinets.

Q 12. Develop a gross material requirements plan for the TOL and HQ cabinets in the previous example.

Q 13. Develop a net material requirements plan for the TOL and HQ file cabinets in the previous problems assuming a current on-hand finished goods inventory of 100 TOL cabinets. The lead times are given below.

- Painting and final assembly of both HQ and TOL requires 2 weeks.
- Both cabinet frames and lock assembly require 1 week for manufacturing.
- Both drawer assemblies require 2 weeks for assembly.
- Both sliding assemblies require 2 weeks for manufacturing.

Q 14. If the TOL file cabinet has a gross material requirements plan as shown below, no inventory and 2 weeks lead time is required for assembly, what are the order release dates and lot sizes when lot sizing is determined using lot-for-lot? Use a holding cost of Rs 2.00 and a setup cost of Rs 20.00, and assume no initial inventory.

Gross material requirements plan

Week	1	2	3	4	5	6	7	8	9	10
TOL			50		100		50			100

Q 15. If the TOL file cabinet has a gross material requirements plan as shown below, no inventory and 2 weeks of lead time is required for assembly, what are the order release dates and lot sizes when lot sizing is determined by EOQ (Economic Order Quantity)? Use a holding cost of Rs 2.00 and a setup cost of Rs 20.00 and assume no initial inventory.

Gross material requirements plan

Week	1	2	3	4	5	6	7	8	9	10
TOL			50		100		50			100

Q 16. What are the types of forcasting

Ans. Chapter 2.1.2

Q 17. Write notes on Qualitative and Quantitative methods of forecasting.

Ans. Chapter 2.1.5 forecasting techniques

Q 18. What are the forecasting errors?

Ans. MAD,MAPE,MSE etc. in the chapter.

Q 19. What are the classification of inventory.

Ans. Inventory in manufacturing companies.

Manufacturing companies produce goods and sell them to customers or merchandising companies. Manufacturing companies normally maintain three inventory accounts. These are: raw materials inventory, work in process inventory and finished goods inventory. These are briefly explained below:

Raw materials inventory: Raw material is the basic material that is processed and converted into finished goods. The cost incurred to obtain raw materials that have not yet been placed into production is reported as raw materials inventory in the current assets section of the balance sheet. Examples of raw materials include wood for the manufacturers of cricket bat and steel for the manufacturers of cars.

Work-in-process inventory: The units that remain incomplete at the end of a period are known as work-in-process inventory. These units need the addition of more materials, labor or manufacturing overhead to be completed into the coming period. Like raw materials, work-in-process inventory is reported in the current assets section of the balance sheet.

Finished goods inventory: Finished goods are completed but unsold goods. The total cost incurred to complete these unsold goods are reported as finished goods inventory along with raw materials and work-in-process inventory in the current assets section of the balance sheet.

Q 20. Catagories the items as per ABC Analysis. Ans. A- item 2,.7,1 and C-rest.

Item number	*Annual quantity used*	*Unit value*
1	75	80
2	150,000	0,9
3	500	3,0
4	18,000	0,20
5	3,000	0,30
6	20,000	0,10
7	10,000	2

Q 21. An auto parts supplier sells hardy-brand batteries to car dealers and auto mechanics. The annual demand is approximately 1,200 batteries. The supplier pays Rs 28 for each battery and estimates that the annual holding cost is 30 percent of the battery's value. It costs approximately Rs 20 to place an order (managerial and clerical costs). The supplier currently orders 100 batteries per month.

a. Determine the ordering, holding and total inventory costs for the current order quantity.
b. Determine the economic order quantity (EOQ).
c. How many orders will be placed per year using the EOQ?
d. Determine the ordering, holding and total inventory costs for the EOQ
e. How has ordering cost changed? Holding cost? Total inventory cost?

Ans. 600tires,18 orders /year,RS900,300 tires,RS900,Rs1800.

Q 22. Distinguish Between P and Q Type of Inventory.

Ans. Continuous Review (Q) Systems, sometimes called reorder point (ROP) systems, track the inventory level each time a withdrawal is made to determine if it is time to reorder. Whenever the inventory level falls to or below a reorder point (R), an order for a fixed quantity (Q) is made. Although the order size is fixed, the time between orders (TBO) will change.

Periodic Review (P) Systems, review the inventory level at fixed periods (e.g., weekly, monthly) in order to determine how large an order to place. An order is placed to take the inventory position (on hand inventory + schedules receipts – backorders) up to a predetermined target level (T). Thus in a P system the TBO is constant but the order quantity will change.

Q 23. Write About Reorder Level and Safety Stock.

Ans. chapter 2.2.1.4

Q 24. Explain Inventory Models.

Ans. 1. EOQ model

This model is applied when objective is to minimize the total annual cost of inventory in the organization. Economic order quantity is that size of the order which helps in attaining the above set objective. EOQ model is applicable under the following conditions.

- Demand per year is deterministic in nature

- Planning period is one year
- Lead time is zero or constant and deterministic in nature
- Replenishment of items is instantaneous
- Demand/consumption rate is uniform and known in advance
- No stockout condition exist in the organization

The total annual cost of the inventory (TC) is given by the following equation in EOQ model.

$$TC = CD + S.\frac{D}{Q} + I.C.\frac{Q}{2}$$

By taking the first partial derivative of T.C. w.r.t. Q

$$\frac{\delta(TC)}{\delta Q} = 0 + \left(-\frac{SD}{Q^2}\right) + \left(\frac{IC}{2}\right)$$

Setting the $\frac{\delta(TC)}{\delta Q} = 0$ and solving for Q

$$Q^* = \sqrt{\frac{2DS}{IC}}$$

where Q* is the optimal order quantity.

Q 25. ABC manufacturers produces 1,25,000 oil seals each year to satisfy the requirement of their client. They order the metal for the bushing in lot of 30,000 units. It cost them Rs 40 to place the order. The unit cost of bushing is Rs 0.12 and the estimated carrying cost is 25% unit cost. Find out the economic order quantity? What percentage of increases or decrease in order quantity is required so that the ordered quantity is economic order quantity.

D = Total amount demand; S = Procurement Cost (per order); I = Carrying cost per unit carried and C = Cost per unit

Economic order quantity

$$Q^* = \sqrt{\frac{2DS}{IC}} = \sqrt{\frac{2(125,000)(40)}{(0.25)(0.12)}} = 18,257.4 = 18258$$

Since the order quantity is 30,000 which is more than EOQ, the quantity should be decreased to reach EOQ. Percentage decrease in order quantity required is

$$= \frac{30,000 - 18,258}{30,000} \times 100\% = 39.14\%$$

MULTIPLE CHOICE QUESTION 2.1

1. **Which of the following is not true for forecasting?**
   a) Forecasts are rarely perfect
   b) The underlying casual system will remain same in the future
   c) Forecast for group of items is accurate than individual item
   d) Short range forecasts are less accurate than long range forecasts
   (*Ans*: d)
2. **Which of the following is not a forecasting technique?**
   a) Judgemental
   b) Time series
   c) Time horizon
   d) Associative
   (*Ans*: c)
3. **In which of the following forecasting technique, subjective inputs obtained from various sources are analyzed?**
   a. Judgemental forecast
   b. Time series forecast
   c. Associative model
   d. All of the above
   (*Ans*: a)
4. **In which of the following forecasting technique, data obtained from past experience is analyzed?**

a. Judgemental forecast
b. Time series forecast
c. Associative model
d. All of the above
(*Ans*: b)

5. **Delphi method is used for**
a. Judgemental forecast
b. Time series forecast
c. Associative model
d. All of the above
(*Ans*: a)

6. **Short term regular variations related to the calendar or time of day is known as**
a. Trend
b. Seasonality
c. Cycles
d. Random variations
(*Ans*: b)

7. **The demand for period t-2 and t-1 is 10 and 12 cases respectively. As per naïve method, the demand for next period 't' is**
a. 10
b. 11
c. 12
d. 14
(*Ans*: d)

8. **Calculate four periods moving average forecast from the last six periods**

Period	*Demand*	*Period*	*Demand*
1	38	2	40
3	42	4	40
5	44	6	38

a) 40

b) 41

c) 42

d) 43

(*Ans*: b)

9. Calculate a weighted average forecast using a weight of.50 to the most recent period,.40 for the next recent period and.30 for the next period

Period	*Demand*	*Period*	*Demand*
1	38	2	40
3	42	4	40
5	44	6	38

a) 46.6

b) 47.6

c) 48.6

d) 49.6

(*Ans*: c)

10. A linear trend equation has the form

a) F=a-bt

b) F=a+bt

c) F=2a-bt

d) F=2a+bt

(*Ans*: b)

11. If the actual demand for a period is 100 units but forecast demand was 90 units. The forecast error is

a. –10

b. +10

c. –5

d. +5

(*Ans*: b)

12. Economies of scale hold when

a) Construction costs do not increase linearly with output levels

b) Production efficiency increases as workers gain experience

c) Quantity discounts are available for material purchases

d) All of the above

(*Ans*: d)

13. Which of the following companies follows a pure chase strategy of aggregate planning?

a) Hershey's

b) Nordstrom's

c) Ford

d) Mars Inc.

(*Ans*: a)

14. A chase demand strategy should be followed when

a) Worker skill qualifications are high

b) Unemployment rates are low

c) Inventory costs are high

d) All of the above

(*Ans*: c)

15. Which of the following aggregate planning techniques guarantees an optimal solution?

a) Linear programming

b) Search decision rule

c) Trial and error with a spreadsheet

d) Management coefficients model

(*Ans*: a)

16. All of the following statements concerning the characteristics of aggregate planning for services is true except

a) Most services cannot be inventoried

b) Demand is difficult to predict

c) Capacity is easy to predict

d) Labor is the most constraining resource

e) All of the above statements are true

(*Ans*: c)

17. All of the following statements concerning level production are true except

a) Level production strategy sets production at a fixed rate

b) The main costs of level production involve hiring and firing

c) Level production strategy uses inventory to absorb variations in demand

d) All of the above statements are true

(*Ans*: b)

18. Using the data above, which of the following statements is true if the company maintains a level production strategy?

a) The total number of units inventoried for the 4 quarters is 40,000 units

b) The cost of the level production plan is Rs18,000

c) There are 12,500 units inventoried in quarter 3

d) A work force of 14 workers is maintained during the 4th quarter period

e) More than one statement above is true

(*Ans*: a)

19. A company wishes to develop a linear programming model that will satisfy demand at a minimum cost. Using the data above, which of the following statements contains the correct formulation of the workforce constraint for quarter 4 for this problem?

a) W4 - W3 + H4 - F3 = 0

b) W4 - W3 - H3 - F3 = 0

c) W4 - W3 + H3 + F3 = 0

d) W4 - W3 - H4 + F4 = 0

e) none of the above

(*Ans*: d)

20. In production planning, the level of detail from highest to lowest is

a) Master production schedule, aggregate plan, material requirements plan

b) Aggregate plan, material requirements plan, master production schedule

c) Aggregate plan, master production schedule, material requirements plan

d) Material requirements plan, master production schedule, aggregate plan

(*Ans*: c)

21. The linear decision rule for aggregate planning is based on the assumption that production costs are linear.

a) True

b) False

(*Ans*: b)

22. Some industries maintain a negative capacity cushion.

a) True

b) False

(*Ans*: a)

23. The capacity lag strategy is the most moderate of the strategies and the least conservative.

a) True

b) False

(*Ans*: b)

24. The costs involved in using a chase strategy are mainly in holding inventory, including the cost of obsolete or perishable items that may have to be discarded.

a) True

b) False

(*Ans*: b)

25. The aggregate planning problem is purely a manufacturing problem and should be solved by manufacturing personnel.

a) True

b) False

(*Ans*: b)

3

Designing of Operational Systems and Control

3.1 PRODUCT DESIGN

Product design in its broadest logic include the entire growth of the product through all the beginning stages until actual manufacturing starts. It refers to the collection of elements or parts that in a group form a product. Product design is the process of shaping all the features and characteristics of a product or service. The design of the product or service must go with the business strategy in order to make the company successful. It means same type of standardized product manufacturing is less costly compared to products of varying nature. The main difference between manufacturing and service is the fact that manufacturing creates a tangible product, while services are in tangible in nature Service design is more complex compared to product because it consists of designing service and its concept. The main center of attention of product brand management lies on the single product or product family. Product design management is related to research and development, marketing and brand management and is coming in the fast-moving consumer goods (FMCG) industry. But service design is accountable for the image expressions of the individual product brand, with its varied customer–brand touch points and the execution of the brand through service design management deals with the newly rising field of service design. It is the action of planning and organizing people, infrastructure, communication and material components of a service. The aim is to develop the quality of the service, the interaction between the service provider and its customers and fulfill the customer's experience. The growing significance and size of the service sector in terms of people employed and economic importance requires that services should be elegant in order to remain competitive and to continue to catch the attention of customers. Design management traditionally focuses in the design and development of manufactured products; service design managers can relate many of the same theoretical and methodological approaches. Systematic and strategic management of service design helps the business gain competitive advantages and beat new markets. Companies that proactively recognize the interests of their customers and use this information to expand services that create good experiences for the customer and it will bring in new and profitable business opportunities.

Companies in the service sector innovate by addressing the intangibility, heterogeneity, inseparability and derivability of service. Goods can be manufactured centrally and delivered around the globe where as services have to be performed at the place of consumption, which makes it difficult to achieve global quality consistency and effective cost control.

3.2 PROCESS DESIGN

It is concerned with the overall series of operations required to attain the design specification of the product. *Example*: Intel's process design for their next generation hub controller demanded an additional factory in Malaysia as well as copious amounts of energy drinks.

Production design: Concept of designing products from the point of view of producibility.

3.3 OBJECTIVES OF PRODUCT DESIGN

(i) The overall objective is profit generation in the long run.

(ii) To achieve the desired product quality.

(iii) To reduce the development time and cost to the minimum.

(iv) To reduce the cost of the product.

(v) To ensure manufacturability (design for manufacturing and assembly).

3.3.1 Steps in Product Design

Idea development: A need is identified and a product idea to satisfy it is put together.

Product screening: Initial ideas are evaluated for difficulty and likelihood of success.

Preliminary design and testing: Market testing and prototype development.

Final design: Product and service characteristics are set.

3.3.1.1 Idea development

Existing and target customers: Customer surveys and focus groups.

Benchmarking: Studying "best in class" companies from your industry or others and comparing their practices and performance to your own.

Reverse engineering: Disassembling a competitor's product and analyzing its design characteristics and how it was made

Suppliers, employees and technical advances

Product Screening Operations:

- Are production requirements consistent with existing capacity?
- Are the necessary labor skills and raw materials available?

Marketing:

- How large is the market niche?
- What is the long-term potential for the product?

Finance:

- Expected return on investment
- Preliminary design and testing
- General performance characteristics are translated into technical specifications

- Prototypes are built and tested (may be offered for sale on a small scale)
- Bugs are worked out and designs are refined final design

Specifications are set and then used to:

- Develop processing and service delivery instructions
- Guide equipment selection
- Outline jobs to be performed
- Negotiate contracts with suppliers and distributors

3.4 APPROACHES TO PRODUCT DESIGN

Designing for the customer

- Industrial design
- Voice of the customer
- Quality function deployment (QFD)
- QFD will help you link the "What's" (needs of the customer) with the "How's" (how the need will be met by the organization).

Understanding the QFD process can help you realize the following benefits:

- Prevention of failure
- Greater teamwork
- Improved communication
- Faster deployment times
- Greater knowledge about customer requirements
- Improved customer satisfaction

Quality function deployment (QFD) is a tool that is sometimes referred to as the "voice of the customer," or as the "house of quality." Quality function deployment has been described as a process to ensure that the customers' wants and, needs are heard and translated into technical characteristics. The technical characteristics are handled by the company through the design function, or better still, through a cross functional team that includes sales, marketing, design engineering, manufacturing engineering and operations. This activity should focus the product or service on satisfying customer requirements. QFD is a tool for the entire organization to use. It is flexible and customized for each case and works well for manufactured products and in the service industry: Fig. 3.1 shows QFD matrix. Where the top matrix is called design requirement matrix, left side matrix is customer need and right side matrix is used to benchmark.

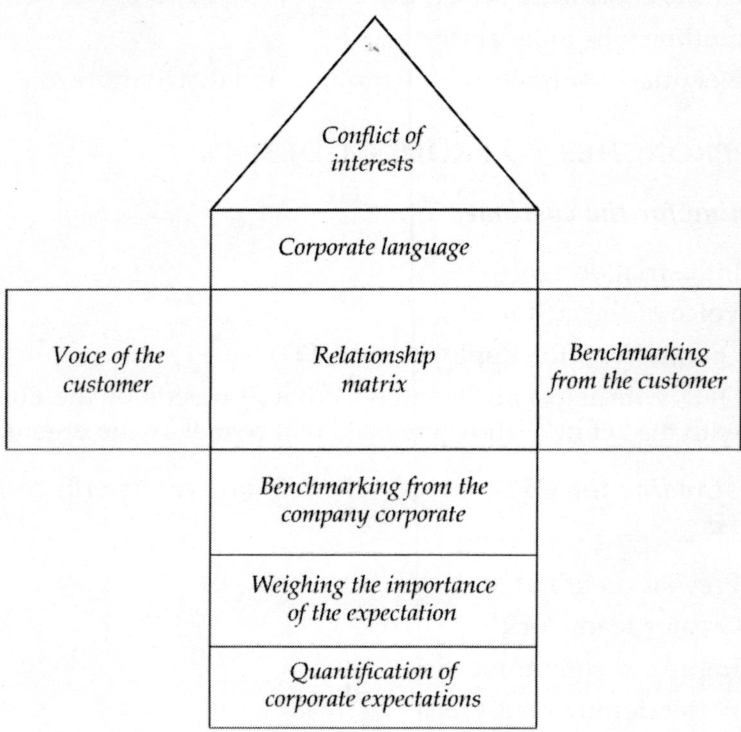

Fig. 3.1 QFD Matrix (*Source*: Google image)

The goal of QFD is to translate often subjective quality criteria into objective ones that can be quantified and measured and which can then be used to design and manufacture the product. It is a complimentary method for determining how and where priorities are to be assigned in product development. The intent is to employ objective procedures in increasing detail throughout the development of the product. The 3 main goals in implementing QFD are:

1. Prioritize spoken and unspoken customer wants and needs.
2. Translate these needs into technical characteristics and specifications.
3. Build and deliver a quality product or service by focusing everybody toward customer satisfaction.

Example:

- Identify customer wants
- Identify how the good/service will satisfy customer wants
- Relate customer wants to product how's
- Identify relationships between the firm's how's
- Develop importance ratings
- Evaluate competing products
- Compare performance to desirable technical attributes

Fig. 3.2 Explains technical attributes of HOQ by showing an example of customer choice of car and design requirement.

Fig. 3.3 shows HOQ calculations of matress selection depending on customer demand where 9,3 and 1 are used for calcuation matrix value.

ii. Designing for Manufacture and Assembly (DFMA)

Over-the-wall approach

Traditional engineering is also renowned as sequential engineering. It is the procedure of marketing, engineering design, manufacturing, testing and production where every stage of the development process is carried out separately and the next stage cannot begin until the previous stage is finished. Therefore the information flow is only in one direction, and it is not until the finish of the chain that errors, changes and corrections can be relayed to the start of the sequence, causing expected costs to be under predicted.

Traditional engineering is also famous as over the wall engineering as each stage blindly throws the development to the next stage over the wall.

Technical Attributes For The Hoq Matrix (1:○ 3:△ 9:□)									
	Importance weights	Stiffness of mattress	Weight	Volume	Design idea	Durability	Base strength	Wood treatment	Wood quality
Good appearance	4		○	△		□			□
Fabric	2		□	△		△		△	○
Versatility	2				□	□	△		○
Comfortable	1	□	□	□	□	□	△	○	□
Long term use	5	△	□	○	□	□	△		
Material	9	□	□	△	□	□	□	□	□
Seating capacity	2			□	○	□			
Easy cleaning	3			□		□	□		
Cost	2			△	□	□	□	□	□
Gaps between matress division	2	□			□	△	□	□	□

Fig. 3.2 Technical attribute for HOQ (*Source*: Paneerselvem)

During the industrial revolution, technology became more difficult. The complexity forced employees of companies to focus in different areas of the product design process. No longer could one person be answerable for the design, manufacture and sales of a product. The age of the craftsmen gave way to the period of the specialist. Large companies begun to organize their into departments with different responsibilities. Some examples of departments and responsibilities are shown below.

1. *Marketing* – Tries to understand the future needs of the customer.
2. *Research* – Develops the technology to meet the wants identified by marketing.

Customer requirements	Importance weights	Stiffness of mattress	Weight	Volume	Design idea	Durability	Base strength	Wood treatment	Wood quality	Current product	Plan	Improvement ratio	Sales point	Absolute weight	Customer need weight
Good appearance	4	0	12.685	38.055	0	114.165	0	0	114.165	7		1.14286	1.5	6.85714	12.685
Fabric	2	0	79.915	26.638	0	26.638	0	26.638	8.8795	3	3	2	1.2	4.8	8.8795
Versatility	2	0	0	0	72.146	72.146	24.049	0	8.0162	3	3	1.6667	1.3	4.3333	8.0162
Comfortable	1	22.476	22.476	22.476	22.476	22.476	7.4921	2.4974	22.476	8	8	1.125	1.2	1.35	2.4974
Long term use	5	48.0973	144.292	16.0324	144.292	144.292	48.0973	0	0	6	6	1.3333	1.3	8.66667	16.0324
Material	9	209.778	209.738	69.926	209.778	209.778	209.778	209.778	209.778	7	7	1	1.4	12.6	23.3087
Seating capacity	2	0	0	46.617	5.1797	46.617	0	0	0	5	5	1	1.4	2.8	5.1797
Easy cleaning	3	0	0	83.245	0	83.245	83.245	0	0	9	9	1.111	1.5	5	9.2495
Cost	2	0	0	17.481	52.445	52.445	52.445	52.445	52.445	8	8	1.125	1.4	3.15	5.8272
Gaps between matress division	2	74.921	0	0	74.921	24.974	74.921	74.921	74.921	6	6	1.5	1.5	4.5	8.3245
Absolute weight		355	469	320	581	797	500	366	491						
Total characteristic weight		9.1568	12.092	8.2598	14981	20.536	12.888	9.4405	12.647						

Fig. 3.3 HOQ (*Source*: Satapathy *et.al.*)

3. Design - Uses the technology developed by research to design products to meet the needs of the customer.
4. Manufacturing – Develops the methods to manufacture the products designed by the design department.
5. Sales – Develop plans and executes the plans to sell the products to the customer.

The design process was then organized into a linear system as shown below.

Concurrent engineering: Concurrent engineering is a work method based on the parallelization of tasks (*i.e.*, performing tasks concurrently), which is sometimes called Simultaneous Engineering or Integrated Product Development (IPD). It refers to an approach used in product development in which functions of design engineering, manufacturing engineering and other functions are incorporated to decrease the elapsed time required to bring a new product to the market.

Design for Manufacturing (DFM), Design for Assembly (DFA)

iii. Designing for Ease of Production (or Manufacturability)

- Specification
- Standardization
- Simplification

iv. Designing for Quality

a. *Designing for robustness (or robust design)*

Robust design method, also called the Taguchi Method, pioneered by Dr. Genichi Taguchi, greatly improves engineering productivity. By intentionally considering the noise factors (environmental variation during the product's usage, manufacturing variation and component deterioration) and the cost of failure in the field the robust design method helps make sure customer satisfaction. Robust Design focuses on improving the fundamental function of the product or process, thus facilitating flexible designs and concurrent engineering. Definitely, it is the most powerful method available to decrease product cost, improve quality and simultaneously reduce development interval.

Robust Parameter design has 4 main steps:

1. ***Problem formulation:*** This step consists of identifying the main function, developing the P-diagram, defining the ideal function and S/N ratio and planning the experiments. The experiments involve changing the control, noise and signal factors systematically using orthogonal arrays.
2. ***Data collection/simulation:*** The experiments may be conducted in hardware or through simulation. It is not necessary to have a full-scale model of the product for the purpose of experimentation. It is sufficient and more desirable to have an essential model of the product that adequately captures the design concept. Thus, the experiments can be done more economically.
3. ***Factor effects analysis:*** The effects of the control factors are calculated in this step and the results are analyzed to select optimum setting of the control factors.
4. ***Prediction/confirmation:*** In order to validate the optimum conditions we predict the performance of the product design under baseline and optimum settings of the control factors. Then we perform confirmation experiments under these conditions and compare the results with the predictions. If the results of confirmation experiments agree with the predictions, then we implement it.

b. *Designing for production*

   i. ***Modular design:*** Modular design, or "modularity in design", is a design approach that subdivides a system into smaller parts called modules or skids, that can be independently created and then used in different systems. A modular system can be characterized by functional partitioning into discrete scalable, reusable modules, rigorous use of well-defined modular interfaces and making use of industry standards for interfaces.

   ii. ***Designing for automation:*** Design automation usually refers to electronic design automation, or design automation which is a product configuration. Extending Computer-Aided Design (CAD), automated design and Computer-Automated Design example. Composite steel construction.

iii. ***Designing for reliability:*** Reliability engineering is engineering that emphasizes dependability in the lifecycle management of a product. Dependability, or reliability, describes the ability of a system or component to function under stated conditions for a specified period of time.

iv. Designing for environmental protection

v. Designing for recycling

vi. Designing of disassembly (DFD)

vii. Designing for mass customization

viii. Delayed differentiation and modular designs are two tactics used to make mass customisation possible.

ix. Other issues in product design are:

(a) *Computer aided design (CAD),*

(b) *Value engineering or value analysis which*

- ***Computer aided design:*** Use of computer graphics for designing the product helps to generate a number of alternative designs and identify the best alternative which meets the designer's criteria.
- ***Value engineering/Value analysis:*** Concerned with the improvement of design and specifications at various stages of product planning and development.
- ***Designing for Ergonomics:*** Human factors and ergonomics (HFandE), also known as comfort design, functional design and systems, is the follow of designing products, systems, or processes to take proper account of the interaction between them and the people who use them.

To achieve best practice design: Ergonomists use the data and techniques of several disciplines:

- *Anthropometry:* Body sizes, shapes, populations and variations
- *Biomechanics:* Muscles, levers, forces, strength

- *Environmental physics:* Noise, light, heat, cold, radiation, vibration body systems: hearing, vision, sensations
- *Applied psychology:* Skill, learning, errors, differences
- *Social psychology:* Groups, communication, learning, behaviors.

According to Safe Work Australia, the total economic cost of work-related injuries and illnesses is estimated to be $60 billion dollars. Recent research has shown that lower back pain is the world's most common work-related disability – affecting employees from offices, building sites and in the highest risk category, agriculture.

Ergonomics aims to create safe, comfortable and productive workspaces by bringing human abilities and limitations into the design of a workspace, including the individual's body size, strength, skill, speed, sensory abilities (vision, hearing), and even attitudes.

3.5 LEGAL, ETHICAL AND ENVIRONMENTAL ISSUES

Legal Aspect of Product Design

- The imposition of rules and acts passed by state and central govt.
- The standards related to code of practice for design, fabrication and testing of products prepared by standards organization.
- The imposition of punitive damages by the courts in product liability cases.
- The resistance of consumer protection forums to badly designed and manufacturing products.
- The resistance of public to damage of their environment.
- The most important law to consider while dealing with the product liability is the consumer protection Act of 1986.
- The sales of goods Act of 1956.

3.5.1 Other Legal Issues

- *Product liability*
- *Intellectual property*

3.5.2 Ethical Issues

- Assessing the impact of the design on consumer
- Protection of Intellectual Property
- Privacy
- Exposure to the undesirable
- Advertising of Design
- Right to alter natural order
- Whether designs should be tested on animals and humans
- Environmental impact
- Sustainable technology
- Minority groups

3.5.3 Environmental

Designer should anticipate environmental trends and design products that are clean enough for future environmental standards.

Process Pollution: Product designer must avoid the process that causing pollution from solvents, combustible products, wastes etc. or he may change the processes at the early stages.

Ease of recycling product: Everyone has a moral obligation about the happens to the product after its useful life is over? Can it be recycled into new even be able to profit in some manner from recycling of its product.

3.6 PROCESS PLANNING AND PROCESS DESIGN

After the final design of the product has been approved and released for production, the production planning and control department takes the responsibility of process planning and process design for converting the product design into a tangible product.

A process is a sequence of activities that is intended to achieve some result, for example, to create added value for the customers.

Process planning: Concerned with planning the conversion processes needed to convert the raw material into finished products.

3.6.1 Steps in Process Planning

- Analysis part print
- Consult with product engineer on product design changes
- List the basic operation
- Determine – economical and practical manufacturing methods
- Combine the operation and put them in to sequence
- Specify the gauging required for process
- *Process design:* Concerned with the overall sequences of operations required to achieve the product specifications
- *Operations design:* Concerned with the design of the individual manufacturing operation.

3.7 PROCESS SELECTION

Process selection refers to the way production of goods or services is organized. Three primary questions to be addressed before deciding on process selection are:

Process selection is based on five considerations:

1. Type of process; range from intermittent to continuous
2. Degree of vertical integration
3. Flexibility of resources
4. Mix between capital and human resources
5. Degree of customer contact

3.8 PROCESS SELECTION DECISION

- Process by market orientation
- Make to stock
- Assemble to order
- Make to order
- Engineer to order

Table 3.1 Shows products from make to stock and make to order where product is made as per producer specified and as per customer requirement respectively.

- Project
- Jobshop
- Batch production
- Assembly line
- Continous flow
- Processes and customer involvement

Table 3.1: Characterized products from. make to stock and make to order.

Characteristics	*Make-to-Stock*	*Make-to-Order*
Product	Producer-specified Low variety Inexpensive	Customer-specified High variety Expensive
Objective	Balance inventory, capacity, and service	Managing delivery lead Times and capacity
Main operations problems	Forecasting Planning production Control of inventory	Delivery promises Delivery Time Process as production system

- Self service
- Product selection
- Partnership

3.8.1 Process Technologies

Automation

The use of various control systems with minimal human interference for operating equipment like machinery, processes in factories, boilers and heat treating ovens, switching on telephone networks, steering and stabilization of ships, aircraft and other applications is called as: *Automated Material Handling*

Example CNC machines.

Automated guided vehicles (AGV)

It is a mobile robot that follows markers or wires in the floor, or uses vision, magnets, or lasers for navigation. They are most often used in industrial applications to move materials around a manufacturing facility or warehouse. Application of the automatic guided vehicle has broadened during the late 20th century.

Example Towing Vehicles

Automated storage and retrieval systems (AS/RS)

It consists of a variety of computer-controlled systems for automatically placing and retrieving loads from defined storage locations. Automated storage and retrieval systems (AS/RS) are typically used in applications where:

- There is a very high volume of loads being moved into and out of storage
- Storage density is important because of space constraints
- No value is added in this process (no processing, only storage and transport)
- Accuracy is critical because of potential expensive damages to the load
- *Example*: Vertical lift module.

Computer-Aided Design (CAD) software

Computer-aided drafting (CAD) is the use of computer systems to aid in the creation, modification, analysis, or optimization of a design. CAD software is used to increase the productivity of the designer, improve the quality of design, improve communications through documentation, and to create a database for manufacturing. CAD output is often in the form of electronic files for print, machining, or other manufacturing operations. The term CADD, (for Computer Aided Design and Drafting) is also used.

Computer-aided design is used in many fields. Its use in designing electronic systems is known as electronic design automation, or EDA. In mechanical design it is known as mechanical design automation (MDA) or computer-aided drafting (CAD), which includes the process of creating a technical drawing with the use of computer software.

CAD is one part of the whole Digital Product Development (DPD) activity within the Product Lifecycle Management (PLM) processes and as such is used together with other tools, which are either integrated modules or stand-alone products, such as:

- Computer-aided engineering (CAE) and Finite element analysis (FEA)
- Computer-aided manufacturing (CAM) including instructions to Computer Numerical Control (CNC) machines
- Photo realistic rendering and motion simulation.
- Document management and revision control using Product Data Management (PDM).

Robotics and Numerically-Controlled (NC) Equipment

Computer Numeric Control (CNC) is the automation of machine tools that are operated by precisely programmed commands encoded on a storage medium (computer command module, usually located on the device. In modern CNC systems, end-to-end component design is highly automated using computer-aided design (CAD) and computer-aided manufacturing (CAM) programs. The programs produce a computer file that is interpreted to extract the commands needed to operate a particular machine by use of a post processor and then loaded into the CNC machines for production. Since any particular component might require the use of a number of different tools – drills, saws, etc. – modern machines often combine multiple tools into a single "cell". In other installations, a number of different machines are used with an external controller and human or robotic operators that move the component from machine to machine. In either case, the series of steps needed to produce any part is highly automated and produces a part that closely matches the original CAD design.

Example: Mils, Lathe, Plasma cutter, Electronics discharge machining.

Flexible Manufacturing Systems (FMS)

The manufacturing system that allows flexibility in the system to react in case of changes, whether predicted or unpredicted, is called as FMS.

This flexibility is generally considered to fall into two categories, which both contain numerous subcategories.

Machine flexibility

It covers the system's ability to be changed to produce new product types, and ability to change the order of operations executed on a part.

Routing flexibility

It consists of the ability to use multiple machines to perform the same operation on a part, as well as the system's ability to absorb large-scale changes, such as in volume, capacity, or capability.

Most FMS consist of three main systems.

- Work machines
- Automated CNC machines
- Material handling system to optimize parts flow and the central control computer which controls material movements and machine flow.

The main advantages of an FMS is its high flexibility in managing manufacturing resources like time and effort in order to manufacture a new product. The best application of an FMS is found in the production of small sets of products like those from a mass production.

Example: Automated material handling.

Computer-Integrated Manufacturing (CIM)

It is the manufacturing approach of using computers to control the entire production process. This integration allows individual processes to exchange information with each other and initiate actions. Through the integration of computers, manufacturing can be faster and less error-prone, although the main advantage is the ability to create automated manufacturing processes. Typically CIM relies on closed-loop control processes, based on real-time input from sensors. It is also known as flexible design and manufacturing.

Example : Electronic design and automation.

3.8.2 Process Strategy

An organization's approach to selection of the process for the conversion of resource inputs into outputs.

Key aspects in process strategy include:

i. Make or buy decisions
ii. Capital intensity and
iii. Process flexibility

Types of Process Designs (or) Process Strategy

- Product –focused (production line or continuous production) - Organised according to the type of product/service being produced general form.

1. Discrete unit manufacturing
2. Process manufacturing

3.9 PRODUCT LIFE CYCLE

Product life cycle

A product life cycle consist of 4 stages through which a product passes that is introduction, growth, maturity, decline.

Introduction: At this stage, sales begin and profit goes from – ve to + ve. In this stage, the demand is low. Because the costumer don't know much about the product. The organization has to invest heavily in advertisement to make the product familiar to the costumers. The volume sales are low and if proper care is not taken, there is chances to product failure.

Growth: The product next enters a stage at rapid growth. Early in this stage (due to acceptability of the product by the costumer) there is drastic jump in sales and profit rise. It is because of limited or no competition. During this stage the mandate for operation is somehow to keep up with demand, efficiency is less of concern.

Maturity: During this stage, sales level off and profit begins to decline. New competition create to cut costs and ultimately on unit profit margin. Now operation must stress on efficiency, although marketing can ease the pressure by intensifying to differentiate the product.

Decline: At last the existing product enters to a declining stage and becomes obsolete. Either demand despisers or a better less expensive product. Life cycle suggest when to eliminate the existing product and introduce a new one. This life cycle varies greatly from product to product. For example it took 15 years for "Xerox" to introduce electrostatic copy m/c. in contrast and computer and microchip industry, products become obsolete in months.

Fig. 3.4 Explains the graph between sales volume and product life cycle. Product life cycle shows three stages like introduction, growth, maturity and decline.

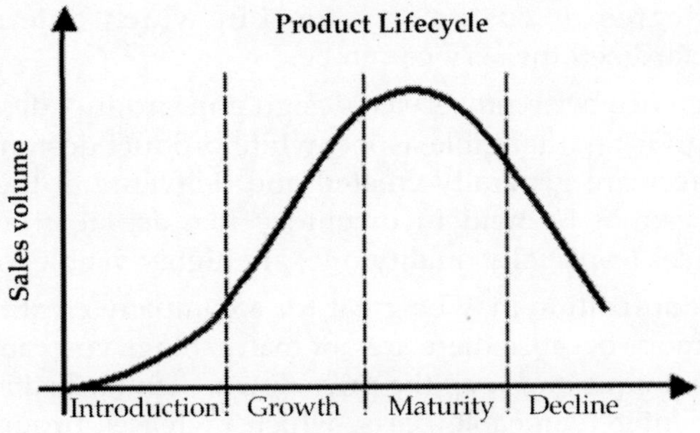

Fig. 3.4: Product life cycle.

KEY NOTE

1. When planning on producing a new product and/or service, the key factor is the product and service design. Successful designs come down to these basic principles: translate customers' wants and needs, refine existing products and services, develop new products and services, formulate quality goals, formulate cost

targets, construct and test prototypes, document specifications and translate products and service specification into process specifications.

2. The process of design has certain steps that include motivation, ideas for improvement, organizational capabilities and forecasting. In the product process innovations, research and development play a significant role. Because of the influence a product and service design can have on an organization, the design process is encouraged to be tied in with the organization's strategy and take into account some key considerations.
3. Service design is an activity of organizing and planning people, communication and material components in order to improve service quality. It is the interaction between the service provider and customers and the customers' experience. A service is anything that is done to or for a client and is created and delivered simultaneously. The two most important issues in service design are the degree of variation in requirements and the degree of customer contact in which determines how standardized the service can be.
4. Difference between service design and product design: Service design is an intangible aspect while product design is tangible. Services are generally created and delivered at the same time and cannot be held in inventory like actual products. Also, services (especially quality one) are highly visible to customers.
5. Standardization may be great for a company creating products like mops because there are not many things you can do to make them unique and keep the price down. Standardization products have interchangeable parts, which increases productivity and lowers the costs of production. Standardization has many important benefits and certain disadvantages. Some advantages are the design costs for standardization products are low. The scheduling of work inventory handling, purchasing and accounting activities are routine, making the quality more consistent. The disadvantages with standardization are that they decrease variety offered to consumers leading to less of an appeal. Also, the high cost of design change makes it relentless to improve.

6. Mass customization is a strategy that some companies can use to incorporate customization while practicing standardization. This strategy keeps costs low while adding variety to a product. The two tactics that make mass customization possible is delayed differentiation and modular design. Some companies may consider *delayed differentiation* if the company chooses to not finish a product due to unknown customer preferences. However, another tactic of modular design is a form of standardization in which component's parts are grouped into modules to allow easy replacement or interchangeability. Producing a computer is an example of modular design.

EXERCISE 3.1

1. **Write about product life cycle with example.**

   Ans. Chapter 3.9 product life cycle

2. **Explain steps of process design.**

   Ans. Chapter 3.6 process planning and process design

3. **Do a case study of product design and new product development.**

   Ans. Chapter 3.3 objectives of product design

4. **Write notes on QFD, FMEA.**

   Ans. Quality Function Deployment (QFD) is a structured approach to defining customer needs or requirements and translating them into specific plans to produce products to meet those needs. The "voice of the customer" is the term to describe these stated and unstated customer needs or requirements.

   Failure mode and effects analysis (FMEA) - also "failure modes", plural, in many publications - was one of the first highly structured, systematic techniques for failure analysis. It was developed by reliability engineers in the late 1950s to study problems that might arise from malfunctions of military systems. An FMEA is often the first step of a system reliability study. It involves reviewing as many components, assemblies and subsystems as possible to identify failure modes and their causes and effects. For each component, the failure modes and their resulting effects on the rest of the system are recorded in a specific FMEA worksheet.

3.1 MULTIPLE CHOICE QUESTION WITH ANSWERS

1. **New product design and development projects transform a new market opportunity and/or new product technology into a set of specifications that define a product.**

   A) True

   B) False

   Ans. A

2. **The _____ phase of the product life cycle is usually the culmination of an intense product design and development effort.**

   A) Launch

   B) Growth

   C) Maturity

   D) Decline

   E) All of the above

   Ans. A

3. **Once demand stabilizes and product refinements become less frequent, the product has reached the ______ stage of the life cycle.**

   A) Launch

   B) Growth

   C) Maturity

   D) Decline

   E) All of the above

   Ans. B

4. **Fast innovators are able to fund more new design and development projects than other firms.**

   A) True

   B) False

   Ans. A

5. **_______________ have fewer problems in launching new products and fewer failures in the market place.**

   A) Fast innovators

   B) High-quality innovators

   C) Efficient innovators

   D) Development projects

   E) Financial managers

   Ans. A

6. **Firms that excel at finding and developing new ideas and opportunities for innovation:**

   A) Hire the best and the brightest

   B) Have an effective reward system in place

   C) Allocate adequate resources

   D) All of the above

   E) None of the above

   Ans. A

7. **____________________ develop products or processes that will employ some entirely new technology.**

   A) Research and advanced development projects

   B) Radical breakthrough development projects

   C) Next generation or platform development projects

   D) Enhancements, hybrid and derivative development projects

   Ans. A

8. **A benefit of involving suppliers in the innovation process is:**

   A) An decreased number of ideas

   B) Fewer successful products

   C) Shared financial risks

   D) More control over intellectual property

   E) More control over goals and innovation timing

   Ans. B

9. **________________ evaluates pilot production units, establishes market channels and an order fulfillment system, and trains sales**

force and field service personnel.

A) Market introduction

B) Product and market testing

C) Detailed design and development

D) Produce and process planning

E) Commercialization

Ans. C

10. **___________ is the simultaneous design and development of all the processes and information needed to produce a product, to sell it, to distribute it, and to service it.**

A) Concurrent engineering (CE)

B) Simultaneous engineering

C) Integrated product development

D) All of the above

E) None of the above

Ans. A

11. **_______ costs are spent to make changes to the product design and to production processes needed to solve problems uncovered both in production and in the field.**

A) Development

B) Sustaining and warranty

C) Production

D) Sales support

E) All of the above

Ans. A

12. **QFD is widely regarded as a useful tool for translating ordinary language used to describe customer needs into engineering language used to set product and process design parameters.**

A) True

B) False

Ans. A

13. The customer requirements planning matrix is also known as the:

A) House of quality

B) Quality function matrix

C) Customer desired flow

D) Beta testing

E) None of the above

Ans. A

4

Production Planning and Control

4.1 INTRODUCTION

- Work study, methods engineering includes work simplification, job design, value analysis and the like.
- Work study method was developed to improve performance of a given work.
- Work study is the body of knowledge concerned with analysis of the work methods and the standard of proposed work methods.
- Objective of work study is to improve operational efficiency.
- The purpose of work study is to determine the best or most effective method of
  - accomplishing a necessary operation.

4.2 RELATIONSHIP OF TIME AND MOTION STUDY TO WORK STUDY

- Time study and motion study are results of practices developed by F.W. Taylor, Frank and Lillian Gilbreth.
- Time study: Exercising control over the output in respect of a job by setting standards for performance.
- Time study may be used to compare the effectiveness of alternative work methods.

Objectives

- To analyze the present method of doing a job, systematically in order to develop a new and better method
- To measure the work content of a job by measuring the time required to do the job for a qualified worker and hence to establish standard time
- To increase the productivity by ensuring the best possible use of human, machine and material resources and to achieve best quality product/service at minimum possible cost.
- To improve operational efficiency

4.3 METHOD STUDY OR METHODS ANALYSIS

- Method study is also known as methods improvement.
- Prime objectives of method study are to eliminate wasteful and inefficient motions.

Steps in Method Study

1. *Select*- Select the work to be studied.
2. *Record*- Record all the relevant facts of the present method of direct observation.
3. *Examine*- Examine the facts critically in sequence, using special critical examination sheet.
4. *Develop*- Develop the best method (*i.e*) the most practical, economic and effective method, under prevailing circumstances.
5. *Install*- Install that method as standard practice.
6. *Maintain*- Maintain the standard practice by regular routine check

Recording techniques:

- Pocess flow chart.
- Process charts are one of the simpler forms of workflow charting and are still in regular usage but are less common than they once were (see Process Mapping). This is unfortunate since it was the ubiquitous nature of the process chart that made it a

common "language" between different groups of people and across different industries.

- A variety of process charts has been designed to meet the needs of a particular level or stage of analysis, they can be used at a detailed level (recording activity at a specific work station or workplace), but also at the wider system, process or procedure level.
- The different kinds of process chart share a common core set of symbols, though some have additional symbols for specific and specialised process steps. The common symbols (of which there are only five) were first promulgated by the American Society of Mechanical Engineers and have become known as the ASME symbols. Table 4.1 shows recording techniques of method study that includes charts, diagrams and photographic aids.

Table 4.1: Recording techniques of method study (*Source*: Aswathappa)

Recording technique	*Information recorded*
(a) *Charts*	
1. Outline process chart	Principle operations and inspection of the processes.
2. Flow process chart	Activities of men, material or equipment are analyzed into five events *viz.*, operation, transport, inspection, delay and storage.
3. Two-handed process chart	Movements of two hands or limbs of the operator.
4. Multiple activity chart	Simultaneous/interrelated activities of operators and/or machines on a common time scale.
5. Simultaneous motion cycle chart (SIMO)	Movement of body members of the operator, expressed in terms of therbligs on a common time scale.
(b) *Diagrams and Models*	
1. Flow diagram	Path of men, materials and equipments on a scale model.
2. String diagram	Same as above except for the variation that it uses string to trace the path.
(c) *Photographic aids*	
1. Cyclegraph	Movement of hand obtained by exposing a photographic plate to the light emitted from small bulbs attached to the operator's fingers.
2. Chrono-cyclegraphs	Modification of cyclegraph in which recording is made using flash light.

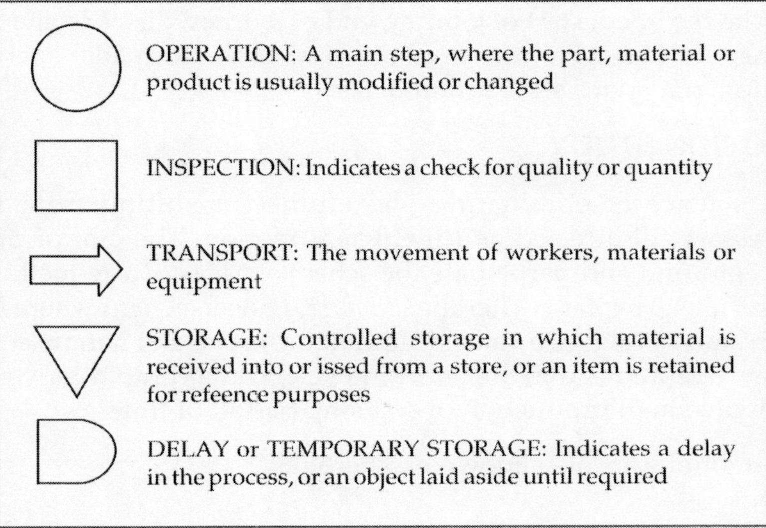

Fig. 4.1: Symbols of operation method study

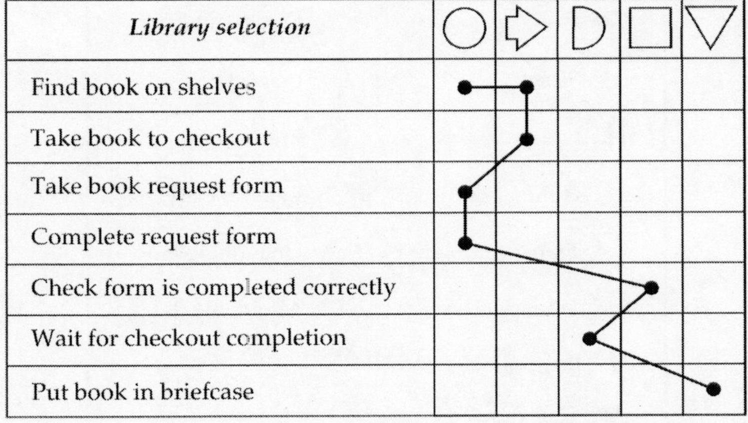

Fig. 4.2: Examples of flow process chart.

Fig. 4.1 and 4.2 shows the movement of materials (book) by showing path and movement within symbols. These symbols are simple linked together in a vertical chart representing the key stages in a process; it is usual to place a commentary in an adjoining column recording contextual/environmental information *e.g.*, against a transport symbol would be recorded, start of journey, end of journey, distance and mode of transport. Fig. 4.1 shows symbols of method study like operation, inspetion, transport, storage and delay.

4.4 MOTION STUDY

Is the science of eliminating wastefulness resulting from using unnecessary; ill-directed and inefficient motion. The aim of motion study is to find and perpetuate the scheme of least waste methods of labour. Fig. 4.3 explains Therbligs (*Source*: Paneerselvem) where Micro motion study provides a valuable technique for making minute analysis of those operations that are short in cycle, contain rapid movements and involve high production over a long period of time.

Micro-motions are also known as Therbligs.

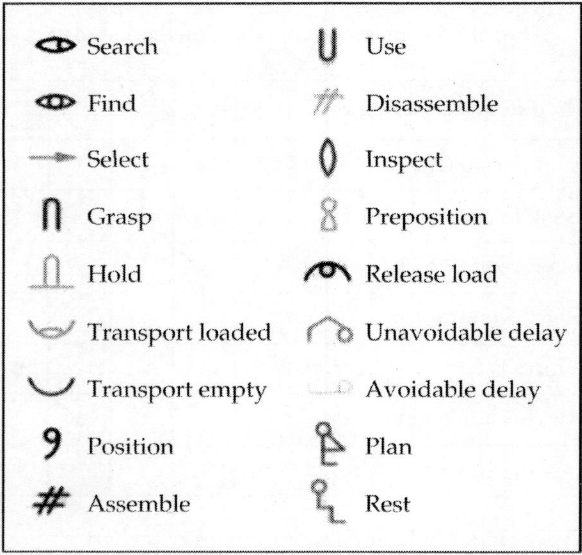

Fig. 4.3 Examples of Therbligs

- Search (Sr)
- Select (St)
- Grasp (G)
- Transport empty (TE)

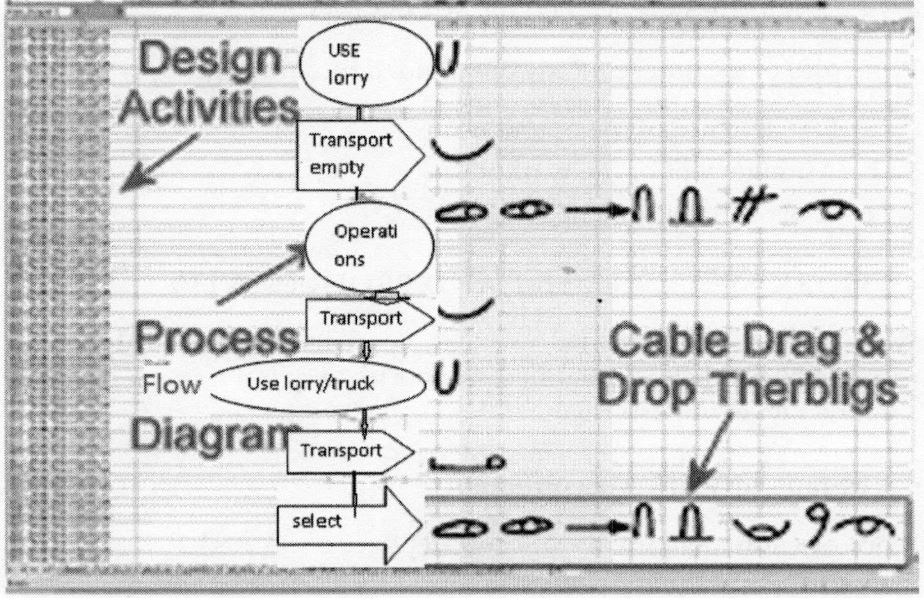

Fig. 4.4: Shows therbligs as per the process flow diagram (*Source*: O. P. Khanna)

- Transport loaded (TL)
- Hold (H)
- Release load (RL)
- Position (P)
- Pre-position (PP)
- Inspect (I)
- Assemble (A)
- Disassemble (DA)
- Use (U)
- Unavoidable delay (UD)
- Avoidable delay (AD)
- Plan (Pn)
- Rest for overcoming fatigue (R)
- Find (F)

4.5 PRINCIPLES OF MOTION ECONOMY

Principles of motion economy are divided into three groups.

a. Effective use of the operator
b. Arrangement of the workplace
c. Tools and equipment

4.6 WORK MEASUREMENT AND PRODUCTIVITY

Work measurement is the application of techniques designed to establish the time for a qualified worker to carry out a specified job at a defined level of performance.

4.6.1 Steps in Work Measurement

Work measurement involves seven steps.

- Break the job into elements.
- Record the observed time for each element by means of either time study, synthesis or analytical estimating.
- Establish elemental time values by extending observed time into normal time for each element by applying a rating factor.
- Assess relaxation allowance for personal needs and physical and mental fatigue involved in carrying out each element.
- Add the relaxation allowance time to the normal time for each element to arrive at the work content.
- Determine the frequency of occurrences of each element in the job, multiply the work content of each element by its frequency (*i.e.,* number of time the element occurs in the job) and add up the times to arrive at the work content for the job.

4.6.2 Techniques of Work Measurement

The following are the principal techniques by which work measurement is carried out:

- Time study
- Activity sampling

- Predetermined motion time systems
- Synthesis from standard data
- Estimating
- Analytical estimating
- Comparative estimating

Of these techniques we shall concern ourselves primarily with time study, since it is the basic technique of work measurement. Some of the other techniques either derive from it or are variants of it.

Time Study

Time Study consists of recording times and rates of work for elements of a specified job carried out under specified conditions to obtain the time necessary to carry out a job at a defined level of performance. In this technique the job to be studied is timed with a stop watch, rated and the basic time calculated. Table 4.2 shows application of each technique and requirements for effective time study and units of measurment.

The requirements for effective time study are:

- Co-operation and goodwill
- Defined job
- Defined method
- Correct normal equipment
- Quality standard and checks
- Experienced qualified motivated worker
- Method of timing
- Method of assessing relative performance
- Elemental breakdown
- Definition of break points

The following table shows the application of each technique and unit of measurement.

Table 4.2 Application of each technique and unit of measurement

Technique	*Application*	*Unit of measurement*
Time study using stop watch	Short cycle repetitive jobs	Centiminute (0.01 min)
PMTS	Manual operations confined to one work centre	TMU (I TMU = 0.006 min)
Work sampling	Long Heterogeneous operation	cycle jobs/Minute
Analytical estimating	Short cycle non-repetitive job	Minute

Time study using stop watch is the most popular technique for determining standard time. The first task of the analyst is to divide the work/job into smaller work elements in such a way that the time for each element should not be less than 3 seconds because for such elements, recording time is difficult. The steps of time study are as follows:

Step 1: First select the job to be studied. Break down the work content of the job into smallest possible elements. Then, inform the worker and define the best method.

Step 2: Observe the time for appropriate number of cycles (such as 25 to 50).

Step 3: Determine the average cycle time (CT)

$$CT = \frac{\sum Times}{\text{No. of cycles}}$$

Step 4: Determine the normal time (NT)

$$\text{NT} = \text{CT (PR)}$$

Where, PR is the performance rating.

Step 5: Determine the standard time using the following formula.

$$ST = \text{NT (AF) where AF} = \frac{1}{I - \%\text{Allowance AF being the allowance factor}}$$

Time Study Equipment

The following equipment is needed for time study work.

- Timing device
- Time study observation sheet
- Time study observation board
- Other equipment

Timing Device: The stop watch is the most widely used timing device used for time study, although electronic timer is also sometimes used. The two perform the same function with the difference that electronic timer can measure time to the second or third decimal of a second and can keep a large volume of time data in memory.

Time Study Observation Sheet: It is a printed form with spaces provided for noting down the necessary information about the operation being studied, like name of operation, drawing number, and name of the worker, name of time study person, and the date and place of study. Spaces are provided in the form for writing detailed description of the process (element-wise), recorded time or stop-watch readings for each element of the process, performance rating(s) of operator, and computation. Fig. 4.5 below shows a typical time study observation sheet.

Time Study Board: It is a light -weight board used for holding the observation sheet and stopwatch in position. It is of size slightly larger than that of observation sheet used. Generally, the watch is mounted at the center of the top edge.

Recording Media

One of the most critical requirements for time study is that of elemental breakdown. There are some general rules concerning the way in which a job should be broken down into elements. They include the following elements should be easily identifiable, with definite beginnings and endings so that, once established, they can be repeatedly recognised. These points are known as the break points and should be clearly described on the study sheet. Elements should be as short as can be conveniently timed by the observer. As far as possible, elements -

OBSERVATION SHEET	
SHEET 1 OF 1 SHEETS	DATE
OPERATION	OP. NO.
PART NAME	PART NO.
MACHINE NAME	MACH. NO.
OPERATOR'S NAME & NO.	MALE ☐ FEMALE ☐
EXPERIENCE ON JOB	MATERIAL
FOREMAN	DEPT. NO.

BEGIN	FINISH	ELAPSED	UNITS FINISHED	ACTUAL TIME PER 100	NO. MACHINES OPERATED

ELEMENTS	SPEED	FEED		1	2	3	4	5	6	7	8	9	10	SELECTED TIME
1.			T											
			R											
2.			T											
			R											
3.			T											
			R											
4.			T											
			R											
5.			T											
			R											
6.			T											
			R											
7.			T											
			R											
8.			T											
			R											
9.			T											
			R											
10. (1)			T											
			R											
11. (2)			T											
			R											
12. (3)			T											
			R											
13. (4)			T											
			R											
14. (5)			T											
			R											
15. (6)			T											
			R											
16. (7)			T											
			R											
17. (8)			T											
			R											
18.			T											
			R											

SELECTED TIME	RATING	NORMAL TIME	TOTAL ALLOWANCE	STANDARD TIME

SKETCH OF COMPONENTS:	TOOLS JIGS GAUGES:
	TIMED BY:

Fig. 4.5: Observation sheet of time study

particularly manual ones - should be chosen so that they represent naturally unified and distinct segments of the operation.

Performance Rating

Time Study is based on a record of observed times for doing a job together with an assessment by the observer of the speed and effectiveness of the worker in relation to the observer's concept of standard rating. This assessment is known as rating, the definition being given in BS 3138 (1979): The numerical value or symbol used to denote a rate of working. Standard rating is also defined (in this British Standard BS3138) as:

"The rating corresponding to the average rate at which qualified workers will naturally work, provided that they adhere to the specified method and that they are motivated to apply themselves to their work. If the standard rating is consistently maintained and the appropriate relaxation is taken, a qualified worker will achieve standard performance over the working day or shift."

Industrial engineers use a variety of rating scales, and one which has achieved wide use is the British Standards Rating Scale which is a scale where 0 corresponds to no activity and 100 corresponds to standard rating. Rating should be expressed as 'X' BS.

Below is an illustration of the Standard Scale: Rating *Walking Pace*

0 = No activity	50 = Very slow
75 = Steady	100 = Brisk (standard rating)
125 = Very fast	150 = Exceptionally fast

The basic time for a task, or element, is the time for carrying out an element of work or an operation at standard rating.

Basic time = Observed Time x Observed Rating the result is expressed in basic minutes - BM's.

Normal time = Observed time x Performance level of worker

Standard performance level

The work content of a job or operation is defined as: basic time + relaxation allowance + any allowance for additional work - *e.g.,* that part of contingency allowance which represents work.

Standard Time: Standard time is the total time in which a job should be completed at standard performance *i.e.,* work content, contingency allowance for delay, unoccupied time and interference allowance, where applicable.

Allowance: Allowance for unoccupied time and for interference may be important for the measurement of machine-controlled operations, but they do not always appear in every computation of standard time. Relaxation allowance, on the other hand, has to be taken into account in every computation, whether the job is a simple manual one or a very complex operation requiring the simultaneous control of several machines. A contingency allowance will probably figure quite frequently in the compilation of standard times; it is therefore convenient to consider the contingency allowance and relaxation allowance, so that the sequence of calculation which started with the completion of observations at the work place may be taken right through to the compilation of standard time.

Contingency allowance: A contingency allowance is a small allowance of time which may be included in a standard time to meet legitimate and expected items of work or delays, the precise measurement of which is uneconomical because of their infrequent or irregular occurrence.

Relaxation allowance: A relaxation allowance is an addition to the basic time to provide the worker with the opportunity to recover from physiological and psychological effects of carrying out specified work under specified conditions and to allow attention to personal needs. The amount of the allowance will depend on the nature of the job. Examples are:

Other allowances: Other allowances include process allowance which is to cover when an operator is prevented from continuing with their work, although ready and waiting, by the process or machine requiring further time to complete its part of the job. A final allowance is that of interference which is included whenever an operator has charge of more than one machine and the machines are subject to random stoppage. In normal circumstances the operator can only attend to one machine, and the others must wait for attention. This machine is then subject to interference which increased the machine cycle time.

It is now possible to obtain a complete picture of the standard time for a straightforward manual operation.

Activity sampling: Activity sampling is a technique in which a large number of instantaneous observations are made over a period of time of a group of machines, processes or workers. Each observation records what is happening at that instant and the percentage of observations recorded for a particular activity or delay is a measure of the percentage of time during which the activity or delay occurs. The advantages of this method are that:

1. It is capable of measuring many activities that are impractical or too costly to be measured by time study.
2. One observer can collect data concerning the simultaneous activities of a group.
3. Activity sampling can be interrupted at any time without effect.

The disadvantages are that:

1. It is quicker and cheaper to use time study on jobs of short duration.
2. It does not provide elemental detail.

The type of information provided by an activity sampling study is:

a. The proportion of the working day during which workers or machines are producing.
b. The proportion of the working day used up by delays. The reason for each delay must be recorded.
c. The relative activity of different workers and machines.

Example 1: In a welding shop, a direct time study was done on a welding operation. One inexperienced industrial engineer and one experienced industrial engineer conducted the study simultaneously. They agreed precisely on cycle time but their opinion on rating the worker differed. The experienced engineer rated the worker 100% and the other engineer rated the worker 120%. They used a 10% allowance.

Cycle time (in minutes)	*Number of times observed*
20	2
24	1
29	1
32	1

From the above statement,

(a) Determine the standard time using the experienced industrial engineer's worker rating.

(b) Find the standard time using the worker rating of inexperienced industrial engineer.

Solution:

(a) Rating of worker at 100% by the experienced industrial engineer Cycle time

(CT) = (20 × 2 + 24 × 1 + 29 × 1 + 32 × 1)/5 = 25 min

Normal time (NT) = CT × P = 25 × 100% = 25 min

Standard time (ST) = NT/(1–%A) = 25/(1–0.10) = 27.78 min

(b) Rating of worker at 120% by the inexperienced industrial engineer Cycle time (CT) = (20 × 2 + 24 × 1 + 29 × 1 + 32 × 1)/5 = 25 min

Normal time (NT) = CT × PR = 25 × 120% = 30 min

Standard time (ST) = NT/(1–%A) = 30/(1–0.10) = 33.33 min

Predetermined Motion Time Systems

A predetermined motion time system is a work measurement technique whereby times established for basic human motions (classified according to the nature of the motion and the conditions under which it is made) are used to build up the time for a job at a defined level of performance. The systems are based on the assumption that all manual tasks can be analysed into basic motions of the body or body members. They were compiled as a result of a very large number of studies of each movement, generally by a frame-by-frame analysis of films of a wide range of subjects, men and women, performing a wide variety of tasks.

The first generation of PMT systems, (Method Time Measurement) MTM1, were very finely detailed, involving much analysis and producing extremely accurate results. This attention to detail was both a strength and a weakness, and for many potential applications the quantity of detailed analysis was not necessary and prohibitively time -consuming. In these cases "second generation" techniques, such as simplified PMTS, Master Standard Data, Primary Standard Data and MTM2, could be used with advantage, and no great loss of accuracy. For even speedier application, where some detail could be sacrificed then a "third generation" technique such as Basic Work Data or MTM3 could be used.

Synthesis

Synthesis is a work measurement technique for building up the time for a job at a defined level of performance by totaling element times obtained previously from time studies on other jobs containing the elements concerned, or from synthetic data. Synthetic data is the name given to tables and formula derived from the analysis of accumulated work measurement data, arranged in a form suitable for building up standard times, machine process times, etc. by synthesis. Synthetic times are increasingly being used as a substitute for individual time studies in the case of jobs made up of elements which have recurred a sufficient number of times in jobs previously studied to make it possible to compile accurate representative times for them.

Estimating

The technique of estimating is the least refined of all those available to the work measurement practitioner. It consists of an estimate of total job duration (or in common practice, the job price or cost). This estimate is made by a craftsman or person familiar with the craft. It normally embraces the total components of the job, including work content, preparation and disposal time, any contingencies etc., all estimated in one gross amount.

Analytical estimating

This technique introduces work measurement concepts into estimating. In analytical estimating the estimator is trained in elemental breakdown, and in the concept of standard performance. The estimate is prepared by first breaking the work content of the job into elements, and then utilising the experience of the estimator (normally a craftsman) the time for each element of work is estimated - at standard performance. These estimated basic minutes are totalled to give a total job time, in basic minutes. An allowance for relaxation and any necessary contingency is then made, as in conventional time study, to give the standard time.

Comparative estimating

This technique has been developed to permit speedy and reliable assessment of the duration of variable and infrequent jobs, by estimating them within chosen time bands. Limits are set within which the job under consideration will fall, rather than in terms of precise capital standard or capital allowed minute values. It is applied by comparing the job to be estimated with jobs of similar work content, and using these similar jobs as "bench marks" to locate the new job in its relevant time band - known as Work Group.

4.7 JOB EVALUATION

Job evaluation is a technique for determining the worth of each job relative to other jobs. The procedure has certain steps. First, the job factors involved in the evaluation are determined. These include training, experience, intelligence, responsibility, working conditions. Secondly, a range of points for each factor are determined. The hourly rate is then adjusted to take into account the total number of points awarded. The advantages of job evaluation are:

1. Job evaluation process helps in the development of rational wage and salary structure because rates are fixed according to the characteristics of the jobs held by the job-holders.
2. It is helpful in developing harmonious relationship between the employer and the employees because no scope is left for personal bias of the employer for fixing the wage rates.
3. It brings into focus the particular needs of a job and a worker who possesses the particular needs is asked to do the job.
4. As job evaluation is followed by job analysis so advantages of job analysis are available with job evaluation. These advantages may be proper recruitment, selection, placement, training, promotion, transfer etc.

5. It helps in job classification and work simplification.
6. It helps in bringing uniformity in wage structure.

4.7.1 Merit Rating

Promotion and placement of workers must be made on their personal performance. The personal performance of an employee is judged by his merit rating. It is a technique for determining any addition that should be made to an individual's normal rate, to reward him for above average service. It should be carefully distinguished from job evaluation which evaluates the employee doing the job. To conduct a merit rating, each employee is rated in respect of a number of personal attributes. These could be initiative, responsibility, attendance, punctuality, accuracy, safety, co-operativeness, etc. He is often- given points for each attribute. The total of his points is then related to some predetermined scale which sets out the merit addition to be made to his rate of pay. The assignment of merit rating should be done periodically, say at quarterly or six-monthly intervals, by the manager or foreman. The following are some important advantages of merit rating:

1. Merit rating helps in determining fair rates of pay for different workers on the basis of their performance.
2. Merit rating is helpful in transfer, promotion, placement and discharge of employees.
3. It helps in judging the effectiveness of the employment office of the company as it reveals the defects, in selection and placement procedures of workers.
4. On the basis of merit rating the right types of employees are recruited by eliminating unfit and misfit workers.
5. On the basis or merit rating permanent disciplinary and performance records of employees are maintained. Such records protect management from the charges of discrimination, favoritism and unfair labor practices.
6. The merit rating distinguishes between the good workers and inefficient workers. Workers with high rating are suitably rewarded while those in the very low rating group are exposed. Such exposure provides them an opportunity to improve their performance.

7. It also helps in developing a sense of competition among the workers, and hence the ultimate result is an increase in production.

1. *Non-quantitative methods:*

(a) Ranking or job comparison

(b) Grading or job classification

2. *Quantitative methods:*

(a) Point rating

(b) Factor comparison

The basic difference between these two methods lies in the sense that, under non-quantitative methods, a job is compared as a whole with other jobs in the organization, whereas in case of quantitative methods, the key factors of a job are selected and, then, measured. The four methods of job evaluation are now discussed one by one.

Ranking method

The ranking method is the simplest form of job evaluation. In this method, each job as a whole is compared with other and this comparison of jobs goes on until all the jobs have been evaluated and ranked. All jobs are ranked in the order of their importance from the simplest to the hardest or from the highest to the lowest.

The importance of order of job is judged in terms of duties, responsibilities and demands on the job holder. The jobs are ranked according to "the whole job" rather than a number of compensable factors. The ranking of jobs in a University, based on ranking method.

The application of the ranking method involves the following procedure

1. Analyze and describe jobs, bringing out those aspects which are to be used for purpose of job comparison.
2. Identify bench-mark jobs (10 to 20 jobs, which include all major departments and functions). The jobs may be the most and least

important jobs, a job midway between the two extremes, and others at the higher or lower intermediate points.

3. Rank all jobs in the organization around the bench-mark jobs until all jobs are placed in their rank order of importance.
4. Finally, divide all the ranked jobs into appropriate groups or classifications by considering the common features of jobs such as similar duties, skills or training requirements. All the jobs within a particular group or classification receive the same wage or range of rates.

Ranking method is appropriate for small-size organizations where jobs are simple and few. It is also suitable for evaluating managerial jobs wherein job contents cannot be measured in quantitative terms. Ranking method being simple one can be used in the initial stages of job evaluation in an organization.

Merits

Ranking method has the following merits

1. It is the simplest method.
2. It is quite economical to put it into effect.
3. It is less time consuming and involves little paper work.

Demerits

The method suffers from the following demerits:

1. The main demerit of the ranking method is that there are no definite standards of judgment and also there is no way of measuring the differences between jobs.
2. It suffers from its sheer unmanageability when there are a large number of jobs.

Grading method

Grading method is also known as 'classification method'. This method of job evaluation was made popular by the U.S. Civil Service Commission. Under this method, job grades or classes are established by an authorized body or committee appointed for this purpose. A job grade is defined as a group of different jobs of similar difficulty or requiring similar skills to perform them. Job grades are determined on the basis of information derived from job analysis.

The grades or classes are created by identifying some common denominator such as skills, knowledge and responsibilities. The example of job grades may include, depending on the type of jobs the organization offers, skilled, unskilled, account clerk, clerk-cum-typist, steno typist, office superintendent, laboratory assistant and so on.

Once the grades are established, each job is then placed into its appropriate grade or class depending on how well its characteristics fit in a grade. In this way, a series of job grades is created. Then, different wage/salary rate is fixed for each grade.

Merits

The main merits of grading method of job evaluation are

1 This method is easy to understand and simple to operate.

2 It is economical and, therefore, suitable for small organizations.

3 The grouping of jobs into classifications makes pay determination problems easy to administer.

4 This method is useful for Government jobs.

Demerits

The demerits of this method include

1. The method suffers from personal bias of the committee members.
2. It cannot deal with complex jobs which will not fit neatly into one grade.
3. This method is rarely used in an industry.

Points Rating

This is the most widely used method of job evaluation. Under this method, jobs are broke down based on various identifiable factors such as skill, effort, training, knowledge, hazards, responsibility, etc. Thereafter, points are allocated to each of these factors.

Weights are given to factors depending on their importance to perform the job. Points so allocated to various factors of a job are then summed. Then, the jobs with similar total of points are placed in similar pay grades. The sum of points gives an index of the relative significance of the jobs that are rated. The procedure involved in determining job points is as follows: Determine the jobs to be evaluated. Jobs should cover all the major occupational and levels of responsibility to be covered by the method. Decide on the factors to be used in analyzing and evaluating the jobs. The number of factors needs to be restricted because too many factors result in an over-complex scheme with overlap and duplication between factors.

Define the factors clearly in written. This is necessary to ensure that different job raters interpret a particular factor in the same sense. Determine degrees of each factor and assign point value to each degree. Point values are assigned to different degrees on the basis of arithmetic progression. Finally, money values are assigned to points. For this purpose, points are added to give the total value of a job. Its value is then translated into money terms with a predetermined formula.

Merits

The method has the following merits

1. It is the most comprehensive and accurate method of job evaluation.
2. Prejudice and human judgment are minimized, *i.e.* the system cannot be easily manipulated.
3. Being the systematic method, workers of the organization favor this method.
4. The scales developed in this method can be used for long time.
5. Jobs can be easily placed in distinct categories.

Demerits

The drawbacks of the method are:

1. It is both time-consuming and expensive method.
2. It is difficult to understand for an average worker.
3. A lot of clerical work is involved in recording rating scales.
4. It is not suitable for managerial jobs wherein the work content is not measurable in quantitative terms.

4.8 FORMULATION OF LINEAR PROGRAMING

When there is two equations and two variables problem can easily solved, if the no of variables are more then number equations, then linear programing problem is useful to solve the problem.

The linear programming problem formulation is illustrated through a product mix problem. The product mix problem occurs in an industry where it is possible to manufacture a variety of products. A product has a certain margin of profit per unit, and uses a common pool of limited resources. In this case the linear programming technique identifies the products combination which will maximize the profit subject to the availability of limited resource constraints.

Objective Function: Is a linear function of the decision variables representing the objective of the manager/decision maker.

Constraints: Are the linear equations or inequalities arising out of practical limitations.

Decision Variables: Are some physical quantities whose values indicate the solution.

Feasible Solution: Is a solution which satisfies all the constraints (including the non-negative) presents in the problem.

Feasible Region: Is the collection of feasible solutions.

Multiple Solutions: Are solutions each of which maximize or minimize the objective function.

Unbounded Solution: Is a solution whose objective function is infinite.

Infeasible Solution: Means no feasible solution

Example 2: Suppose an industry is manufacturing two types of products P1 and P2. The profits per kg of the two products are Rs. 30 and Rs. 40 respectively. These two products require processing in three types of machines. The following table shows the available machine hours per day and the time required on each machine to produce one kg of P1 and P2. Formulate the problem in the form of linear programming model.

Ans.

Profit/kKg	P1	P2	Total available machine
	Rs. 30	Rs. 40	hours/day
Machine 1	3	2	600
Machine 2	3	5	800
Machine 3	5	6	1100

Solution:

The procedure for linear programming problem formulation is as follows:

Introduce the decision variable as follows: Let x_1 = amount of P1

x_2 = amount of P2

In order to maximize profits, we establish the objective function as

$$30x_1 + 40x_2$$

Since one kg of P1 requires 3 hours of processing time in machine 1 while the corresponding requirement of P2 is 2 hours. So, the first constraint can be expressed as

$$3x_1 + 2x_2 \leq 600$$

Similarly, corresponding to machine 2 and 3 the constraints are

$$3x_1 + 5x_2 \leq 800$$

$$5x_1 + 6x_2 \leq 1100$$

In addition to the above there is no negative production, which may be represented algebraically as

$$x_1 \geq 0 \quad ; \quad x_2 \geq 0$$

Thus, the product mix problem in the linear programming model is as follows:

Maximize

$$30x_1 + 40x_2$$

Subject to:

$$3x_1 + 2x_2 \leq 600$$

$$3x_1 + 5x_2 \leq 800$$

$$5x_1 + 6x_2 \leq 1100 \; x_1 \geq 0,$$

$$x_2 \geq 0$$

The constraints in the previous example 4.1 are of "less than or equal to" type. In this section we are going to discuss the linear programming problem with different constraints, which is illustrated in the following

Example 3: A company owns two flour mills *viz.* A and B, which have different production capacities for high, medium and low quality flour. The company has entered a contract to supply flour to a firm every month with at least 8, 12 and 24 quintals of high, medium and low quality respectively. It costs the company Rs. 2000 and Rs. 1500 per day to run mill A and B respectively. On a day, Mill A produces 6, 2 and 4 quintals of high, medium and low quality flour, Mill B produces 2, 4 and 12 quintals of high, medium and low quality flour respectively. How many days per month should each mill be operated in order to meet the contract order most economically.

Solution:

Let us define x1 and x2 are the mills A and B. Here the objective is to minimize the cost of the machine runs and to satisfy the contract order.

The linear programming problem is given by

Minimize

$$2000x_1 + 1500x_2$$

Subject to:

$$6x_1 + 2x_2 \geq 8$$

$$2x_1 + 4x_2 \geq 12$$

$$4x_1 + 12x_2 \geq 24$$

$$x_1 \geq 0,\ x_2 \geq 0$$

Graphical method

The graphical method is applicable to solve the LPP involving two decision variables x_1, and x_2, we usually take these decision variables as x, y instead of x_1, x_2. To solve an LP, the graphical method includes two major steps.

a. The determination of the solution space that defines the feasible solution. Note that the set of values of the variable x_1, x_2, x_3,....x_n which satisfy all the constraints and also the non-negative conditions is called the feasible solution of the LP.
b. The determination of the optimal solution from the feasible region.

Example 4: Let us find the feasible solution for the problem of a decorative item dealer whose LPP is to maximize profit function

$$Z = 50x + 18y \qquad (1)$$

Subject to the constraints

$$2x + 7 \leq 100$$

$$x + y \leq 80$$

$$x \geq 0,\ y \geq 0$$

Ans.

Step 1: Since $x \geq 0$, $y \geq 0$, we consider only the first quadrant of the xy - plane

Step 2: We draw straight lines for the equation

$$2x + y = 100 \quad (2)$$

$$x + y = 80$$

To determine two points on the straight line $2x + y = 100$

Put $y = 0, 2x = 100$

$x = 50$

(50, 0) is a point on the line (2)

put $x = 0$ in (2), $y = 100$

(0, 100) is the other point on the line (2)

Plotting these two points on the graph paper draw the line which represent the line $2x + y = 100$.

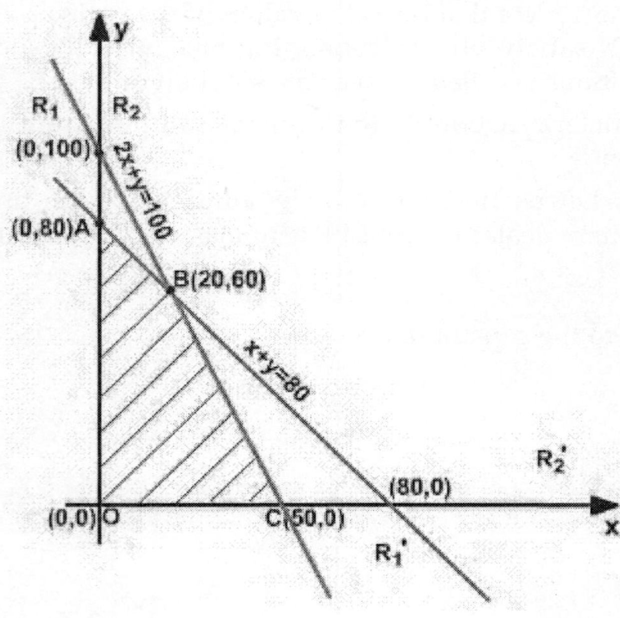

This line divides the 1st quadrant into two regions, say R1 and R2. Choose a point say (1, 0) in R1. (1,0) satisfy the inequality $2x + y \leq 100$. Therefore R1 is the required region for the constraint $2x + y \leq 100$.

Similarly draw the straight line $x + y = 80$ by joining the point (0, 80) and (80, 0). Find the required region say R1', for the constraint $x + y \leq 80$.

The intersection of both the region R1 and R1' is the feasible solution of the LPP. Therefore every point in the shaded region OABC is a feasible solution of the LPP, since this point satisfies all the constraints including the non-negative constraints.

Example 5: Solve the following LPP graphically using ISO- profit method.

Maximize $\qquad Z = 100 + 100y$

Subject to the constraints

$$10x + 5y \leq 80$$

$$6x + 6y \leq 66$$

$$4x + 8y \leq 24$$

$$5x + 6y \leq 90$$

$$x \geq 0,\ y \geq 0$$

Ans: Since $x \geq 0$, $y \geq 0$, consider only the first quadrant of the plane graph the following straight lines on a graph paper

$$10x + 5y = 80 \quad \text{or} \quad 2x + y = 16$$

$$6x + 6y = 66 \quad \text{or} \quad x + y = 11$$

$$4x + 8y = 24 \quad \text{or} \quad x + 2y = 6$$

$$5x + 6y = 90$$

Identify all the half planes of the constraints. The intersection of all these half planes is the feasible region as shown in the figure.

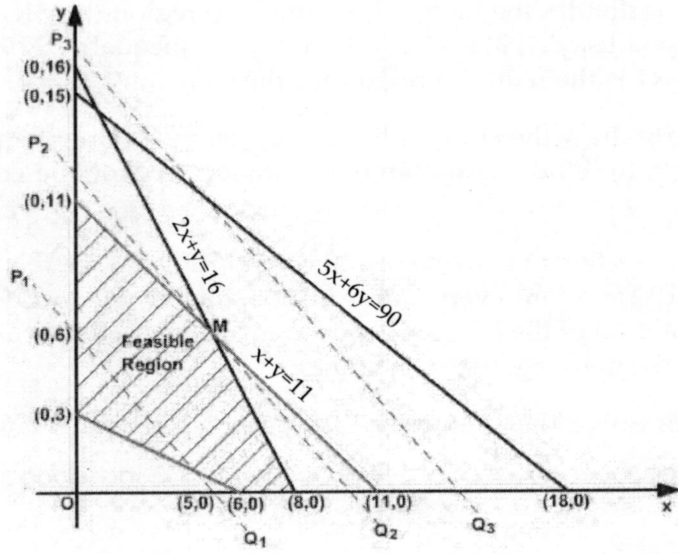

Give a constant value 600 to Z in the objective function, then we have an equation of the line

$$120x + 100y = 600 \qquad (1)$$

or $6x + 5y = 30$ (Dividing both sides by 20)

P1Q1 is the line corresponding to the equation $6x + 5y = 30$. We give a constant 1200 to Z then the P2Q2 represents the line.

$$120x + 100y = 1200$$

$$6x + 5y = 60$$

P2Q2 is a line parallel to P1Q1 and has one point 'M' which belongs to feasible region and farthest from the origin. If we take any line P3Q3 parallel to P2Q2 away from the origin, it does not touch any point of the feasible region.

The co-ordinates of the point M can be obtained by solving the equation $2x + y = 16$

$x + y = 11$ which give $x = 5$ and $y = 6$

The optimal solution for the objective function is $x = 5$ and $y = 6$

The optimal value of Z

$$120\ (5) + 100\ (6) = 600 + 600 = 1200$$

4.9 TRANSPORTATION MODEL

A special class of linear programming problem is transportation problem, where the objective is to minimize the cost of distributing a product from a number of sources (e.g., factories) to a number of destinations (e.g., warehouses) while satisfying both the supply limits and the demand requirement. The model assumes that the distributing cost on a given rout is directly proportional to the number of units distributed on that route. Generally, the transportation model can be extended to areas other than the direct transportation of a commodity, including among others, inventory control, employment scheduling, and personnel assignment.

The transportation problem special feature is illustrated here with the help of following:

Example 6: Suppose a manufacturing company owns three factories (sources) and distribute his products to five different retail agencies (destinations). The following table shows the capacities of the three factories, the quantity of products required by the various retail agencies and the cost of shipping one unit of the product from each of the three factories to each of the five retail agencies.

			Retail Agency			
Factories	1	2	3	4	5	Capacity
1	1	9	13	36	51	50
2	24	12	16	20	1	100
3	14	33	1	23	26	150
Requirement	100	60	50	50	40	300

Usually the above table is referred as transportation table, which provides the basic information regarding the transportation problem. The quantities inside the table are known as transportation cost per unit of product. The capacity of the factories 1, 2, 3 is 50, 100 and 150 respectively. The requirement of the retail agency 1, 2, 3, 4, 5 are 100, 60, 50, 50 and 40 respectively.

In this case, the transportation cost of one unit from factory 1 to retail agency 1 is 1, from factory 1 to retail agency 2 is 9, from factory 1 to retail agency 3 is 13, and so on.

A transportation problem can be formulated as linear programming problem using variables with two subscripts.

Let

x_{11} = Amount to be transported from factory 1 to retail agency 1

x_{12} = Amount to be transported from factory 1 to retail agency 2

....

....

....

....

x_{35} = Amount to be transported from factory 3 to retail agency 5.

Let the transportation cost per unit be represented by C_{11}, C_{12}, ... C_{35} that is C_{11}=1, C_{12}=9, and so on. Let the capacities of the three factories be represented by a_1=50, a_2=100, a_3=150.

Let the requirement of the retail agencies are b_1=100, b_2=60, b_3=50, b_4=50, and b_5=40.

Thus, the problem can be formulated as

Minimize

$$C_{11}x_{11} + C_{12}x_{12} + \ldots\ldots\ldots\ldots + C_{35}x_{35}$$

Subject to:

$$x_{11} + x_{12} + x_{13} + x_{14} + x_{15} =$$

$$a_1\ x_{21} + x_{22} + x_{23} + x_{24} + x_{25} =$$

$$a_2\ x_{31} + x_{32} + x_{33} + x_{34} + x_{35} = a_3$$

$$x_{11} + x_{21} + x_{31} = b_1\ x_{12} + x_{22} + x_{32} =$$

$$b_2\ x_{13} + x_{23} + x_{33} = b_3\ x_{14} + x_{24} + x_{34} =$$

$$b_4\ x_{15} + x_{25} + x_{35} = b_5$$

$$x_{11}, x_{12}, \ldots\ldots, x_{35} \geq 0.$$

Thus, the problem has 8 constraints and 15 variables. So, it is not possible to solve such a problem using simplex method. For two equations and two variables graphical method is used for no of variables and equation more than two simplex is usefull, but for more equations (constraints) and variables simplex will be complex to solve. This is the reason for the need of special computational procedure to solve transportation problem. There are varieties of procedures, which are described in the next section.

4.9.1 Transportation Algorithm

The transportation problem is a special class of the linear programming problem. It deals with the situation in which a commodity is transported from Sources to Destinations. The objective is to determine the amount of commodity to be transported from each source to each destination so that the total transportation cost is minimum.

The steps of the transportation algorithm are exact parallels of the simplex algorithm, they are:

Step 1: Determine a starting basic feasible solution, using any one of the following three methods

1. North west corner method
2. Least cost method

3. Vogel approximation method

Step 2: Determine the optimal solution using the following method

1. MODI (Modified Distribution Method) or UV Method.

Generally, any basic feasible solution with m sources (such as factories) and n destination (such as retail agency) has at most m + n - 1 non-zero Xij.

The special structure of the transportation problem allows securing a non artificial (without using any artificial variable) basic feasible solution using one the following three methods.

1. North west corner method
2. Least cost method
3. Vogel approximation method

The difference among these three methods is the quality of the initial basic feasible solution they produce, in the sense that a better initial solution yields a smaller objective value. Generally the Vogel Approximation Method produces the best initial basic feasible solution, and the North West Corner Method produces the worst, but the North West Corner Method involves least computations and the transportation cost is also optimum.

North West corner method:

The method starts at the North West (upper left) corner cell of the tableau (variable x11).

Step 1: Allocate as much as possible to the selected cell, and adjust the associated amounts of capacity (supply) and requirement (demand) by subtracting the allocated amount.

Step 2: Cross out the row (column) with zero supply or demand to indicate that no further assignments can be made in that row (column). If both the row and column becomes zero simultaneously, cross out one of them only, and leave a zero supply or demand in the uncrossed out row (column).

Step 3: If exactly one row (column) is left uncrossed out, then stop. Otherwise, move to the cell to the right if a column has just been crossed or the one below if a row has been crossed out. Go to step -1.

Example 7: Consider the problem discussed in North West Corner Method of determining basic feasible solution.

	Retail Agency					
Factories	1	2	3	4	5	Capacity
1	1	9	13	36	51	50
2	24	12	16	20	1	100
3	14	33	1	23	26	150
Requirement	100	60	50	50	40	300

The allocation is shown in the following tableau:

Capacity

1 9 13 36 51

. 50 50

50 24 50 12 16 20 1 100 50

14 10 33 50 1 50 23 40 26

150 140 90 40

Requirement 100 60 50 50 40

50 10

The arrows show the order in which the allocated (bolded) amounts are generated. The starting basic solution is given as

$$x_{11} = 50,$$

$$x_{21} = 50, \; x_{22} = 50$$

$$x_{32} = 10, \; x_{33} = 50, \; x_{34} = 50, \; x_{35} = 40$$

The corresponding transportation cost is:

50 * 1 + 50 * 24 + 50 * 12 + 10 * 33 + 50 * 1 + 50 * 23 + 40 * 26 = 442

Factor Comparison Method

This method is a combination of both ranking and point methods in the sense that it rates jobs by comparing them and makes analysis by breaking jobs into compensable factors. This system is usually used to evaluate white collar, professional and managerial positions.

The mechanism for evaluating jobs under this method involves the following steps:

1. First of all, the key or benchmark jobs are selected as standards. The key jobs selected should have standards contents, well accepted pay rates in the community, and should consist of a representative cross-section of all jobs that are being evaluated-from the lowest to the highest paid job, from the most important to the least important-and cover the full range of requirements of each factor, as agreed upon by a committee representing workers and management.
2. The factors common to all jobs are identified, selected and defined precisely. The common factors to all jobs are usually five, *viz.*, mental requirements, physical requirements, skill requirements, working conditions and responsibility.
3. Once the key jobs are identified and also the common factors are chosen, the key jobs are, then, ranked in terms of the selected common factors.
4. The next step is to determine a fair and equitable base rate (usually expressed on an hourly basis) and, then, allocate this base rate among the five common factors as mentioned earlier. Following is a specimen of base rate and its allocation scheme:
5. The final step in factor comparison method is to compare and evaluate the remaining jobs in the organisation. To illustrate, a 'toolmaker' job is to be evaluated. After comparison, it is found that its skill is similar to electrician (5), mental requirements to welder (10) Physical requirements to again electrician (12), working conditions to mechanist (24) and responsibility also to

mechanist (3). Thus, the wage rate for the job of toolmaker will be Rs. 54 (Rs.5 + Rs. 10 + Rs. 12 + Rs.24 + Rs.3).

Merits

This method enjoys the following merits

1. It is more objective method of job evaluation.
2. The method is flexible as there is no upper limit on the rating of a factor.
3. It is fairly easy method to explain to employees.
4. The use of limited number of factors (usually five) ensures less chances of overlapping and over-weighting of factors.
5. It facilitates determining the relative worth of different jobs.

Demerits

The method, however, suffers from the following drawbacks

1. It is expensive and time-consuming method.
2. Using the same five factors for evaluating jobs may not always be appropriate because jobs differ across and within organizations.
3. It is difficult to understand and operate

4.9.2 Assignment Problem

The assignment problem is a special case of transportation problem as it is a special type of LPP where the objective is to minimize the cost of distributing a product from a number of sources or origins to a number of destinations but in assignment problem the objective is to assign 'm' jobs or workers to 'n' machines such that the cost incurred is minimized. JOBS 1 2 -------- n 1 2 -- WORKERS -- -- n the element Cij represents the cost of assigning worker I to job (I,j= 1,2,---n). There is no loss in generality in assuming that the number of workers always equals the number of jobs because we can always add fictitious (untrue or fabricated) workers or fictitious jobs to effect this result. The assignment model is actually a special case of the transportation model in which the workers represent the sources and the jobs represent the destinations. The supply amount at each source and the demand amount at each destination exactly equal 1. The cost of transporting workers I to job j is Cij . The assignment model can be solved directly as a regular transportation model. The fact that all the supply and demand amounts equal 1 has led to the development of a simple solution algorithm called the Hungarian method.

4.9.2.1 Assignment algorithm (Hungarian Method)

Assignment method seeks to minimize the opportunity cost of not using the cheapest cells.

Step 1: Create Zero elements in the cost matrix by subtract the smallest element in each row column for the corresponding row and column.

Step 2: Drop the least number of horizontal and vertical lines so as to cover all zeros if the no of their lines are 'N' i If N = n (n=order of the square matrix) then an optimum assignment has been obtained ii) If N < n then the numbers crosed ones remain same, double crossed are added with minimum number and uncrossed numbers are subtracted from minimum number, then further steps are repeated from step 1.

Step 3: We now have exactly one encircled zero in each row and each column of the cost matrix. The assignment schedule corresponding to their zeros is the optimum (maximal) assignment. Note: the above procedure for assignment is Hungarian assignment method problem 1. Three jobs A B C are to be assigned to three machines X Y Z. The processing costs are as given in the matrix shown below. Find the allocation which will minimize the overall processing cost.

Example 8: Three jobs A B C are to be assigned to three machines X Y Z. The processing costs are as given in the matrix shown below. Find the allocation which will minimize the overall processing cost.

		X	Y	Z
Jobs	A	19	28	31
	B	11	17	16
	C	12	15	13

Ans. ***Solution:***

Step 1: Create zero in each row or column by subtracting by selecting least number in each row and column

Row Minimization

0	9	12
0	6	5
0	3	1

Column Minimization

0	6	11
0	3	4
0	0	0

Now draw Horizontal and vertical lines

0	6	11
0	3	4
0	0	0

Here, no of horizontal lines is one and vertical line is one.

The order of matrix is 3 × 3, therefore, $N \neq n$

Now, in the uncrossed cell the least cost is selected and subtracted for the remaining uncrossed cell by the least value and for the intersection of the horizontal line and vertical line the least value should be added and the resulting matrix.

0	3	8
0	0	1
3	0	0

The above matrix has two horizontal line and one vertical line which satisfies our condition N= n

{0}	3	8
0	{0}	1
3	0	{0}

The assignment are	A	X	=	19
	B	Y	=	17
	C	Z	=	13
				49

Example 9: Solve of the assignment problem

	I	II	III	IV	V
1	11	17	8	16	20
2	9	7	12	6	11
3	13	16	15	12	16
4	21	24	17	28	26
5	14	10	12	11	15

Ans:

Row minimization

3	9	0	8	12
3	1	6	0	5
1	4	3	0	4
4	7	0	11	9
4	0	2	1	5

Column minimization

2	9	0	8	8
2	1	6	0	1
0	4	3	0	0
3	7	0	11	5
3	0	2	1	1

$N' \neq n$ $5' \neq 4$

2	9	0	8	8
2	1	6	0	0
0	4	3	0	0
3	7	0	11	5
3	0	2	1	1

The least value in the uncrossed cell is 1, it is subtracted for the uncrossed cell and added for intersection of the vertical line and horizontal.

The least value in the uncrossed cell is 1, it is subtracted for the uncrossed cell and added for intersection of the vertical line and horizontal.

1	9	0	8	7
1	1	6	0	0
0	4	3	0	0
2	7	0	11	4
2	0	2	1	0

least value is one again

Again N′ ≥ n

0	8	0	7	6
1	1	6	0	0
0	4	3	0	0
1	6	0	10	3
2	0	2	1	0

Here, it satisfies our condition N = n

Now, the assignment for the optimum table

[0]	8	0̶	7	6
1	1	6	[0]	0̶
0̶	4	3	0̶	[0]
1	6	[0]	10	3
2	[0]	2	1	0̶

Assignment

1	I	=	11
2	IV	=	6
3	V	=	16
4	III	=	17
5	II	=	10
			50

Example 10: Using the following cost matrix, determine a (optimal job assignment b) the cost of assignments

JOB	1	2	3	4	5
A	10	3	3	2	8
B	9	7	8	2	7

MECHANIC

C	7	5	6	2	4
D	3	5	8	2	4
E	9	10	9	6	10

Row Minimization

8	1	1	0	6
7	5	6	0	5
5	3	4	0	2
1	3	6	0	2
3	4	3	0	4

Column minimization

7	0	0	0	4
6	4	5	0	3
4	2	3	0	0
0	2	5	0	0
2	3	2	0	2

Draw the horizontal and vertical lines

7	~~0~~	~~0~~	~~0~~	~~4~~
6	4	5	~~0~~	~~3~~
4	2	3	~~0~~	~~0~~
0	2	5	~~0~~	~~0~~
2	3	2	~~0~~	~~2~~

Here, N′ ≠ n, 4′ ≠ 5

Then, we have to select the least value in the uncrossed cell *i.e,* 2 the result table.

~~9~~	~~0~~	~~0~~	2	~~6~~
6	2	2	0	3
4	~~0~~	~~1~~	0	~~0~~
~~0~~	~~0~~	~~3~~	0	~~0~~
~~2~~	~~1~~	~~0~~	0	~~2~~

N=n satisfies our condition, so optimal assignment can be done

9	[0]	~~0~~	2	6
6	2	2	[0]	3
4	~~0~~	1	~~0~~	[0]
[0]	~~0~~	3	~~0~~	~~0~~
2	1	[0]	~~0~~	2

A— — 2	=	3	
B— — 4	=	2	
C— — 5	=	4	
D— — 1	=	3	
E— — 3	=	9	
		21	the minimum cost is Rs. 21

Example 11: Job shop needs to assign 4 jobs to 4 workers. The cost of performing a job is a function of the skills of the workers. Table summarizes the cost of the assignments. Worker1 cannot do job3, and worker 3 cannot do job 4. Determine the optimal assignment using the Hungarian method.

Worker \ Job	1	2	3	4
1	Rs. 50	Rs. 50	—	Rs. 20
2	Rs. 70	Rs. 40	Rs. 20	Rs. 30
3	Rs. 90	Rs. 30	Rs. 50	—
4	Rs. 70	Rs. 20	Rs. 60	Rs. 70

Row minimization

30	30	—	0
50	20	0	10
60	0	20	—
50	0	40	50

Column minimization

0	30	—	0
20	20	0	10
30	0	20	—
20	0	40	50

N′ ≠ n 3′ ≠ 4

The least value in the uncrossed cell is 10 and the resulting table will be as follows

~~0~~	40	—	~~0~~
~~10~~	20	~~0~~	~~0~~
20	0	20	—
10	0	40	40

N′ ≠ n 3=4

The least value in the uncrossed cell is 10

0	50	—	0
10	20	0	0
10	0	10	—
0	0	30	30

N = n

The given problem satisfies the condition, the assignment can be made for the optimal table.

~~0~~	50	—	[0]
10	20	[0]	~~0~~
10	[0]	10	—
[0]	~~0~~	30	30

1—— 4	=	20
2—— 3	=	20
3—— 2	=	30
4—— 1	=	70
		140

Example 12: Four different jobs can be done on four different machines and take down time costs are prohibitively high for change overs. The matrix below gives the cost in rupees of producing job on machine j;

Jobs	Machine			
	M1	M2	M3	M4
J1	5	7	11	6
J2	8	5	9	6
J3	4	7	10	7
J4	10	4	8	3

How the jobs should be assigned to the various machines so that the total cost is minimized.

Ans. Row minimization

0	2	6	1
3	0	4	1
0	3	6	3
7	1	5	0

Column minimization

0	2	2	1
3	0	0	1
0	3	2	3
7	1	1	0

Draw the horizontal and vertical lines which covers max no of zeros

θ	2	2	1
3	θ	θ	1
θ	3	2	3
7	1	1	0

N′ ≠ n 3′ ≠ 4

The least value is 1, the resulting table

0	1	1	1
4	θ	θ	2
0	2	1	3
7	θ	θ	θ

N′ ≠ n 3′ ≠ 4

The least value is 1, the resulting table

0	0	0	0
5	0	0	2
0	1	0	2
8	0	0	0

N=n 16

4=4 The assignment can be made for the above optimal table

θ	θ	θ	[0]
5	[0]	0	2
[0]	1	θ	2
8	θ	[0]	θ

J1—————— M4 = 6

J2—————— M2 = 5

J3—————— M1 = 4

J4—————— M3 = 8

23

Alternate solution

[0]	θ	θ	θ
5	[0]	θ	2
θ	1	[0]	2
8	θ	θ	[0]

J1—————— M1 = 5

J2—————— M2 = 5

J3—————— M3 = 10

J4—————— M4 = 3

23

Example 13: A company has 5 jobs to be done the following matrix shows the return in Rs. of assigning the machine (i = 1, 2, 3, —5) to the jth job (j = 1, 2, 3,——n). Assign the 5 jobs to the 5 machines so as to maximize the expected profit.

JOB

1	2	3	4	5	
1	5	11	10	12	4
2	2	4	6	3	5

Machine

3	3	12	5	14	6
4	6	14	4	11	7
5	7	9	8	12	8

Since, the given problem is maximum

Step 1: To convert the problem to a minimum by multiply all elements C_{ij} of the assignment matrix by –1

Then the given problem will in the form as shown below

JOB

1	2	3	4	5	
1	–5	–11	–10	–12	–4
2	–2	–4	–6	–3	–5

Machine

3	–3	–12	–5	–14	–6
4	–6	–14	–4	–11	–7
5	–7	–9	–8	–12	–8

Step 2: Select the most –ve and subtract with other elements of the matrix min z = –(–max Z) in the matrix the most –ve value is –14. Using this value the matrix is subtracted and the resulting is the minimization matrix. This can be used for finding the optimal assignment table using usual procedure to solve the problem.

JOB

1	2	3	4	5	
1	9	3	4	2	10
2	12	10	8	11	9

Machine

3	11	2	9	0	8
4	8	0	10	3	7
5	7	5	6	2	6

Example: C11 = –5 – (–14) = 9 and continued for all other element

Step 3: Using the above table *i.e.,* min Z matrix table and all cost elements non –ve. The Hungarian method can be applied to find the optimal assignment problem.

Row minimization

7	1	2	0	8
4	2	0	3	1
11	2	9	0	8
8	0	10	3	7
5	3	4	0	4

Column minimization

3	1	2	0	7
0	2	0	3	0
7	2	9	0	7
4	0	10	3	6
1	3	4	0	3

N = 3, n = 5 × 5

N' ≠ n, select the minimum value from the uncrossed cell and subtract for all the elements of uncrossed cell and add for the intersection of horizontal and vertical.

~~2~~	1	1	0	6
~~0~~	3	~~0~~	4	~~0~~
~~6~~	2	8	0	6
~~3~~	0	9	3	5
~~0~~	3	3	0	2

N = 4 n = 5 × 5 N′ ≠ n

The least value in the uncrossed cell is 1 again and subtracts using this value for all other elements and add for intersection of horizontal and vertical

~~2~~	1	~~0~~	0	5
~~1~~	4	~~0~~	5	0
~~6~~	2	7	0	5
~~3~~	0	8	3	4
~~0~~	3	2	0	1

N = n, for assignment the optimal table is obtained

2	1	[0]	~~0~~	5
1	4	~~0~~	5	[0]
6	2	7	[0]	5
3	[0]	8	3	4
[0]	3	2	~~0~~	1

Now the assignment is

1——	3	=	10
2——	5	=	5
3——	4	=	14

4—— 2 = 14

5—— 1 = 7

50

4.10 QUEUEING THEORY

Introduction

A flow of customers from finite or infinite population towards the service facility forms a queue (waiting line) an account of lack of capability to serve them all at a time. In the absence of a perfect balance between the service facilities and the customers, waiting time is required either for the service facilities or for the customers arrival. In general, the queueing system consists of one or more queues and one or more servers and operates under a set of procedures. Depending upon the server status, the incoming customer either waits at the queue or gets the turn to be served. If the server is free at the time of arrival of a customer, the customer can directly enter into the counter for getting service and then leave the system. In this process, over a period of time, the system may experience "Customer waiting" and /or "Server idle time"

4.10.1 Queueing System

A queueing system can be completely described by

(1) The input (arrival pattern)
(2) The service mechanism (service pattern)
(3) The queue discipline and
(4) Customer's behaviour

4.10.2 The Input (Arrival Pattern)

The input described the way in which the customers arrive and join the system. Generally, customers arrive in a more or less random manner which is not possible for prediction. Thus the arrival pattern can be described in terms of probabilities and consequently the probability distribution for inter-arrival times (the time between two successive arrivals) must be defined. We deal with those queueing system in which the customers arrive in poisson means probability of an arrival at any one instant of time is the same as at any other instant of time process.

Mean arrival rate (ë)

It is rate at which customers arrive at a service facility. It is expressed in flow (customers/hr or vehicles/hour in transportation scenario) or time headway (seconds/customer or seconds/vehicle in transportation scenario). If inter arrival time that is time headway (h) is known, the arrival rate can be found out from the equation:

$$\ddot{e} = 3600$$

4.10.3 The Service Mechanism

This means the arrangement of service facility to serve customers. If there is infinite number of servers, then all the customers are served instantaneously or arrival and there will be no queue. If the number of servers is finite then the customers are served according to a specific order with service time a constant or a random variable. Distribution of service time follows' *Exponential distribution* means number of customers served per unit time is Poisson from where distribution of service time becomes exponential'_ defined by

$$f(t) = e^{-t}, t > 0$$

Mean arrival rate (μ)

It is the rate at which customers (vehicles in transportation scenario) depart from a transportation facility. It is expressed in flow (customers/ hr or vehicles/hour in transportation scenario) or time headway (seconds/customer or seconds/vehicle in transportation scenario). If inter service time that is time headway (h) is known, the service rate can be found out from the

Equation: $\mu = 3600/600$

$\mu = h$

4.10.4 Queuing Discipline

It is a rule according to which the customers are selected for service when a queue has been formed. The most common disciplines are

1. First come first served – (FCFS)
2. First in first out – (FIFO)
3. Last in first out – (LIFO)
4. Selection for service in random order (SIRO)
5. Priority service
6. Process sharing

1. ***First in first out (FIFO):*** If the customers are served in the order of their arrival, then this is known as the first-come, first-served (FCFS) service discipline. Prepaid taxi queue at airports where a taxi is engaged on a first-come, first-served basis is an example of this discipline.
2. ***First in last out (FILO):*** Sometimes, the customers are serviced in the reverse order of their entry so that the ones who join the last are served first. For example, assume that letters to be typed, or order forms to be processed accumulate in a pile, each new addition being put on the top of them. The typist or the clerk might process these letters or orders by taking each new task from the top of the pile. Thus, a just arriving task would be the next to be serviced provided that no fresh task arrives before it is picked up. Similarly, the people who join an elevator first are the last ones to leave it.
3. ***Served in random order (SIRO):*** Under this rule customers are selected for service at random, irrespective of their arrivals in the service system. In this every customer in the queue is equally likely to be selected. The time of arrival of the customers is, therefore, of no relevance in such a case.
4. ***Priority Service:*** Under this rule customers are grouped in priority classes on the basis of some attributes such as service time or urgency or according to some identifiable characteristic and FIFO rule is used within each class to provide service. Treatment of VIP's in preference to other patients in a hospital is an example of priority service.

5. ***Processor (or Time) Sharing:*** The server is switched between all the queues for a predefined slice of time (quantum time) in a round-robin manner. Each queue head is served for that specific time. It doesn't matter if the service is complete for a customer or not. If not then it'll be served in its next turn. This is used to avoid the server time killed by customer for the external activities (*e.g.*, Preparing for payment or filling half-filled form).

4.10.5 Customer's Behavior

1. Generally, it is assumed that the customers arrive into the system one by one. But in some cases, customers may arrive in groups. Such arrival is called bulk arrival.
2. If there is more than one queue, the customers from one queue may be tempted to join another queue because of its smaller size. This behavior of customers is known as jockeying.
3. If the queue length appears very large to a customer, he/she may not join the queue. This property is known as balking of customers.
4. Sometimes, a customer who is already in a queue will leave the queue in anticipation of longer waiting line. This kind of departure is known as reneging.

4.10.6 List of Variables

The following notation assumes that the system is in a steady-state condition (At a given time t):

1. Utilization factor p = λ / μ
2. Pn = Probability of exactly n customers in queuing system (waiting + service).
3. L= Expected (avg) number of customers in queuing system. [sometimes denoted as Ls]
4. Lq = Expected (avg) queue length (excludes customers being served) or no of Customers.
5. W = Expected waiting time in system (includes service time) for each individual customer or time a customer spends in the system. [sometimes denoted as Ws]

6. Wq = Waiting time in queue (excludes service time) for each individual customer or Expected time a customer spends in a queue

4.10.7. Traffic Intensity (or Utilization Factor)

An important measure of a simple queue is its traffic intensity .Trafic intensity means the ratio of average occupancy of a server or a resource out of time the facility is available for occupancy. This leads to the ratio of mean arrival time to mean service time.

$$\text{Traffic intensity} = \frac{\text{Mean arrival time}}{\text{Mean service time}} \quad (\geq 1)$$

queue delay will grow without bound and the unit of traffic intensity is Erlang.

4.10.8 Classification of Queuing Models

Generally, queuing models can be classified into six categories using Kendall's notation with six parameters to define a

Model: The parameters of this notation are:

P- Arrival rate distribution *i.e.,* probability law for the arrival / inter – arrival time.

Q - Service rate distribution, *i.e.,* probability law according to which the customers are being served.

R - Number of Servers (*i.e.,* number of service stations)

X - Service discipline

Y - Maximum number of customers permitted in the system.

Z - Size of the calling source of the customers.

A queuing model with the above parameters is written as (P/Q/R: X/Y/Z)

4.10.9 Model 1 : (M/M/1) : (GD/1 / ∝) Model

In this model

(i) The arrival rate follows Poisson (M) distribution.

(ii) Service rate follows Poisson distribution (M)

(iii) Number of servers is 1

(iv) Service discipline is general disciple (*i.e.*, GD)

(v) Maximum number of customers permitted in the system is infinite ( )

(vi) Size of the calling source is infinite ( )

Some general relations hold in queuing, regardless of the specific system under consideration. The first is

$$W_s = W_q + 1/m \quad (1)$$

Another useful relation, known as little's formula (based on work published by J.D.C. little in 1961) is

$$L_\bullet = \lambda W_\bullet$$

where the "•" stand for either the subscript "s" or the subscript "q".

The simplest queuing model is the M/M/1, for which key formulas are:

$P_0 = 1 - \rho$	$L_s = \dfrac{\lambda}{\mu - \lambda}$	$W_s = \dfrac{1}{\mu - \lambda}$
$P_n = P_0\rho^n$	$L_q = \dfrac{\rho\lambda}{\mu - \lambda} = \dfrac{\rho^2}{1-\rho}$	$W_q = \dfrac{\rho}{\mu - \lambda}$

Example 14: The arrival rate of customers at a banking counter follows a Poisson distribution with a mean of 30 per hours. The service rate of the counter clerk also follows Poisson distribution with mean of 45 per hour.

a) What is the probability of having zero customer in the system?

b) What is the probability of having 8 customer in the system?

c) What is the probability of having 12 customer in the system?

d) Find Ls, Lq, Ws and Wq.

Solution:

Given arrival rate follows Poisson distribution with mean = 30

= 30 per hour

Given service rate follows Poisson distribution with mean = 45

= 45 Per hour Utilization factor

= 30/45 = 2/3 = 0.67

a. The probability of having zero customer in the system

Po = 1 – 0.67 = 0.33

b. The probability of having 8 customers in the system

$P8 = (1 - 0.67)^8 (1 - 0.67) = 0.0134$

c. Probability of having 12 customers in the system is

$P12 = (1 - 0.67)^{12} (1 - 0.67) = 0.002760$

d. Ls = 0.67/1 – 0.67 = 2.03 (2 customer)

e. Lq = 0.67^2/1 – 0.67 = 1.36 (1 customer)

f. Ws = 1/45 – 30 = 0.066 hrs

g. Wq = 0.67/45 – 30 = 0.467 hrs

Example 15: At one-man barber shop, customers arrive according to Poisson dist with mean arrival rate of 5 per hour and the hair cutting time was exponentially distributed with an average hair cut taking 10 minutes. It is assumed that because of his excellent reputation, customers were always willing to wait. Calculate the following:

(i) Average number of customers in the shop and the average numbers waiting for a haircut.

(ii) The percentage of time arrival can walk in straight without having to wait.

(iii) The percentage of customers who have to wait before getting into the barber's chair.

Solution

(i) Mean arival of customer = 5/60

Mean time of server = 1/10

Trafic intensity = 5/60/1/10 = 0.83

(ii) Average number of customers in the system (numbers in the queue and in the service station)

L_s = / 1-(1-p) = 0.83/1 – 0.83 = 0.83/0.17 = 4.88 = 5 Customers

(iii) The percentage of time arrival can walk straight into barber's chair without waiting is

Service utilization = 0.833 × 100 = 83.3

(iv) The percentage of customers who have to wait before getting into the barber's chair = (1–)%

(1 – 0.833)% = 0.167 × 100 = 16.7%

Example 16: Vehicles are passing through a toll gate at the rate of 70 per hour. The average time to pass through the gate is 45 seconds. The arrival rate and service rate follow Poisson distribution. There is a complaint that the vehicles wait for a long duration. The authorities are willing to install one more gate to reduce the average time to pass through the toll gate to 35 seconds if the idle time of the toll gate is less than 9% and the average queue length at the gate is more than 8 vehicle, check whether the installation of the second gate is justified?

Solutions

Arrival rate of vehicles at the toll gate = 70 per hour

Time taken to pass through the gate = 45 Seconds

Service rate = 1 hours/45 seconds = 3600/45 = 80 = 80 Vehicles per hour

Utilization factor = p = 70 / 80 = 0.875

(a) Waiting no. of vehicles in the queue = Ls = $0.875^2/(1 – 0.875)$ = 6.125 = 6

(b) Revised time taken to pass through the gate = 30 seconds

The new service rate after installation of an additional gate

= 1 hour/35 seconds

= 3600/35 = 102.8 Vehicles/hour

Utilization factor = p = 70/102.8

= 0.681

Percentage of idle time of the gate = (1 – p)%

= (1 – 0.681)% = 0.319% = 31.9 = 32%

This idle time is not less than 9% which is expected.

Therefore, the installation of the second gate is not justified since the average waiting number of vehicles in the queue is less than 8 but the idle time is not less than 32%. Hence idle time is far greater than the number of vehicles waiting in the queue.

4.11 SIMULATION

Simulation is an experiment conducted on a model of some system to collect necessary information on the behavior of that system.

4.12 INTRODUCTION

The representation of reality in some physical form or in some form of mathematical equations are called simulations. Simulations are imitation of reality.

For example:

1. Children cycling park with various signals and crossing is a simulation of a read model traffic system
2. Planetarium
3. Testing an air craft model in a wind tunnel.

4.13 NEED FOR SIMULATION

Consider an example of the queuing system, namely the reservation system of a transport corporation. The elements of the system are booking counters (servers) and waiting customers (queue). Generally the arrival rate of customers follow a Poisson distribution and the service time follows exponential distribution. Then the queuing model (M/M/1): (GD/ /) can be used to find the standard results. But in reality, the following combinations of distributions my exist.

1. Arrived rate does not follow Poisson distribution, but the service rate follows an exponential distribution.
2. Arrival rate follows a Poisson distribution and the service rate does not follow exponential distribution.
3. Arrival rate does not follows Poisson distribution and the service time also does not follow exponential distribution. In each of the above cases, the standard model (M/M/1): (G/D/ /) cannot be used. The last resort to find the solution for such a queuing problem is to use simulation.

4.14 SOME ADVANTAGE OF SIMULATION

1. Simulation is Mathematically less complicated.
2. Simulation is flexible.
3. It can be modified to suit the changing environments.
4. It can be used for training purpose.
5. It may be less expensive and less time consuming in a quite a few real world situations.

4.15 SOME LIMITATIONS OF SIMULATION

1. Quantification or Enlarging of the variables maybe difficult.
2. Large number of variables make simulations unwieldy and more difficult.
3. Simulation may not. Yield optimum or accurate results.
4. Simulation are most expensive and time consuming model.
5. We cannot relay too much on the results obtained from simulation models.

4.16 STEPS IN SIMULATION

1. Identify the measure of effectiveness.
2. Decide the variables which influence the measure of effectiveness and choose those variables, which affects the measure of effectiveness significantly.

3. Determine the probability distribution for each variable in step 2 and construct the cumulative probability distribution.
4. Choose an appropriate set of random numbers.
5. Consider each random number as decimal value of the cumulative probability distribution.
6. Use the simulated values so generated into the formula derived from the measure of effectiveness.
7. Repeat steps 5 and 6 until the sample is large enough to arrive at a satisfactory and reliable decision.

4.17 USES OF SIMULATION

Simulation is used for solving

1. Inventory problem
2. Queuing problem
3. Training programs etc.

Example 17: Customers arrive at a milk booth for the required service. Assume that inter – arrival and service time are constants and given by 1.5 and 4 minutes respectively. Simulate the system by hand computations for 14 minutes.

1. What is the waiting time per customer?
2. What is the percentage idle time for the facility? (Assume that the system starts at t = 0)

Solution:

- First customer arrives at the service center at t = 0
- His departure time after getting service = 0 + 4 = 4 minutes. Second customer arrives at time t = 1.5 minutes
- He has to wait = 4 – 1.5 = 2.5 minutes.
- Third customer arrives at time t = 3 minutes he has to wait for = 8 – 3 = 5 minutes
- Fourth customer arrives at time t = 4.5 minutes and he has to wait for 12 – 4.5 = 7.5 minutes.

- During this 4.5 minutes, the first customer leaves in 4 minutes after getting service and the second customer is getting service.
- Fifth customer arrives at t = 6 minutes he has to wait 14 – 6 = 8 minutes. Sixth customer arrives at t = 7.5 minutes he has to wait 14 – 7.5 = 6.5 minutes Seventh customer arrives at t = 9 minutes he has to wait 14 – 9 = 5 minutes
- During this 9 minutes the second customer leaves the service in 8th minute and third person is to get service in 9th minute. Eighth customer arrives at t = 10.5 minutes
- He has to wait 14 – 10.5 = 3.5 minutes, Nineth customer arrives at t = 12 minutes he has to wait 14 – 12 = 2 minutes
- But by 12th minute the third customer leaves the Service 10th Customer arrives at t = 13.5 minutes
- He has to wait 14 – 13.5 = 0.5 minute

From this calculation it is clear that

(i) Average waiting time for 10 customers

= 2.5 + 5 + 7.5 + 8 + 6.5 + 5.0 + 3.5 + 2 + 0.5/10 = 4.05

(ii) Average waiting time for 9 customers who are in waiting for service 40.5/9 = 4.5 minutes.

But the average service time is 4 minutes which is less that the average waiting time, the percentage of idle time for service = 0%

4.18 LINE BALANCING

Line: an assembly line composed of several work stations, at which specific operations are performed.

Line Balancing is the process of assigning tasks to workstations in such a way that the workstations (operations) have approximately equal time requirements.

For Product Layouts (Sequence of tasks!)

Multiple tasks can be assigned to one workstation.

Cycle Time of Workstation

The time a workstation needs to complete its set of assigned tasks once.

Example: Workstation A is assigned 2 tasks, task one need 0.5 minute and task two 1 minute. So the cycle time (CT) of workstation A is?

Solution: The CT of a product line containing multiple workstations is the longest CT of the workstations. (Line CycleTime)

(Line Cycle Time) An Assembly Line Balancing Example

$$\text{Cycle Time} = \frac{\text{Production Time Available per Day}}{\text{Units Required per Day}}$$

$$\text{Min. Num. of Workstations} = \frac{\sum \text{Task Times}}{\text{Cycle Time}}$$

$$\text{Efficiency} = \frac{\sum \text{Task Times}}{\text{Actual Number of Workstations} \times \text{Cycle Time}}$$

Line balancing procedure:

- Calculate CT and N_{Min}.
- Assign tasks to workstations moving from left to right through the precedence diagram.
- Tasks eligible for assignment are tasks where all preceding tasks have been assigned and tasks with times that do not exceed the remaining time at the work station.

Select an eligible task for assignment using one or more of the following rules:

- Assign the task with the greatest number of tasks following it.
- Assign the task with the longest task time.
- After each task assignment calculate time remaining at the current work station.
- Continue this until all tasks have been assigned to workstations.
- Compute appropriate measures (*e.g.,* line percent idle time and line efficiency) for the set of assignments.

Example 18: Design the work stations for an assembly line shown below. Use RPW method. Desired cycle time is 10 minutes.

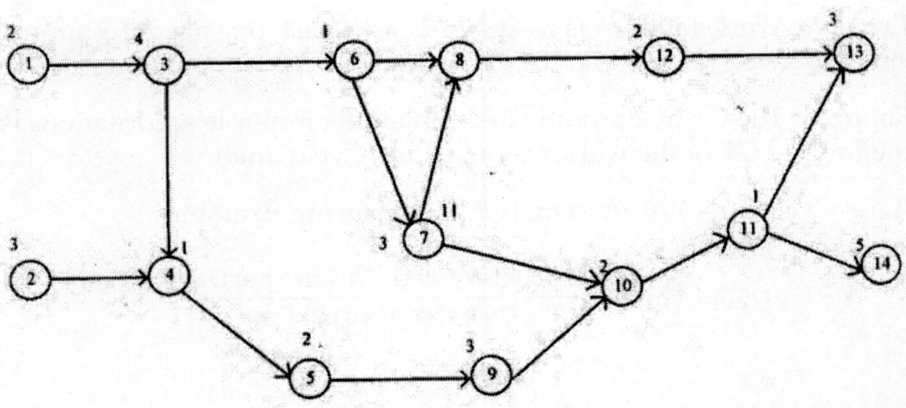

Solution: $T_{we} = S^{N}{}_{i=1}\ T_{iN} =$

Total work content = 2+4 + 1 + 2 + 2 + 3 + 3 + 2+ 1 + 5 + 3 + 2 + 1 + 3 = 34

Range of cycle time:

$$\text{Max}\ (T_{iN}) < T_c < \Sigma^{N}{}_{i=1}\ T_{iN} \quad \text{or} \quad 5 < T_c < 34$$

Desired cycle time C = 10 min.

Minimum Rank Position Weight (RPW) method: Rank positional weight means the processing time of the machine and the connectors if present. It is the total time on the longest path from the beginning of the operation to the last operation of the network.

As in 14 the processing time is 5, So RPW=5,

for 13 RPW = 3,

for 12 RPW = 3 + 2 = 5,

for 11 RPW = 5 + 1 = 6,

for 8 RPW = 3 + 2 + 3 = 7

for 10 RPW = 5 + 1 + 2 = 8,

for 7 RPW = 5 + 1 + 2 + 3 = 11,

for 6 RPW = 5 + 12 + 2 + 3 + 1 = 12,

for 9 RPW = 5 + 1 + 2 + 3 = 11,

for 5 RPW = 5 + 1 + 2 + 3 + 2 = 13

for 4 RPW = 5 + 1 + 2 + 3 + 2 + 1 = 14

for 2 RPW = 5 + 1 + 2 + 3 + 2 + 1 + 3 = 17

for 3 RPW = for 4 + 4 = 14 + 4 = 18

for 1 RPW = for 3 + 2 = 18 + 2 = 20

Task	RPW	Task	RPW	Task	RPW
1	(20)	3	(18)	2	(17)
4	(14)	5	(13)	9	(11)
6	(12)	7	(11)	10	(8)
8	(7)	11	(6)	12	(5)
14	(5)	13	(3)		

Now, grouping on the basis of weight:

(a) *Balance delay* $= [I = \Sigma N_{i=1}\ T_{iN}/nT_c]$

= Total ideal time / cycle time × no. of stations

= [1 – 34/4*10] * 100 = 15%

(b) *Linee efficiency* = [1 – Balance delay] * 100

= [1 – 0.15] * 100 = 85%

(c) *Smoothness index* $= \sqrt{\Sigma N_{i=1}}\ [(T_s)_{max} - T_{si}]^2$

$= \sqrt{\Sigma(10-10)^2 + (10-19)^2 + (10-10)^2 + (10-5)^2}$

$= \sqrt{\Sigma 0 + 1 + 0 + 25}$

$= \sqrt{26} = 5.1$

Example 19: Consider the assembly network as shown .The number by side of each node represents the processing time in minutes. The required production volume in 8hr-shift is 24 completed assembly line using RPW method.

Ans. Cycle time = Production time/production volume

= 8*60/24 = 20 minutes.

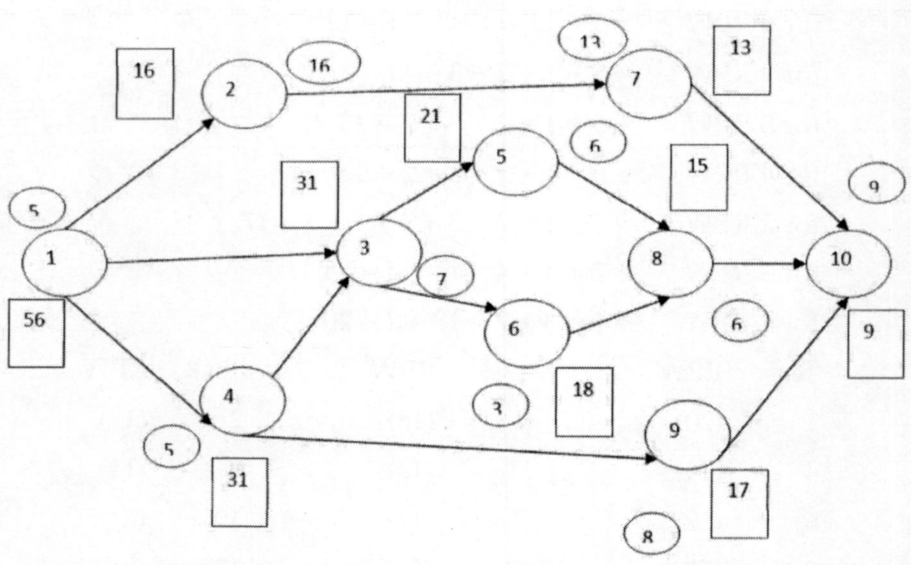

Station number	List	Work element selected	Unassigned cycle time	Sum of unassigned cycle time
1	-	-	20	
	1	1	15	
	2,3,4	4	10	
	2,3,9	3	3	
	2,6	6	0	
2	-	-	20	3
	2,5,9	5	14	
	2,8,9	9	6	
	2,8	2	3	
	-	-	3	
3	-	-	20	1
	7,8	8	14	
	7	7	10	
	10	10	1	

Balancing efficiency = [1 – SUACT/CT*SN]*100

= [1 – 4/20*3]*100

= 93.33% (*Ans.*)

4.19 OVERVIEW OF JIT

Just-in-time is the philosophy of manufacturing based on planned elimination of all waste and continuous improvement of productivity.

Just in time is a pull system of production, so actual orders provide a signal for when a product should be manufactured. Demand-pull enables a firm to produce only what is required, in the correct quantity and at the correct time.

This means that stock levels of raw materials, components, work in progress and finished goods can be kept to a minimum. This requires a carefully planned scheduling and flow of resources through the production process. Modern manufacturing firms use sophisticated production scheduling software to plan production for each period of time, which includes ordering the correct stock. Information is exchanged with suppliers and customers through EDI (Electronic Data Interchange) to help ensure that every detail is correct.

Supplies are delivered right to the production line only when they are needed. For example, a car manufacturing plant might receive exactly the right number and type of tyres for one day's production, and the supplier would be expected to deliver them to the correct loading bay on the production line within a very narrow time slot.

Overview of JIT manufacturing

1. Inventory reduction
2. Quality improvement
3. Lead time reduction
4. Continuous improvement
5. Total preventive maintenance
6. Strategic gain

Advantages of JIT

- Lower stock holding means a reduction in storage space which saves rent and insurance costs.
- As stock is only obtained when it is needed, less working capital is tied up in stock.
- There is less likelihood of stock perishing, becoming obsolete or out of date.
- Avoids the build-up of unsold finished product that can occur with sudden changes in demand.
- Less time is spent on checking and re-working the product of others as the emphasis is on getting the work right first time.

Disadvantages of JIT

- There is little room for mistakes as minimal stock is kept for re-working faulty product.
- Production is very reliant on suppliers and if stock is not delivered on time, the whole production schedule can be delayed.
- There is no spare finished product available to meet unexpected orders, because all product is made to meet actual orders–however, JIT is a very responsive method of production.

His chapter focuses on this idea of using different approaches and systems. The overall philosophy of Lean/JIT is to pursue a system that functions efficiently with minimal levels of inventories, space and transactions. The main benefits of lean operations systems are:

1. Reduced cost through reduced inventory levels
2. Higher quality
3. Reduced lead time
4. Increased productivity
5. Reduced amounts of wastes

Inventories should never be used as the solution to fix machine malfunctions. One method that JIT systems uses to minimize inventory is to have suppliers deliver goods directly to the production floor. Overall, carrying low inventories offers many benefits such as less carrying cost, less space needed and less rework to complete in case of a product recall. Lean systems can also be referred to as "just-in-time" (JIT) systems. The object of a lean system is to create a system that is demand driven, and provides supply based on demand at any given point. Lean systems tend to concentrate on waste reduction and have continuous improvement. There are four building blocks that contribute to the building of a lean system. They are:

1. Product design
2. Process design
3. Personnel/organizational elements
4. Manufacturing planning and control

Each process is crucial and contributes to an effective lean system. **Product design** consists of standard parts (workers have fewer parts to deal with), modular design (an extension of standard parts, they are separate parts clustered together and treated as one unit), highly capable production systems with quality built in (JIT requires highly capable production systems), and concurrent engineering (keeping engineering practices shouldn't change to avoid disruptions). **Process Design** consists of small lot sizes (optimal one unit), setup time reductions, manufacturing cells (specialized and efficient production centers, quality improvement, production flexibility, a balanced system (distributing workload evenly among the workstations), little inventory storage, and fail safe methods (incorporate ways to reduce or eliminate the potential for errors during the process). Lean systems have an extremely effective production method. **Personnel/organizational** elements includes workers as assets **(A JIT philosophy)**, cross-trained workers (perform several parts of the process and operate several machines), cost accounting, and leadership/project management (a two-way communication process between managers and workers). The last building block is manufacturing planning and control. It includes level loading, (achieving stable, level daily mix schedules) pull systems (work moves on in response to demand from the next stage in the process), visual systems (A kanban card used as authorization to move or work on parts), limited work-in-process, close vendor relationships, reduced transaction processing (logistical, balancing, quality, or change transactions), preventive maintenance and housekeeping (keeping the workplace clean and free of unneeded material.

4.20 LEAN OPERATION

Lean operations began as lean manufacturing in the 1900's, and was developed by the Japanese automobile manufacturer, Toyota. The Japanese were sensitive to waste and inefficiency issues. The goal was to eliminate all waste from the process. Waste was identified by them as anything that interfered with the process or simply did not add value. Companies began adopting the lean approach and to do so realized that they had to do major changes in their organization and with their culture in the organization. Lean methods have demand-based operations, flexible operations with rapid change over capability, effective worker behaviors, and continuous improvement efforts. The terms used in the lean approach are the following:

Muda: Waste and inefficiency. The philosophy that waste and inefficiency can be minimized using the following tactics.

Kanban: Manual system used to control the movement of parts and materials responding to the need to deliver them.

Pull System: To produce only what is needed

Heijunka: Volume and variety must be leveled

Kaizen: Continuous improvement

Jidoka: Quality at the source

Poka-yoke: Safeguards built into the process to reduce error

Team concept: Use small team workers for process improvements

Key notes

I. Performance measures for Model I: (M/M/1): ("/ FCFS)
   This model is based on the following assumptions.
   (i) Arrivals follow poisson distribution
   (ii) Service time follow exponential distribution
   (iii) Single server
   (iv) Infinite capacity.

(v) First come first served service discipline.

1. Expected number of customers in the system (Ls) = λ / ($\mu - \lambda$)
2. Expected number of customers in the queue (Lq) = λ^2 / μ ($\mu - \lambda$)
3. Expected waiting time for a customer in the queue (Wq) = λ / μ ($\mu - \lambda$)
4. Expected waiting time for a customer in the system (Ws) = = 1 / ($\mu - \lambda$)
5. Probability that the queue is non-empty P(n>1) = $(\lambda / \mu)^2$
6. Probability that the number of customers, n in the system exceeds a given number, k

$$P(n > =k) = =(\lambda / \mu)^k$$

7. Expected length of non-empty queue = μ / ($\mu - \lambda$).

Solved problems 4.1

Problems 21: A television repairman finds that the time spent on his jobs has an exponential distribution with a mean of 30 minutes. If he repairs sets in the order in which they came in, and if the arrival of sets follow a Poisson distribution with an average rate of 10 per 8 hour day, what is the repairman's expected idle time each day? How many jobs are ahead of the average set just brought in?

Solution: λ = 10/8 = 5/4 sets/hr; μ = (1/30) 60 = 2 sets/hr.

Number of hours for which the repairman remains busy in 8-hour day

$$= 8^* (\lambda / \mu) = 8(5/8)= 8 \text{ hrs.}$$

Repairman's expected idle time in an 8-hour day = 8 – 5 = 3 hrs.

Expected number of T.V sets in the system = (Ls) = λ / ($\mu - \lambda$)

$$= (5/4)/[2 - (5/4)] = 5/3 = 2 \text{ sets (approx.)}$$

Problem 22: Arrivals at telephone booth are considered to be poisson with an average time of 10 minutes between one arrival and the next. The length of phone call is assumed to be distributed exponentially, with mean 3 minutes.

(a) What is the probability that a person arriving at the booth will have to wait?

(b) The telephone department will install a second booth when convinced that an arrival would expect waiting for at least 3 minutes for a phone call. By how much should the flow of arrivals increase in order to justify a second booth?

(c) What is the average length of the queue that forms from time to time?

(d) What is the probability that it will take him more than 10 minutes altogether to wait for the phone and complete his call.

Solution: $\lambda = 1/10$ person/minute; $\mu = 1/3 = 0.33$ person/minute.

(a) Probability that a person arriving at the booth will have to wait $= 1 - P0 = 0.3$

(b) The installation of the 2nd booth will be justified only if the arrival rate is more than the waiting time.

Let λ' be the increased arrival rate. Then expected waiting time in the queue will be $(Wq) = \lambda' / \mu (\mu - \lambda')$

$$3 = \lambda' / 0.33(0.33 - \lambda')$$

$$\text{Or } \lambda' = 0.16$$

Hence the increase in the arrival rate is 0.16-0.10 = 0.06 arrivals / minute.

(c) Average length of non-empty queue

$$= \mu / (\mu - 1) = 0.33/0.23 = 2 \text{ customers(approx.)}$$

(d) Probability of waiting for 10 minutes or more = $P(t >= 10)\infty$

$$= \int(\lambda / \mu)\ (\mu - \lambda)\ e^{-(\mu - ë)t}\ dt$$

10

∞

$$= \int 0.3 * 0.23 * e^{-0.23\,t}\ dt$$

10

$$= 0.03$$

Key note

1. To describe the general model for the transportation problem, we need to use terms that are considerably less specific than those for the components of the prototype example. In particular, the general transportation problem is concerned (literally or figuratively) with distributing any commodity from any group of supply centers, called sources, to any group of receiving centers, called destinations, in such a way as to minimize the total distribution cost.

EXERCISE 4.1

1. a. Least Cost Method
   b. Vogel Approximation Method (VAM)

	Warehouses			
Company	*A*	*B*	*C*	*Supply*
W	10	8	9	15
X	5	2	3	20
Y	6	7	4	30
Z	7	6	9	35
Requirement	25	26	49	100

Ans.

a. $x_{11} = 15$, $x_{21} = 10$, $x_{22} = 10$, $x_{32} = 16$, $x_{33} = 14$, $x_{43} = 35$
   Minimum Cost is: 753

b. $x_{13} = 15$, $x_{22} = 20$, $x_{33} = 30$, $x_{41} = 25$, $x_{42} = 6$, $x_{43} = 4$
   Minimum Cost is: 542

c. $x_{13}= 15$, $x_{22}= 20$, $x_{33}= 30$, $x_{41}= 25$, $x_{42}= 6$, $x_{43}= 4$
   Minimum Cost is: 542

2. Find the optimum Solution of the following Problem using MODI method.

Source	*Destination* 1	2	3	*Capacity*
A 42	8	9	10	30
B	9	11	11	28
C	10	12	9	
Demand	35	40	25	100

Ans. $x_{11} = 2, x_{12} = 40, x_{21} = 30, x_{31} = 3, x_{33} = 25$

Minimum Transportation Optimal cost is: 901

3. The ABT transport company ships truckloads of food grains from three sources *viz.* X, Y, Z to four mills viz. A, B, C, D respectively. The supply and the demand together with the unit transportation cost per truckload on the different routes are described in the following transportation table. Assume that the unit transportation costs are in hundreds of dollars. Determine the optimum minimum shipment cost of transportation using MODI method.

Source	*Mill* A	*B*	*C*	*D*	*Supply*
X	10	2	20	11	15
Y	12	7	9	20	25
Z	4	14	16	18	10
Demand	5	15	15	15	

Ans. $x_{12} = 5, x_{14} = 10, x_{22} = 10, x_{23} = 15, x_{31} = 5, x_{34} = 5$

Minimum Optimal Cost is: $435

4. An organization has three plants at X, Y, Z which supply to warehouses located at A, B, C, D, and E respectively. The capacity of the plants is 800, 500 and 900 per month and the requirement of the warehouses is 400, 400, 500, 400 and 800 units respectively. The following table shows the unit transportation cost.

	A	B	C	D	E
X	5	8	6	6	3
Y	4	7	7	6	6
Z	8	4	6	6	3

Determine an optimum distribution for the organization in order to minimize the total cost of transportation.

Ans. $x_{15} = 800$, $x_{21} = 400$, $x_{24} = 100$, $x_{32} = 400$, $x_{33} = 200$, $x_{34} = 300$, $x_{43} = 300$ (supply shortage) Minimum Cost of Transportation is: $9200

5. The arrival rate of customers at a banking counter follows a Poisson distribution with a mean of 10 per hours. The service time per customer is exponential distribution with a mean of 5 minutes. One service door can accomodate 3 persons at a time.
   (a) What is the probability that an arriving customer can drive directly to the space in front of window.
   (b) What is the probability of waiting of arrival customer out side the system.
   (c) How long the arriving customer expected to wait before starting of service.

Ans. 0.42, 0.48, 25 minute.

6. Vehicles pass through a toll gate at a rate of 30 trains per day. The average time to pass through the gate is 36 seconds. The arrival rate and service rate follow Poisson distribution. There is a complaint the vehicles wait for long duration. Calculate mean queue size, the probability that queue size exceeds.

Ans. 3,0.06.

7. Cars arrive at a drive-in restaurant with mean arrival rate of 30 cars per hours and the service rate of the cars is 22 per hours. The arrival rate and the service rate follow Poisson distribution. The number parking space for cars is only 5. Find the standard results.

Ans: $L_q = 2.38$ cars, $L_s = 3.3133$ cars, $W_q = 0.116$ hours and $W_s = 0.1615$ hours

8. In a harbor, ship arrive with a mean rate of 24 per week. The harbor has 3 docks to handle unloading and loading of ships. The service rate of individual dock is 12 per week. The arrival rate and the service rate follow Poisson distribution. At any point of time, the maximum no. of ships permitted in the harbor is 8. Find P_0, Lq, L_s, W_q, W_s

Ans: P_0 = 0.1998, L_q = 1.0371 ships, L_s = 2.9671 ships, W_q = 0.04478 week and W_s = 0.1281 week

9. Define simulation and its advantages.
10. Discuss the steps of simulation.
11. The Basic Block Company needs to produce 4000 boxes of blocks per 40-hours week to meet upcoming holiday demand. The process of making blocks can be broken down into six work elements. The precedence and time requirements for each element are as follows. Draw a precedence diagram for the production process. Set up a balanced assembly line and calculate the efficiency of the line.

Ans. 83.4%

Work Element	*Precedence*	*Performance Time (Minutes)*
A	–––––	0.10
B	A	0.40
C	A	0.50
D	–––––	0.20
E	C, D	0.60
F	B, E	0.40

12. Consider the assembly network which shows the precededence relationship in assembling a product. The no. of shifts per day is two and number of working hours per shift is 8. The company aims to produce 80 units of the product per day. Find balancing efficiency by rank positional weight method.

Operation number	*Immediate preceding task*	*Duration*
1	-	7
2	1	2
3	1	2
4	1	5
5	2,3	8
6	3,4	3
7	5	4
8	5,6	7
9	4,6	9
10	7,8,9	8

Ans. CT = 12 minutes, balancing efficiency = 76.39%

13. Consider the following assembly network relationship of a product. The number of shifts per day is two and the number of working hours per shift is 8. The company aims to produce 24 assemblies.

Ans. CT = 20 minutes, balancing efficiency = 75%

Operation No.	*Immediate Task*	*Duration (Min)*	*Operation No.*	*Immediate Task*	*Duration (Min)*
1	-	5	6	3,4	3
2	1	3	7	2	4
3	1	7	8	5,6	6
4	1	5	9	4,	12
5	3	6	10	7,8,9	9

Group the activities into work stations using RPW method and compute balancing efficiency.

MULTIPLE CHOICE QUESTION AND ANSWER 4.1

1. **Work study consists of**
   a. Effective use of plant and equipment
   b. Effective use of human effort
   c. Evaluation of human work
   d. All of the above
   Ans: d
2. **Work study examines**
   a. Method
   b. Duration of work
   c. Both 'a' and 'b'
   d. None of the above
   Ans: c
3. **Work study is also recognised as**
   a. Time study
   b. Motion study
   c. Both 'a' and 'b'
   d. None of the above
   Ans: c
4. **The correct order of procedure in method study is**
   a. Select – Record – Examine – Develop – Define – Install – Maintain
   b. Select – Define – Examine – Develop – Record – Install – Maintain
   c. Select – Record – Develop – Examine – Define – Install – Maintain
   d. Select – Record – Examine – Define – Develop – Install – Maintain
   Ans: a
5. **The following factor(s) must be considered while selecting the work for method study**
   a. Economic considerations

b. Technical considerations

c. Human reactions

d. All of the above

Ans: d

6. In process charts, the symbol used for storage is

a. Circle

b. Square

c. Arrow

d. Triangle

Ans: d

7. In process charts, the symbol used for inspection is

a. Circle

b. Square

c. Arrow

d. Triangle

Ans: b

8. Delay occurs when

a. Someone stops the process

b. Product wait for next event (operation)

c. Both 'a' and 'b'

d. None of the above

Ans: c

9. A milk powder tin is being weighed as it is filled is an example of

a. Operation cum transportation

b. Operation cum inspection

c. Transportation cum inspection

d. None of the above

Ans: b

10. In outline process chart, the horizontal lines represents

a. General flow of process

b. Materials being introduced

c. Both 'a' and 'b'

d. None of the above

Ans: b

11. The outline (operation) process chart, the following symbols are used

a. Operation and inspection

b. Operation and transportation

c. Inspection and transportation

d. Operation and storage

Ans: a

12. The following is (are) the type(s) of flow process chart

i. Man type

ii. Material type

iii. Equipment type

The correct answer is

a. only i

b. i and ii

c. ii and iii

d. All of the above

Ans: d

13. Key concept under which technique are network of events and activities, resource allocation, time and cost considerations, network paths and critical paths?

a. Game theory

b. Network analysis

c. Decision theory

d. None of the above

Ans: b

14. Which technique is used to imitate an operation prior to actual performance?

a. Simulation

b. Integrated production models

c. Inventory control

d. Game theory

Ans: b

15. Graphic method can be applied to solve a LPP when there are only variable

a. One

b. More than One

c. Two

d. Three

Ans: c

16. If the feasible region of a LPP is empty, the solution is

a. Infeasible

b. Unbounded

c. Alternative

d. None of the above

Ans: a

17. A minimization problem can be converted into a maximization problem by changing the sign of coefficients in the

a. Constraints

b. Objective functions

c. Both A and B

d. None of the above

Ans: a

18. In maximization cases, are assigned to the artificial variables as their coefficients in the objective function.

a. +m

b. –m

c. 0

d. None of the above

Ans: b

19. In simplex method, we add variables in the case of '='

a. Slack variable

b. Surplus variable

c. Artificial variable

d. None of the above

Ans: c

20. In simplex method, if there is tie between a decision variable and a slack (or surplus) variable, should be selected.

a. Slack variable

b. Surplus variable

c. Decision variable

d. None of the above

Ans: d

21. Every LPP is associated with another LPP is called

a. Primal

b. Dual

c. Non linear programming

d. None of the above

Ans: b

22. As for maximization in assignment problem, the objective is to maximize the

a. Profit

b. Optimization

c. Cost

d. None of the above

Ans: a

23. If there are more than one optimum solution for the decision variable the solution is

a. Infeasible

b. Unbounded

c. Alternative

d. None of the above

Ans: c

24. Dual of the dual is

a. Primal

b. Dual

c. Alternative

d. None of the above

Ans: a

25. Operations research approach is

a. Multi disciplinary

b. Scientific

c. Initiative

d. All of the above

Ans: a

26. MODI method is used to obtain

a. Optimal solutions

b. Optimality test

c. Both A and B

d. Optimization

Ans: c

27. For solving an assignment problem, which method is used?

a. Hungarian

b. American

c. German

d. Both are incorrect

Ans: a

28. A feasible solution is called a basic feasible solution if the number of non negative allocations is equal to

a. m n+1

b. m n 1

c. m+n 1

d. None of the above

Ans: c

REFERENCES

Hamdy A Taha. 1999. Introduction to operations research, PHI Limited, New Delhi.

Mustafi, C.K. 1988. Operations research methods and practice, Wiley Eastern Ltd., New Delhi.

Mittal, K.V. 1976. Optimization methods in operations research and systems analysis, Wiley Eastern Ltd., New Delhi.

5

Productivity Management and Quality Management

5.1 PRODUCTIVITY

Productivity is a relationship between the output (product/service) and input (resources consumed in providing them) of a business system. The ratio of aggregate output to the aggregate input is called productivity.

$$\text{Productivity} = \text{Output} / \text{Input}$$

For survival of any organization, this productivity ratio must be at least 1. If it is more than 1, the organization is in a comfortable position. The ratio of output produced to the input resources utilized in the production.

5.2 BENEFITS DERIVED FROM HIGHER PRODUCTIVITY ARE AS FOLLOWS

It helps to cut down cost per unit and thereby improve the profits. Gains from productivity can be transferred to the consumers in form of lower priced products or better quality products. These gains can also be shared with workers or employees by paying them at higher rate. A more productive entrepreneur can have better chances to exploit expert opportunities. It would generate more employment opportunity. Overall productivity reflects the efficiency of production system. More output is produced with same or less input. The same output is produced with lesser input. More output is produced with more input. The proportional increase in output being more than the proportional increase in input.

5.3 PRODUCTIVITY MEASUREMENT

Productivity may be measured either on aggregate basis or on individual basis, which are called total and partial measure.

Total productivity Index / measure = Total output / Total input

= Total production of goods and services / (Labour + material + capital + Energy + management)

Partial productivity indices, depending upon factors used, it measures the efficiency of individual factor of production.

Labour productivity Index / Measure = Output in unit / Man hours worked

Management productivity Index / Measure = Output / Total cost of management

Machine productivity Index / Measure = Total output / Machine hours worked

Land productivity Index / Measure = Total output / Area of Land used

Partial Measure = Output / labour; Output/capita; Output / Materials; Output / Energy

Example 1: The input and output data for an industry is given in the table. Find out various productivity measures like total, multifactor and partial measure. Output and Input production data in dollar ($)

Output		*Input*	
Finished units	10,000	Human	3000
Work in progress	2500	Material	153
Dividends	1000	Capital	10000
Bonds	Energy	540	
Other income	Others	1500	
Total	13,500	15,193	

Solution:

Total measure = Total Output / Total input = 13,500 / 15,193 = 0.89

Multi factor measure = Total Output / Human + Material

= 13,500/3500 = 3.85

Multi factor measure = Finished units / Human + Material

= 10,000/3153 = 3.17

Partial Measure 1 = Total Output / Energy

= 13,500/540 = 25

Partial Measure 2 = Finished units / Energy

= 10,000/540 = 18.52

For multifactor and partial measures it is not necessary to use total output as numerator. Often, it is described to create measures that represent productivity as it relates to some particular output of interest.

5.4 PRODUCTIVITY MEASUREMENT APPROACHES AT THE ENTERPRISES LEVEL

As stated above total productivity is expressed as the ratio of aggregate output to the aggregate input. That the total overall performance is captured in this ratio, becomes apparent, if we examine the relationship between this ratio and the age-old performance measure of profit. If the outputs and input for the period for which productivity is measured, are expressed in rupees, then under such restrictive assumptions one can write:

Aggregate output = Gross sales = G

Aggregate input = Cost = C

Total productivity = P = G/ C

From the definition of profit, we have; Profit = π = G – C

Dividing by C, $\pi/c = G/C - 1$

$\pi/c = p - 1$

For Zero profit (p = 0), P = 1

For a Loss, (p < 0),

P < 1 For a profit, π > 0, P > 1

Zero profit will give a productivity value of 1, while a loss will give productivity value less than 1. The profit to cost ratio will determine the increase in productivity. The above relationship that demonstrates that increased profit to cost ratio will lead to increased overall productivity, is constituent with our expectation on how an overall performance measure should behave. However it suffers from a number of drawbacks. Some of which are listed here,

a) Given that our objective in productivity measurement is to capture the efficiency of utilization of resources, the effect of price variations over time need to be corrected. Thus aggregate output should be equal to gross sales suitably inflated or deflated with respect to a base year.

b) Equating output to sales implies, whatever is produced in the particular period is sold. Possibility of inventory, material manufactured for own use, etc. are not taken in to consideration.

c) Equating aggregate input to cost raises a host of problems and involves several restrictive assumptions. How to account for the fixed investment and working capital, whether to take the fringe benefits in to account etc. are some of the problems. The different approaches to measurement have arisen mainly in the context of correcting the above drawbacks.

5.5 TECHNIQUES FOR PRODUCTIVITY IMPROVEMENT

Higher productivity in organization leads to national prosperity and better standard of living for the whole community. The methods contribute to the improvement of productivity are method study and work measurement by reducing work content and ineffective time. Work content means the amount of work "contained in" a given product or process measured in man-hour or machine-hour. Except in some cases like in processing industries, actual operation times are far in excess of the theoretical minimum. Ineffective time is the time for which the worker or machine or both are idle due to the shortcomings of the management or the worker.

5.6 ISO 9000

ISO stands for international organization for standardization. It is an international body consists of representatives from more than 90 countries. The national standard bodies of these countries are the member of this organization. These are non-governmental organizations and can provide common standards of goods and services on international trades. ISO 9000 series has 5 numbers of international standards on quality management which are listed below with different objectives. ISO 9000: Provides guide lines on selection and use of quality management and quality assurance standards. ISO 9001: This is applicable for industries doing their own design and development, production, installation and servicing. It has 20 elements.

ISO 9002: It has 18 elements. It is same as ISO 9001 without the 1st two tasks *i.e.,* design and development.

ISO 9003: It has 12 elements covering final inspection and testing for laboratories and warehouses.

ISO 9004: This provides guidelines to interpret the quality management and quality assurance. It also has suggestions which are not mandatory.

Benefits of ISO 9000 Series

1. This gives competitive advantage in the global market.
2. Consistency in quality, as ISO helps in detecting non-conforming early which makes it possible to rectify.
3. Documentation of quality procedure adds clarity to quality system.
4. It ensures adequate and regular quality training for all members of the organization.
5. It helps in customers to have cost effective purchase procedure.
6. The customers during purchase from firm holding ISO certificate need not spend much on inspection and testing. This will reduce quality cost and lead time.
7. This will aid to improved morale and involvement of workers.
8. The level of job satisfaction will be more.
9. This will help in increasing productivity.

Steps in ISO 9000 Registration

1. Selection of appropriate standard from ISO 9001/9002/9003 using guidelines given in ISO 9000.
2. Preparation of quality manual to cover all the elements in the selected model.
3. Preparation of procedure and shop floor instruction which are used at the time of implementing the system. Also document these items.
4. Self-auditing to check compliance of the selected module.
5. Selection of a registrar (an independent body with knowledge and experience to evaluate any one of the three quality systems *i.e.,* ISO 9001 / 9002 / 9003) and the application is to be submitted to obtain certificate for the selected quality system / model.

5.7 TQM BASIC TOOLS

The totality of features and characteristics of a product or service that bear on its ability to satisfy stated or implied needs- ASQC

- User-based
- Product-based
- Manufacturing-based

Five TQM concepts:

- Continuous improvement
- Employee empowerment
- Benchmarking
- Just-in-Time
- Develop proper tools

Deming's 14 points:

1. Create consistency of purpose
2. Lead to promote change
3. Quality through design instead of inspection
4. Reduce # of suppliers, don't buy on price alone
5. Continuously improve product, quality, and service
6. Institute modern training methods
7. Emphasize leadership
8. Drive out fear
9. Break down barriers between departments
10. Eliminate numerical goals, slogans, posters for the work force
11. Using statistical methods to improve quality and productivity
12. Remove barriers to pride of workmanship
13. Institute a program for retraining people in new skills
14. Put everybody to work on the transformation

Improving Quality

Fig. 5.1 shows plan, do, study and act (PDSA) cycle.

- Also called the deming wheel after originator
- Circular, never ending problem solving process

Plan

- Evaluate current process
- Collect procedures, data, identify problems
- Develop an improvement plan, performance objectives

Do

- Implement the plan – trial basis

Study

- Collect data and evaluate against objectives

Act

- Communicate the results from trial
- If successful, implement new process

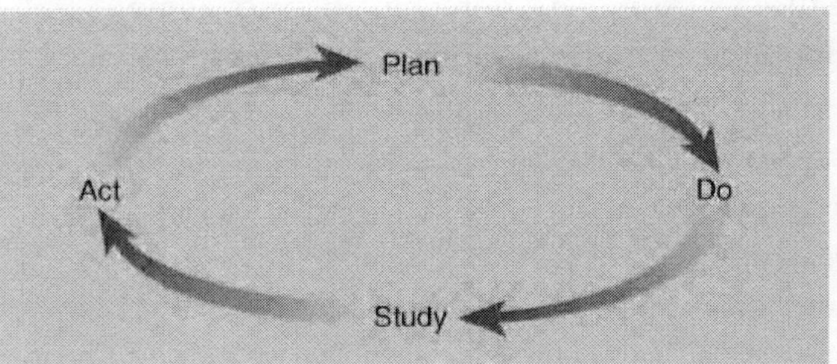

Fig 5.1: PDSA (Google)

Fig. 5.1 shows plan, do, study and act.

Seven Tools of Quality Control

- Tools typically taught to problem solving teams

Tools for TQM

- Simple tools for TQM.

5.7.1 Flowcharts

- Remember system theory: (Input, Output, customer supplier and their interactions).
- Divide complex processes into simple sub-processes.
- A Qualitative tools

Flow chart is divided into two parts:

1. *Layout flowchart*: Example staff movement
2. *Data flow diagrams*: Fig. 5.2 shows Data flow diagram and shows example of leave approval process

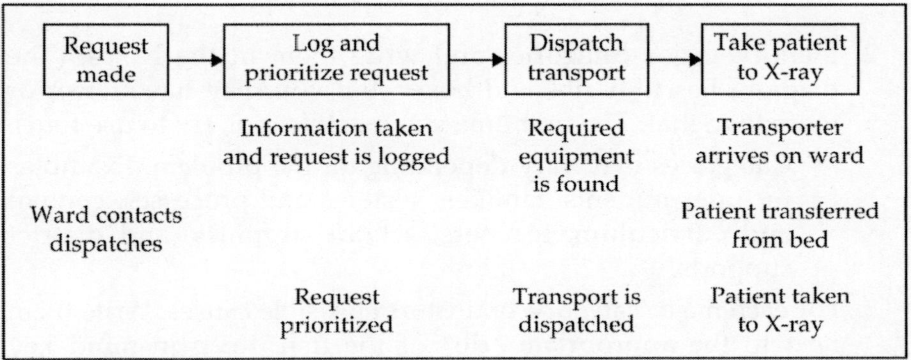

Fig. 5.2: Data flow diagram (O.P. Khana)

5.7.2. Cause and Effect (Ishikawa/fishbone)

Fig. 5.3 cause and effect diagram which shows as fishbone diagram

1. Also known as fishbone or cause-and-effect diagrams
2. Non-quantitative tools (qualitative)
3. Sometimes called the 5M diagram (men, machine, materials, measurements and methods)

For example

1. Write the problem in the box at the "head" of the fish.

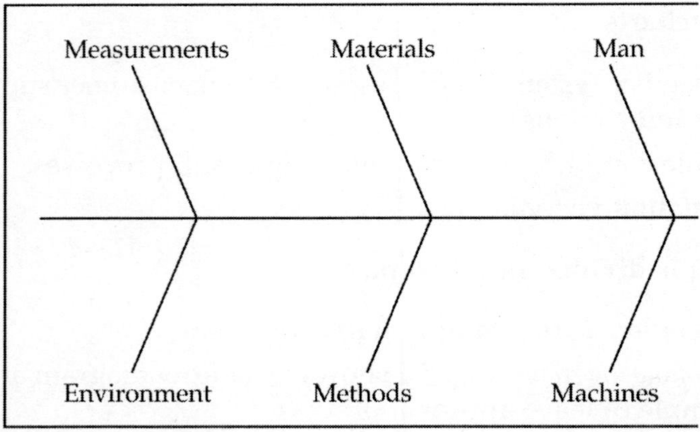

Fig. 5.3 Cause and effect diagram(Google)

2. Identify major categories and write them in the boxes. (The diagram has four ribs and boxes, but you may have fewer or more than that. The first time you use this tool, try to use four).
   - Categories may vary depending on the problem. Examples include: students, families, systems and processes, content and curriculum, teachers, school supports, and district supports.
3. For each major category, brainstorm possible causes. Write them next to the appropriate "rib" of the fish. Keep in mind key guidelines for brainstorming[1]:
   - Let questions flow freely. Generate as many as possible, saying the first thing that comes to your mind. Do not censor your ideas.
   - Share brainstormed questions without discussing them. The point of this exercise is to generate questions, not to evaluate or sort them (yet).
   - Bolder, unexpected questions are best. Break out of old patterns.
   - Even if your idea is similar to something else that has been said, say it anyway. It will keep the creative energies going.
   - Do not debate, discuss, sort, or evaluate ideas at this time; do not even say "great idea!"
   - Make sure everyone contributes.

Participants may come up with possible causes that do not fit easily into one of the previously identified categories. This can indicate a need to identify a new category or broaden an existing category. Do not discard an idea solely because it does not fit into a previously identified category. The purpose of the major categories is to provide a structure to guide the brainstorming. Categories should be used to inspire, rather than restrict, participants' thinking.

In the early stages of the process, participants often use this activity as an opportunity to vent frustrations and criticisms. This can be acceptable in the beginning, but be sure to steer them in a more constructive direction as the activity progresses.

4. Analyze each possible cause identified to determine whether it is a root cause by asking:
   - Would the problem have occurred if the cause had not been present?
   - Would the problem reoccur if the cause were corrected?

   If the answer to both of these questions is "no," you have found a likely root cause.
5. Circle root causes. Cross off ideas that are not root causes.

As a group, identify 1–3 root causes that are within the realm of control of the school. These will be the focus of further action planning. Figure 5.4 shows the fish bone diagram of teachers and families and student reading process.

5.7.3 Check Sheets

Fig. 5.5 explains the example of check sheet of patient transport problem sheet

- Central tool for quality assurance programs
- Specially useful for operational procedures
- Could be derived from the flowchart and fishbone diagrams

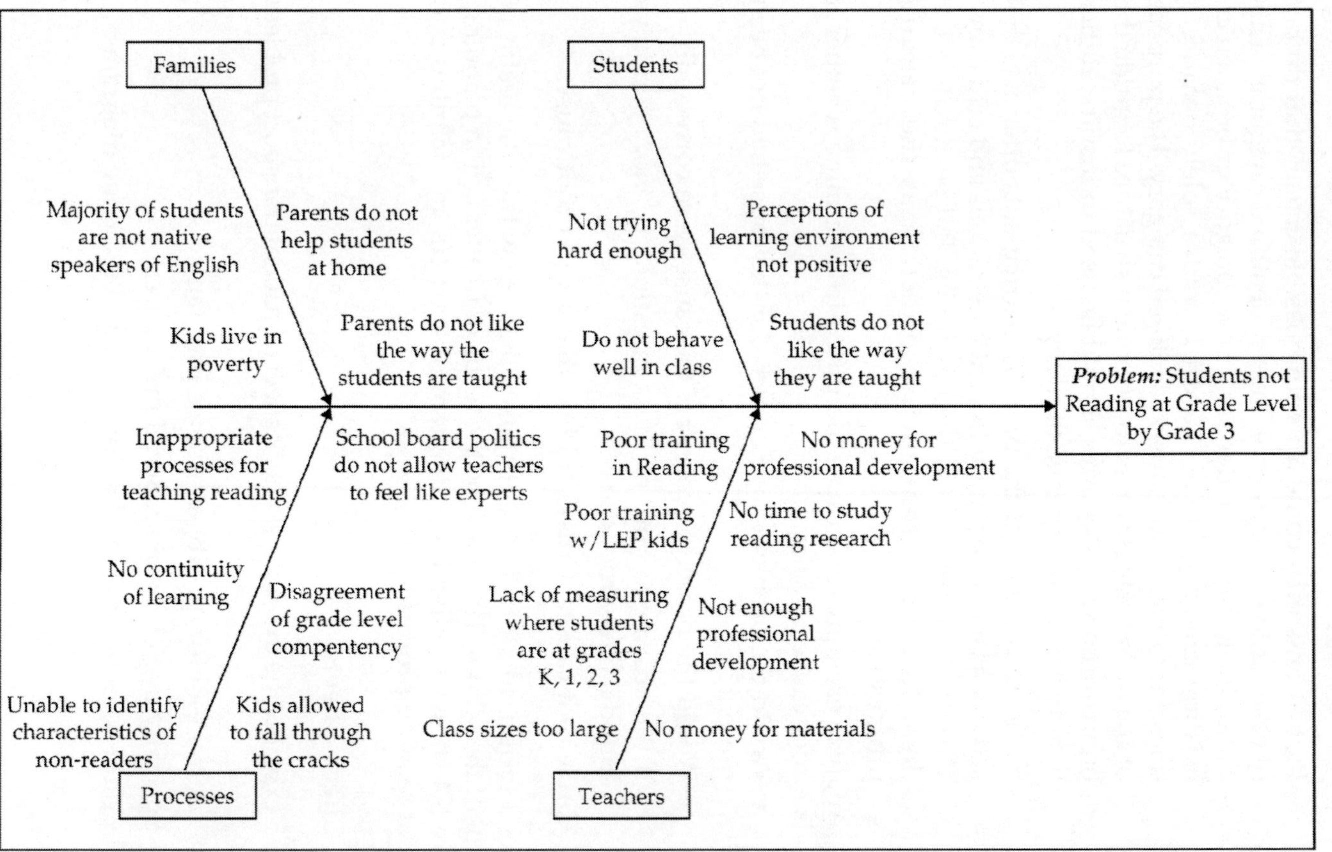

Fig. 5.4: Fish bone diagram (Google)

Patient transport problem sheet		
Area: Ward 3b	Period: June 1996	
Type	Tally	Subtotal
Equipment broken	IIIII	5
Patient not ready	IIIII II	7
Not enough staff	III	3
Patient having another exam etc.	IIIII IIIII II	12

Fig. 5.5: Checksheet (*Source*: O.P.Khanna)

5.7.4 Pareto Charts

Fig. 5.6 shows example of Pareto chart by taking component A, B, C, D, E with respect to %.

- Technique that displays the degree of importance for each element
- Named after the 19th century Italian economist often called the 80-20 rule
- Principle is that quality problems are the results of only a few problems *e.g.*, 80% of the problems caused by 20% of causes

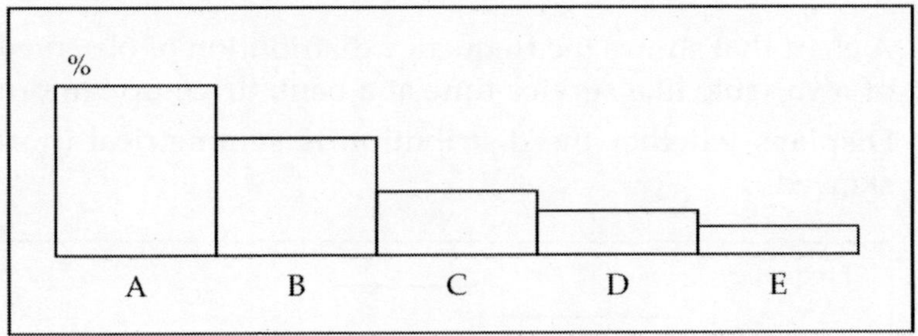

Fig. 5.6 Pareto chart

For example: Fig. 5.7 shows pareto chart of work type of unplanned maintenance accounts for over 61% of the work load, far ahead of planned maintenance work orders which fall into second place.

Source: www.Juran.com

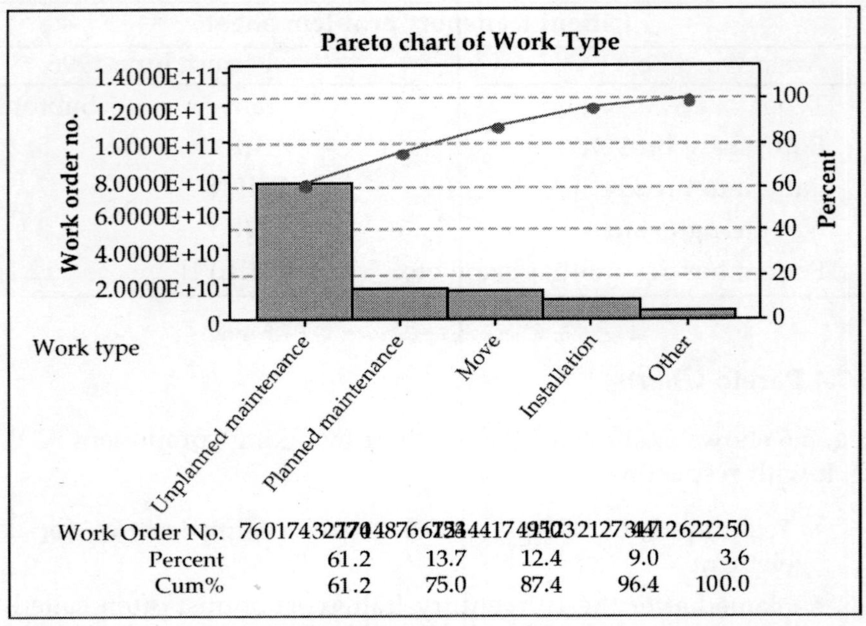

Fig. 5.7: Pareto chart of work type

5.7.5 Histograms

Fig. 5.8 shows the histogram drawn frequency *verses* sample

- A chart that shows the frequency distribution of observed values of a variable like service time at a bank drive-up window
- Displays whether the distribution is symmetrical (normal) or skewed

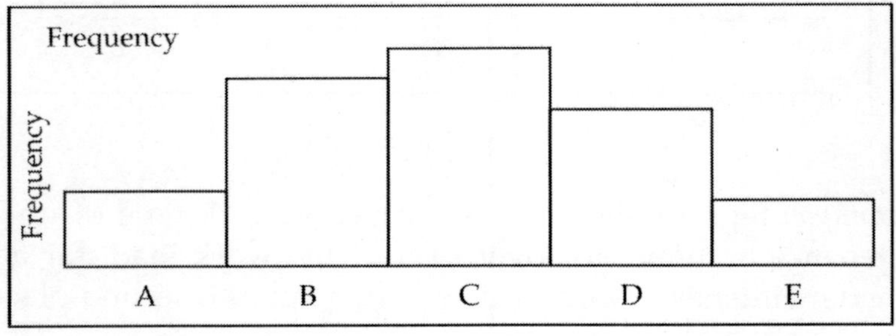

Fig. 5.8: Histogram

Example: Fig. 5.9 explains barriers of sustainable supply chain management by histogram For sustainable supply chain management the barriers data are collected for thermal sector and histograms are plotted. The 10 bars are the barriers of SSCM got by expert analysis.

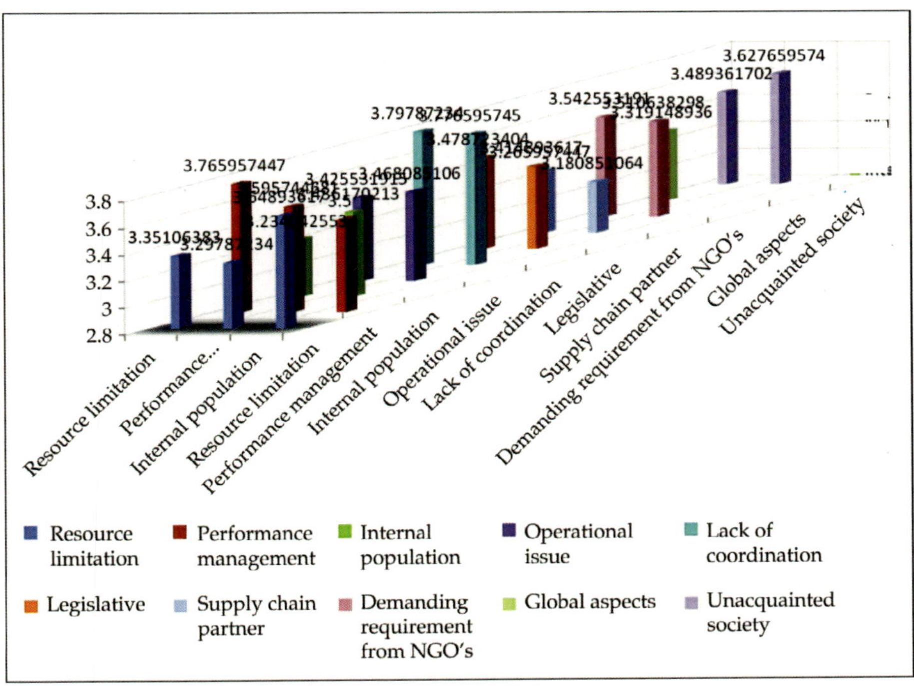

Fig. 5.9: Barriers of sustainable supply chain management by histogram (Satapathy *et.al*)

5.7.6 Run Charts and Control Charts

Important tool used in statistical process control. Fig. 5.10 shows statistical process control upper control and lower control limit.

- The UCL and LCL are calculated limits used to show when process is in or out of control

  Scatter plots and correlation analysis Fig. 5.11 shows the statistical control chart by taking month and data
- A graph that shows how two variables are related to one another

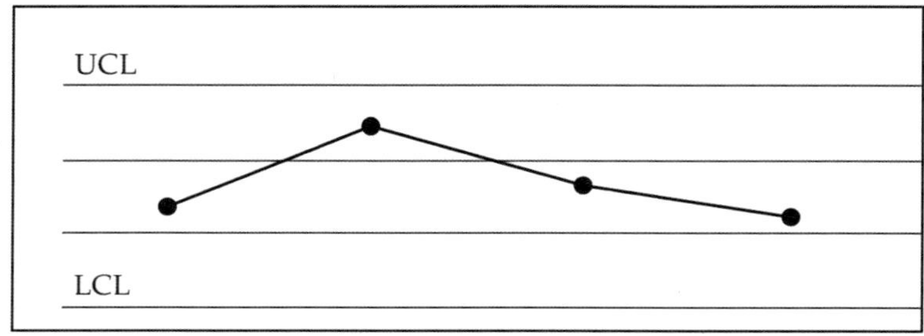

Fig. 5.10 Statistical process control(Amitav Mitra)

- Data can be used in a regression analysis to establish equation for the relationship

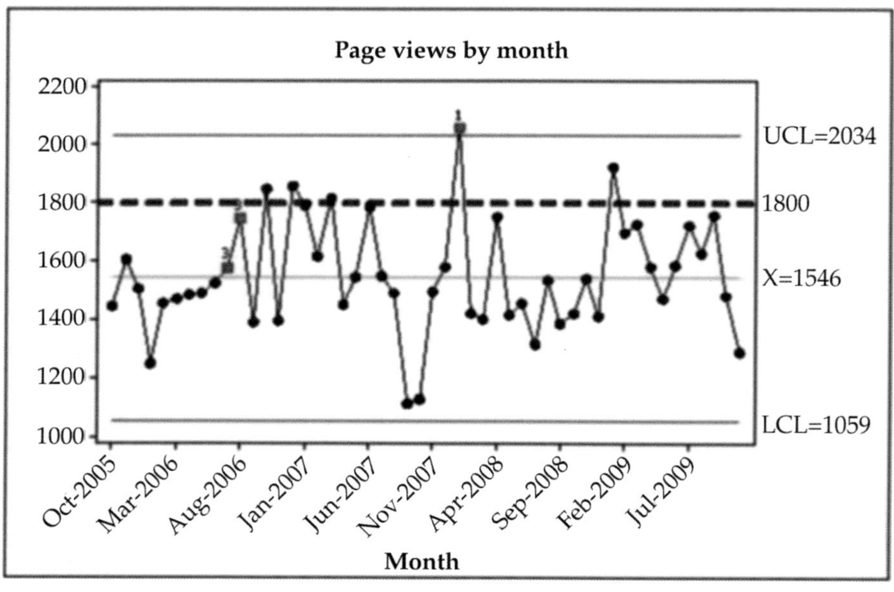

Fig. 5.11 Statistical control chart for Page views by month(Google)

5.7.7 Other Tools of TQM

- Process map identifies the *sequence of activities* or the flow in a process.
- Objectively provides a *picture of the steps* needed to accomplish a task.

- Helps all employees understand *how they fit into the process* and who are their suppliers and customers.
- Can also pinpoint places where quality-related measurements should be taken.
- Also called process mapping and analysis.
- Very successfully implemented in various organizations. *e.g.*, Motorola reduced manufacturing time for pagers using flow harts.

Example: Fig. 5.12 shows flow chart of algorithim and the steps for interpretive structural modeling implemented in electricity sector to establish linear relation between the customer satisfaction factors are shown by process map.

5.7.8 Cost of Quality

1. Framework for identifying quality components that are related to producing both high quality products and low quality components, with the goal of minimizing the total cost of quality.
2. Costs of poor quality:
    - Detection/appraisal costs
    - Internal failure costs
    - External failure costs

5.7.9 Quality Circle

- *Teams of workers and supervisors* that meet regularly to address work-related problems involving quality and productivity.
- Developed by *Kaoru Ishikawa* at University of Tokyo.
- Became immediately popular in Japan as well as USA.
- *Lockheed Missiles and Space Division* was the leader in implementing Quality circles in USA in 1973 (after their visit to Japan to study the same).
- Typically *small day-to-day problems* are given to quality circles. Since workers are most familiar with the routine tasks, they are asked to identify, analyze and solve quality problems in the routine processes.

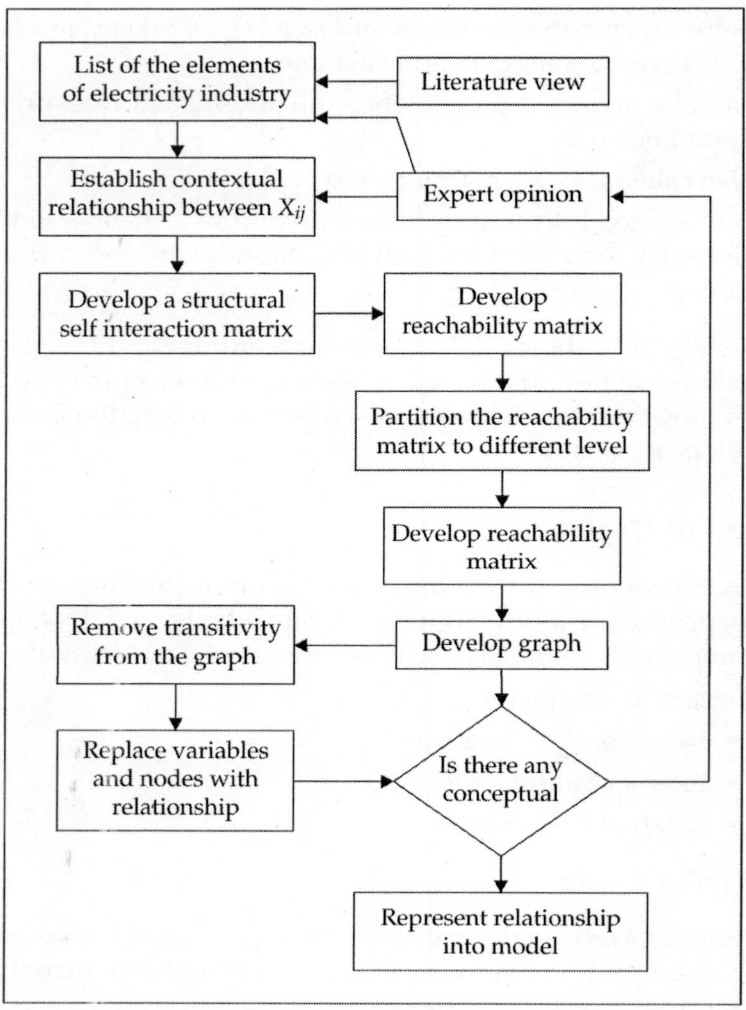

Fig. 5.12: Flow chart (Satapathy *et.al*)

5.7.10 Kaizen Blitz

- An intense and rapid improvement process in which a team or a department throws all its resources into an improvement project over a short period of time.
- Short time "burst" rather than long range simmer- hence the name.

- Blitz teams usually comprise of employees from all areas involved in the process who *understand* it and can *implement the changes on the spot.*

5.7.11 Poka-Yoke (Mistake Proofing)

- Approach for mistake-proofing processes using automatic devises or methods to avoid simple human error.
- Developed and refined in the 1960s by the late Shigeo Shingo, a Japanese manufacturing engineer who developed the Toyota production system.

Focused on two aspects:

- *Prediction* – Recognizing that a defect is about to occur and provide a warning.
- *Detection* – Recognizing that a defect has occurred and stop the process.

5.8 QUALITY MANAGEMENT AWARDS

- ISO 9000: 2000
- Created by *International Organization for Standardization* (IOS) which was created in 1946 to standardize quality requirement within the European market.
- ISO initially composed of representatives from 91 countries: probably most wide base for quality standards.
- *Adopted a series of written quality standards* in 1987 (first revised in 1994, and *more recently (and significantly) in 2000*).
- Prefix "ISO" in the name refers to the scientific term *"iso" for equal*. Thus, certified organizations are assured to have quality equal to their peers.

The International Organization for Standardization (ISO)

Table 5.1 ISO and ISO 9000 series of quality standards

- An international set of standards for documenting the processes that an organization uses to produce its goods and services. ISO 9000 certification.

- First party certification—A firm audits itself.
- Second party certification—Customers audit their suppliers.
- Third party assessment—Company is assessed by outside registrars from ASQ's Registration Accreditation Board (RAB).
- ISO 9000/Q90 registration process
- Application to registrar
- Preliminary assessment
- Full audit

Table 5.1 ISO

ISO 9001:2000	Quality Management Systems: Requirements
ISO 9004:2000	Quality Management Systems: Guidelines for Performance Improvement
ISO 9000:2000	Quality Management Systems: Fundamentals and Standards

ISO 9000: 2000 structure ISo-Consists of three documents

1. ISO 9000 – Fundamentals and vocabulary.
2. ISO 9001 – Requirements.

Organized in four sections: Management Responsibility; Resource Management; Product Realization; and Measurement, Analysis and Improvement.

ISO 9004 – Guidelines for performance improvements

- Principle 1: Customer Focus
- Principle 2: Leadership
- Principle 3: Involvement of people
- Principle 4: Process approach
- Principle 5: Systems approach for management
- Principle 6: Continual improvement
- Principle 7: Factual approach to decision making
- Principle 8: Mutually beneficial supplier

Six Sigma

1. Business improvement approach that seeks to *find and eliminate causes of defects and errors in processes* by focusing on outputs that are critical to customers.
2. The term Six Sigma is based on a statistical measure that equates *3.4 or fewer errors or defects per million opportunities*.
3. Motorola pioneered the concept of Six Sigma.
4. The late Bill Smith, a reliability engineer is credited with conceiving the idea of Six Sigma.

GE (specifically CEO Jack Welch) Extensively Promoted

Core philosophy based on key concepts:

- Think in terms of key business processes and customer requirements with focus on strategic objectives.
- Focus on corporate sponsors responsible for championing projects.
- Emphasize quantifiable measures such as defects per million opportunities (*dpmo*).
- Ensure appropriate metrics is identified to maintain accountability.
- Provide extensive training.
- Create highly qualified process improvement experts -"belts".

Set Stretch Objectives for Improvement

Contrasts between traditional TQM and Six Sigma (SS) -

- TQM is based largely on worker empowerment and teams; SS is owned by business leader champions.
- TQM is process based; SS projects are truly cross-functional.
- TQM training is generally limited to simple improvements tools and concepts; SS is more rigorous with advanced statistical methods.
- TQM has little emphasis on financial accountability; SS requires verifiable return on investment and focus on bottom line.

Awards: Malcolm Baldrige National Quality Award, EFQM Model, Deming Prize

Promotion of high quality goods and services

1. Malcolm Baldrige National Quality Award (MBNQA) (United States)
2. Deming Prize (Japan)
3. European Quality Award (European Union)
4. ISO : 9000 certification

Background

- Established in 1987 to recognize total quality management in American industry.

Purpose

- Stimulate U.S. companies to improve quality and productivity.
- Establish guidelines and criteria to evaluate quality.
- Recognize those firms that improve their quality.
- Provide guidance in how to achieve quality.

Baldrige guidelines can be used to:

- Help define and design a total quality system.
- Evaluate ongoing internal relationships among department, divisions, and functional units within an organization.
- Assess and assist outside suppliers of goods and services to a company.
- Assess customer satisfaction.

Deming Prize

- Initiated by Japan in 1951 to recognize the importance of high quality products.
- Name after W. Edwards Deming
- Categories of the deming prize:
- The deming prize for individuals

- The deming application prize
- The quality control award for operations/ business units
- European Foundation for Quality Management (EFQM)
- Stimulate and assist European organizations in quality improvement activities.
- Support managers in the adoption of TQM.

EFQM Excellence Model

- A non-prescriptive frame work based on nine criteria that recognizes that there are many approaches to achieving sustainable excellence.

Lean verses Six Sigma

1. Lean is focused on the process. Six Sigma focuses on the output. In practice, this difference isn't nearly as significant as it sounds. Both methodologies work toward very similar ultimate goals. However, in a Lean implementation you'll find yourself highly focused on process improvements for efficiency, while Six Sigma often starts with tools to perfect the outputs.
2. Many lean tools reflect common sense put into action. By adding "fool proofing" to your processes, you can catch production errors before they become common sense. By adding monitoring to your problem-solving, you'll see better solution implementations. Most importantly, the customer's point-of-view drives an entire lean organization.

   In contrast, Six Sigma is inherently quantitative. Varied inputs lead to varied outputs. Constant measurement is key. Depending on the structure of your enterprise, you may find that one method is easier to adopt due to it's resonance among employee
3. Six Sigma you can expect to immediately start progressing toward the major metric of high quality. In lean, many organizations choose to target "low hanging fruit" that are causing visible problems in the enterprise. By increasing safety, eliminating obvious inefficiencies from the process, and accomplishing other "small steps" with the help of lean tools, your quality will improve and you'll continue to progress toward exceptional client satisfaction.

4. Lean is about moving the mean, it takes steps towards reducing waste, response times, and production times. Six Sigma is about reducing variation, through focus on the defect rate.

Reference

1. These brainstorming guidelines are drawn from two sources: *Moving Beyond Icebreakers*, by Stanley Pollack and Mary Fusoni (2005, www.teenempowerment.org), and *Facilitation at a Glance, 2nd Edition*, by Ingrid Bens (2008, www.participative-dynamics.com)

Key Note

2. Teams of workers and supervisors that meet regularly to address work-related problems involving quality and productivity = Quality circle
3. ISO stands for international organization for standardization. It is an international body consists of representatives from more than 90 countries

QUESTIONS

1. Write measurement techniques of productivity index.

Ans. Chapter 5.3 productivity measurement:

2. What are the techniques for productivity improvement.

Ans. Chapter 5.5 techniques for productivity improvement

3. Write short notes on TQM, IS0. 2000.

Ans. Chapter 5.6 ISO 9000

4. Write about TQM basic tools.

5. What are the tools of total quality management.

Ans. Chapter 5.7. TQM basic tools and certification.

6. Briefly discuss the diferent ways to improve productivity.

Ans. Improved or higher productivity meaning clearer.

- *Improved productivity of land*: If by using better seed, better methods of cultivation and more fertilizer, the yield of corn from a particular hectare of land can be increased from 4 quintals to 6 quintals, the productivity of that land, in the agricultural sense is increased (improved) by 50 percent. The productivity of land used for industrial purposes is said to have been increased if the output of goods or services within that area of land is increased by whatever means.

- *Improved productivity of materials*: A skilled tailor is able to cut 12 suits from a bale of cloth where an unskilled labour is able to cut only 10 suits from a bale of cloth, then the productivity of the bale used by skilled worker is 16.6 percent greater than unskilled labour.
- *Improved productivity of machines*: A machine tool is producing 90 pieces per working day (*i.e.,* 8 hours). Considering that through the use of improved cutting tools, the output is increased to 120 pieces, then the productivity of that machine will be increased by 33.33 percent.
- *Improved productivity of Men (Labour)*: The worker is producing 32 plates per hour. Considering that with the improved methods of work, he will be able to produce 42 plates per hour, then productivity of worker will be improved by 31.25 percent. Thus it can be said that more output results into higher productivity or improvement from same amount of resources which means lower money costs and higher net money returns per unit of output. Another productivity concept known as Japanese Holistic view of productivity explains productivity as a comprehensive holistic phenomenon encompassing all elements required to improve products/ services (output). Productivity in the future must be concern itself with seeking affluence of a kind which will provide people with material wealth as well as spiritual satisfaction. Also 72 the outputs particularly in the form of physical pollution must be controlled in the context of increasing concern of society for clean environment and sustainable development. To improve productivity products must be designed to satisfy customer need with optimum consumption of resources without generation of waste in the manufacturing process

6. Discuss the benifits of ISO 9000 sweries.

Ans. The advantages associated with ISO 9000 certification are numerous, as both business analysts and business owners will attest. These benefits, which can impact nearly all corners of a company, range from increased stature to bottom-line operational savings. They include:

- *Increased marketability*—Nearly all observers agree that ISO 9000 registration provides businesses with markedly heightened credibility with current and prospective clients alike. Basically, it proves that the company is dedicated to providing quality to its customers, which is no small advantage whether the company is negotiating with a long-time customer or endeavoring to pry a potentially lucrative customer away from a competitor. This benefit manifests itself not only in increased customer retention, but also in increased customer acquisition and heightened ability to enter into new markets; indeed, ISO 9000 registration has been cited as being of particular value for small and mid-sized businesses hoping to establish a presence in international markets.
- *Reduced operational expenses*—Sometimes lost in the many discussions of ISO 9000's public relations cache is the fact that the rigorous registration process often exposes significant shortcomings in various operational areas. When these problems are brought to light, the company can take the appropriate steps to improve its processes. These improved efficiencies can help companies garner savings in both time and money. "The cost of scrap, rework, returns, and the employee time spent analyzing and troubleshooting various products are all considerably reduced by initiating the discipline of ISO 9000," confirmed Richard B. Wright in *Industrial Distribution.*
- *Better management control*—The ISO 9000 registration process requires so much documentation and self-assessment that many businesses that undergo its rigors cite increased understanding of the company's overall direction and processes as a significant benefit.

- *Increased customer satisfaction*—Since the ISO 9000 certification process almost inevitably uncovers areas in which final product quality can be improvėd, such efforts often bring about higher levels of customer satisfaction. In addition, by seeking and securing ISO 9000 certification, companies can provide their clients with the opportunity to tout their suppliers' dedication to quality in their own business dealings.
- *Improved internal communication*—The ISO 9000 certification process's emphasis on self-analysis and operations management issues encourages various internal areas or departments of companies to interact with one another in hopes of gaining a more complete understanding of the needs and desires of their internal customers.
- *Improved customer service*—The process of securing ISO 9000 registration often serves to refocus company priorities on pleasing their customers in all respects, including customer service areas. It also helps heighten awareness of quality issues among employees.
- *Reduction of product-liability risks*—Many business experts contend that companies that achieve ISO 9000 certification are less likely to be hit with product liability lawsuits, etc., because of the quality of their processes.
- *Attractiveness to investors*—Business consultants and small business owners alike agree that ISO-9000 certification can be a potent tool in securing funding from venture capital firms.

7. Explain the steps in obtaining ISO 9000 registration.

Ans. These eight steps-along with their sub-steps-are based on what many major companies have followed to achieve their own ISO 9000 registration. These steps are also useful for companies simple seeking to conform to the ISO 900 standards, but not formally become certified.

These steps are a good guide for establishing a timeline, schedule, and potential costs for the process of becoming ISO 9000 certified.

(NOTE: Also see *Simple Plan for ISO 9000 Certification* for another outlook on this process.)

1. Get top management commitment
   a. Top management considers ISO 9000 registration
   b. Quality steering committee meets to evaluate process
   c. Committee informs top management of ISO 9000 costs, schedule, etc.
   d. Top management commits to pursue ISO 9000 registration
2. Train personnel
   a. Hold basic quality and ISO 9000 training for all employees
   b. Select and train personnel to be internal auditors
3. Prepare quality policy manual
   a. Study and understand ISO 9000 requirements as they apply to your company
   b. Write (or re-write) company vision and mission statements
   c. Write basic quality policy manual outline
   d. Complete first draft of quality policy manual
   e. Send copy of manual to customer desiring ISO 9000 compliance (if necessary)
4. Prepare operating procedures
   a. Define responsibilities, using quality manual as a guide
   b. Have those responsible for functions outline their procedures
   c. Interview managers and fine-tune procedures
   d. Compare operating procedures with quality manual for consistency
5. Hold internal audit
   a. Hold internal audit of ISO 9000 manual vs. ISO 9000 compliance
   b. Implement corrective action items from audit
6. Select registrar
   a. Research registrars and their cost
   b. Qualify possible registrars
   c. Select third party registrar

7. Go through registration process
   a. Apply for registration and audits
   b. Agree to audit process etc. with registrar
   c. Hold pre-assessment audit
   d. Take any needed corrective action
   e. Have ISO 9000 registration audit
   f. Take any needed corrective action
   g. Re-audit as needed
   h. Take any needed corrective action
8. Obtain ISO 9000 registration
   This verifies that you operate your business in compliance to the ISO 9000 requirements.
9. Explain tools of TQM with example.

Ans. Chapter 5.7. TQM basic tools and certification.

MULTIPLE CHOICE QUESTION AND ANSWER 5.1

1. Malcolm Baldrige National Quality Award is for (MBNQA)
   a. Total quality management
   b. International standard organization
   c. Total productive maintenance
   d. Total quality control

   Ans: a

2. The process mapping is a ______ diagram.
   a. Data flow
   b. Work flow
   c. Circular
   d. Audit

   Ans: b

3. Control chart is a
   a. Process monitoring tool
   b. Process control tool
   c. Both (a) and (b)

d. None of the above

Ans: c

4. The objective of ISO-9000 family of quality management is

a. Customer satisfaction

b. Employee satisfaction

c. Skill enhancement

d. Environmental issues

Ans: a

5. Total Quality Management (TQM) focuses on

a. Employee

b. Customer

c. Both (a) and (b)

d. None of the above

Ans: c

6. Which of the following is responsible for quality objective?

a. Top level management

b. Middle level management

c. Frontline management

d. All of the above

Ans: a

7. The following is (are) the machine down time.

a. Waste

b. No material

c. Breakdown

d. All of the above

Ans: d

8. TQM and ISO both focuses on

a. Customer

b. Employee

c. Supplier

d. All of the above

Ans: a

9. According to deming, quality problems are

a. Due to management
b. Due to method
c. Due to machine
d. Due to material

Ans: a

10. While setting quality objective, ________ to be considered.

a. Material quality
b. Customer need
c. Market demand
d. All of the above

Ans: b

11. Match the following

A. TQM promotes	1. Small change
B. Kaizen is	2. Continuous improvement
C. Quality circle can solve problem related to	3. Employee participation
D. Quality circle benefit to	4. Employee

The correct order is

a. A-3, B-1, C-2, D-4
b. A-1, B-3, C-2, D-4
c. A-3, B-1, C-4, D-2
d. A-3, B-2, C-1, D-4

Ans: a

12. _______ helps organization reduce employee turnover and absenteeism.

a. Job design
b. Training and development
c. Wage revision
d. All of the above

Ans: b

13. CMM stands for

a. Capability maturity model

b. Capability monitoring model

c. Capability measuring model

d. Capability matching model

Ans: a

14. While setting Quality objective, ________ to be considered.

a. Customer need

b. Organizational need

c. Supplier need

d. Worker need

Ans: a

15. Which of the following is for Environment management?

a. ISO-9000

b. ISO-14000

c. ISO-26000

d. ISO-31000

Ans: b

16. The so-called 'quality gurus' of Total Quality Management (TQM) do not include one of the following

a. Kavoru ishikawa

b. Joseph M juran

c. Bill cushy

d. W. Edward Deming

Ans: c

17. Which of the following would not normally be considered as a 'costs of quality'

a. Marketing costs

b. Prevention costs

c. Warranty costs

d. R and D costs

e. All

Ans: e

6

Project Management

6.1 INTRODUCTION

A project is a temporary effort undertaken to produce a unique product or service. Project management means overall planning and co-ordination of a project from commencement to completion. It is intended at meeting the declared requirements and ensuring achievement on time, within cost and to required quality standards.

6.2 STEPS IN PROJECT MANAGEMENT

The various ladders in a project management are:

1. Project definition and scope
2. Technical design
3. Financing
4. Contracting
5. Implementation
6. Performance monitoring

6.3 PROJECT LIFE CYCLE

The various elements of project management life cycle are

- Need identification
- Initiation

- Planning
- Executing
- Controlling

Need Identification

It is the procedure to identify components of the project. Projects may be identified both internally and externally: Fig. 6.1 explains the steps of project life cycle like initiation, planning etc.

Internal detection takes place when the energy manager identify a package of energy reduction opportunities during the day-to-day energy management actions, or from facility audits.

External discovery of energy savings can take place through regular energy audits undertaken by a trustworthy energy auditor or energy service company.

Initiation

Project, and stake holders of the project are required to reach an agreement on its beginning. Involving all stakeholders in the project phases generally improves the probability of satisfying customer requirements by mutual ownership of the project by the stakeholders. The success of the project team depends upon starting with complete and accurate information, management support, and the authorization necessary to manage the project.

Planning

The planning phase is considered as the most important phase in project management. Project planning defines project activities that will be performed; the products that will be produced, and describes how these activities will be able and managed. Project planning means showing each major task, estimates the time, resources and cost required, and provides a structure for management appraisal, organize and control. Planning means identifying and documenting scope, tasks, schedules, cost, risk, quality, and staffing needs.

At last project planning gives an organized project plan, That will be an accepted, comprehensive manuscript that allows a project team to start and compile the work which is essential to accomplish the project targets and objectives. The project plan will deal with the way the project team will manage the project essentials. It will grant a high level of self-assurance and confidence in the organization's ability to meet the scope, timing, cost, and quality requirements.

Executing

Once a project moves into the implementation stage, the project team and all essential resources to carry out the project should be in place and prepared to perform project activities. The project plan is completed and base lined by this time as well. The project team and the project manager's focuses participating, observing, and analyzing the work being done.

The execution phase is when the work activities of the project plan are executed, resulting in the completion of the project deliverables and achievement of the project objectives. This phase brings together all of the project management disciplines, resulting in a product or service that will meet the project deliverable requirements and the customers need. During this phase, elements completed in the planning phase are implemented, time is expended, and money is spent.

Controlling

Project Control function that means comparing actual performance with planned performance and taking corrective action to get the desired outcome when there are significant differences. By monitoring and measuring progress regularly, identifying variances from plan, and taking corrective action if required, project control ensures that project goals are met.

Closing Out

Project closeout is performed after all defined project objectives have been met and the customer has formally accepted the project's deliverables and end product or, in some instances, when a project has been cancelled or ended early. Although, project closeout is a scheduled process, still it is very important. The project closeout phase is comprised of contract closeout and administrative closure.

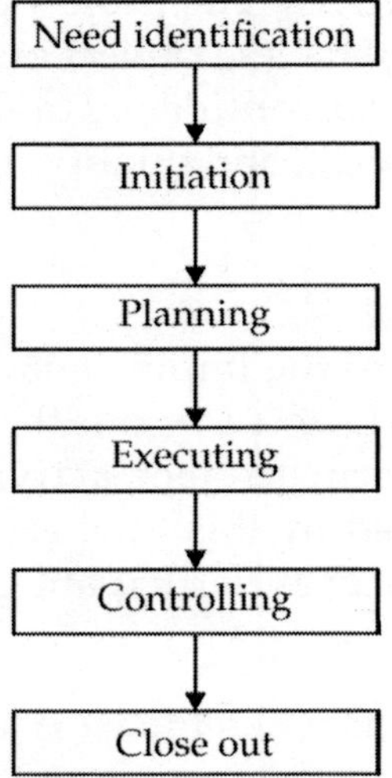

Fig. 6.1 Project life cycle.

6.4 PROJECT PLANNING TECHNIQUES

The three basic project planning techniques are Gantt chart, CPM and PERT. All monitor progress and costs against resource budgets.

6.4.1 Gantt Chart

Gantt charts are also called bar charts. The use of gantt charts started during the industrial revolution of the late 1800's. An early industrial engineer named Henry Gantt developed these charts to improve factory efficiency. Fig. 6.2 shows gantt chart which is commonly used for scheduling the tasks and tracking the progress of energy management projects. Gantt charts are developed using bars to represent each task. The length of the bar shows how long the task is expected to take to complete. Duration is easily shown on gantt charts. Sequence is not well shown on gantt charts shown below.

If, for example, the start of task C depends on both activity B and activity E, then any delay to task E will also delay task C. We just don't have enough information on the gantt chart to know this information.

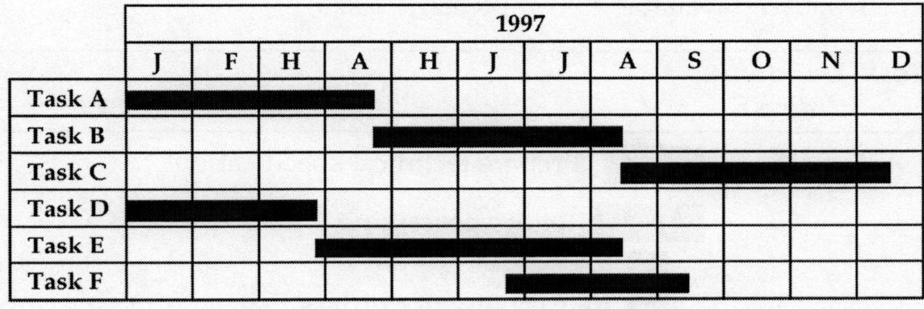

Fig. 6.2 Gantt chart (Google)

Example 1:

Activity code	*Activity*	*Duration in days*	*Depends on*
A	Prepare technical specifications	15	-
B	Tender processing	25	A
C	Release of work orders	3	B
D	Supply of boiler equipment	60	C
E	Supply of ancillary for boiler	20	C
F	Supply of pipes and pipe fittings	10	C
G	Civil work	15	C
H	Installation of ancillary pipes and equipments	5	E, F and G
I	Installation of boiler	10	D and H
J	Testing and commissioning	2	I

Ans. **Drawing a Gantt chart requires information on:**

The logic of the tasks.

The duration of the tasks.

The resources available to complete the tasks.

Task	*Duration (days)*	
A	15	Prepare technical specifications
B	25	Tender processing
C	3	Release of work orders
D	60	Supply of boiler equipment
E	20	Supply of auxiliaries
F	10	Supply of pipes and pipe fittings
G	15	Civil work
H	5	Installation of auxiliary equipment and piping
I	10	Installation of boiler
J	2	Testing and ommissioning

6.4.2 CPM

DuPont developed a Critical Path Method (CPM) designed to address the challenge of shutting down chemical plants for maintenance and then restarting the plants once the maintenance had been completed.

Complex project, like the above example, require a series of activities, some of which must be performed sequentially and others that can be performed in parallel with other activities. This collection of series and parallel tasks can be modeled as a network.

CPM models the activities and events of a project as a network. Activities are shown as nodes on the network and events that signify the beginning or ending of activities are shown as arcs or lines between the nodes.

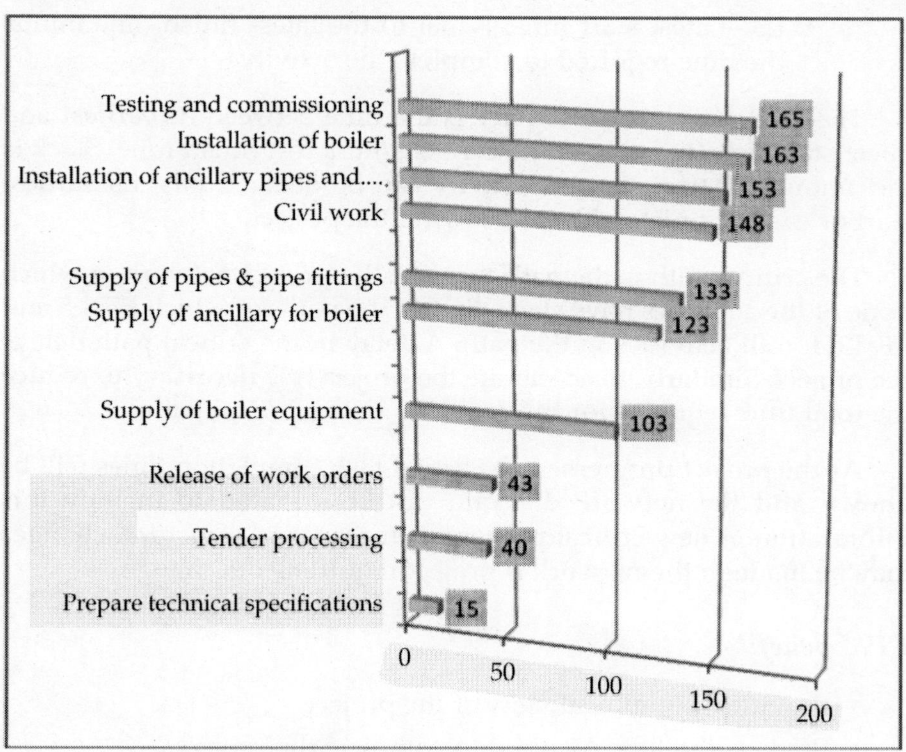

Steps in CPM project planning

1. Specify the individual activities.
2. Determine the sequence of those activities.
3. Draw a network diagram.
4. Estimate the completion time for each activity.
5. Identify the critical path (longest path through the network)
6. Update the CPM diagram as the project progresses.
   - ES - Earliest start time: The earliest time at which the activity can start given that its precedent activities must be completed first.

- EF - Earliest finish time: Equal to the earliest start time for the activity plus the time required to complete the activity.
- LF –Latest finish time: The latest time at which the activity can be completed without delaying the project.
- LS –Latest start time: Equal to the latest finish time minus the time required to complete the activity.

The slack time for an activity is the time between its earliest and latest start time, or between its earliest and latest finish time. Slack is the amount of time that an activity can be delayed past its earliest start or earliest finish without delaying the project.

The critical path is the path through the project network in which none of the activities have slack, that is, the path for which ES=LS and EF=LF for all activities in the path. A delay in the critical path delays the project. Similarly, to accelerate the project it is necessary to reduce the total time required for the activities in the critical path.

As the project progresses, the actual task completion times will be known and the network diagram can be updated to include this information. A new critical path may emerge, and structural changes may be made in the network if project requirements change.

CPM benefits

- Provides a graphical view of the project.
- Predicts the time required to complete the project.
- Shows which activities are critical to maintaining the schedule and which are not.

CPM limitations

While CPM is easy to understand and use, it does not consider the time variations that can have a great impact on the completion time of a complex project. CPM was developed for complex but fairly routine projects with minimum uncertainty in the project completion times. For less routine projects there is more uncertainty in the completion times, and this uncertainty limits its usefulness.

6.4.3. PERT

The Program Evaluation and Review Technique (PERT) is a network model that allows for randomness in activity completion times. PERT was developed in the late 1950's for the U.S. Navy's Polaris project having thousands of contractors. It has the potential to reduce both the time and cost required to complete a project.

In a project, an activity is a task that must be performed and an event is a milestone marking the completion of one or more activities. Before an activity can begin, all of its predecessor activities must be completed. Project network models represent activities and milestones by arcs and nodes. PERT is typically represented as an activity on arc network, in which the activities are represented on the lines and milestones on the nodes.

Steps in the PERT planning process

PERT planning involves the following steps:

1. Identify the specific activities and milestones.
2. Determine the proper sequence of the activities.
3. Construct a network diagram.
4. Estimate the time required for each activity.
5. Determine the critical path.
6. Update the PERT chart as the project progresses.

The critical path is determined by adding the times for the activities in each sequence and determining the longest path in the project. The critical path determines the total time required for the project. To take care of uncertainty, PERT takes three time estimates into account: optimistic, most likely, and pessimistic time. PERT time estimates follow beta distribution.

Optimistic time (to): This is the shortest time taken by an activity if everything goes exceptionally well.

Most likely time (tm): It is the time in which the activity is normally expected to complete under normal contingencies.

Pessimistic time (tp): It is the maximum time that would be required to complete the activity if bad luck were encountered at every turn. This does not include catastrophes like earthquakes, floods, fires, etc.

These time estimates are not always easy to prepare, but together they give useful information about the expected uncertainties of an activity. For standard activities, the three time estimates should not vary much from each other. But the greater the uncertainty of an activity, the wider will be the range of the estimated completion times.

PERT calculates the expected value of duration as a weighted average of three time estimates. It assumes that *to* and *tp* are equally likely to occur, and *tm* is four times more likely to occur than the other two. Hence, the expected time $te = (to + 4tm + tp)/6$

The expected time is the time that we would expect if the activity were repeated a large number of times. But in reality, activities do not get repeated many times; they usually occur just once.

PERT simplifies the calculation of Te (standard deviation) and Vt (variance) as follows:

$T_e = (tp - to)/6$ and $V_t = \{(tp - to)/6\}^2$

If activities outside the critical path speed up or slow down (within limits), the total project time does not change. The amount of time that a non-critical path activity can be delayed without delaying the project is referred to as slack time.

If the critical path is not immediately obvious, it may be helpful to determine the following four quantities for each activity:

- EST - Earliest Start time
- EFT - Earliest Finish time
- LST - Latest Start time
- LFT - Latest Finish time

These times are calculated using the expected time for the relevant activities. The EST and EFT of each activity are determined by working forward through the network and determining the earliest time at which an activity can start and finish considering its predecessor activities.

The latest start and finish times are the latest times that an activity can start and finish without delaying the project. LS and LF are found by working backward through the network. The difference in the latest and earliest finish of each activity is that activity's slack. The critical path then is the path through the network in which none of the activities have slack.

The variance in the project completion time can be calculated by summing the variances in the completion times of the activities in the critical path. Given this variance, one can calculate the probability that the project will be completed by a certain date.

Since the critical path determines the completion date of the project, the project can be accelerated by adding the resources required to decrease the time for the activities in the critical path. Such a shortening of the project sometimes is referred to as project crashing.

Make adjustments in the PERT chart as the project progresses. As the project unfolds, the estimated times can be replaced with actual times. In cases where there are delays, additional resources may be needed to stay on schedule and the PERT chart may be modified to reflect the new situation.

Benefits of PERT

PERT is useful because it provides the following information:

- Expected project completion time.
- Probability of completion before a specified date.
- The critical path activities that directly impact the completion time.
- The activities that have slack time and that can lend resources to critical path activities.
- Activities start and end dates.

Limitations of PERT

The following are some of PERT's limitations:

- The activity time estimates are somewhat subjective and depend on judgment. In cases where there is little experience in performing an activity, the numbers may be only a guess. In other cases, if the person or group performing the activity estimates the time there may be bias in the estimate.
- The underestimation of the project completion time due to alternate paths becoming critical is perhaps the most serious.

PERT / CPM networks contain two major components

Basis for Comparison	*PERT*	*CPM*
Meaning	PERT is a project management technique, used to manage uncertain activities of a project.	CPM is a statistical technique of project management that manages well defined activities of a project.
What is it?	A technique of planning and control of time.	A method to control cost and time.
Focus on	Event	Activity
Model	Deterministic model	Probabilistic model
Estimates	Three time estimates	One time estimate
Appropriate for	High precision time estimate	Reasonable time estimate
Management of	Unpredictable activities	Predictable activities
Nature of jobs	Non-repetitive nature	Repetitive nature
Critical and Non-critical activities	No differentiation	Differentiated

Suitable for	Research and development project	Non-research projects like civil construction, ship building etc.
Crashing concept	Not Applicable	Applicable

i. ***Activities and activity:*** Fig. 6.3A shows an activity represents an action and consumption of resources (time, money, energy) required to complete a portion of a project. Activity is represented by an arrow,

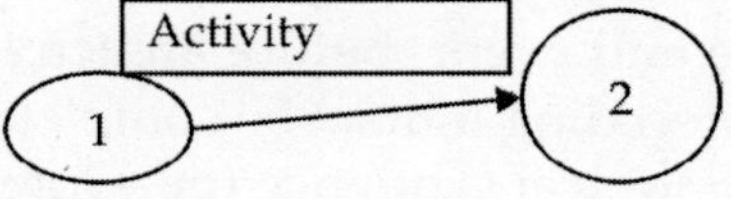

Fig. 6.3A: Activity

ii. ***Events:*** Fig. 6.3B Shows, an event (or node) will always occur at the beginning and end of an activity. The event has no resources and is represented by a circle.

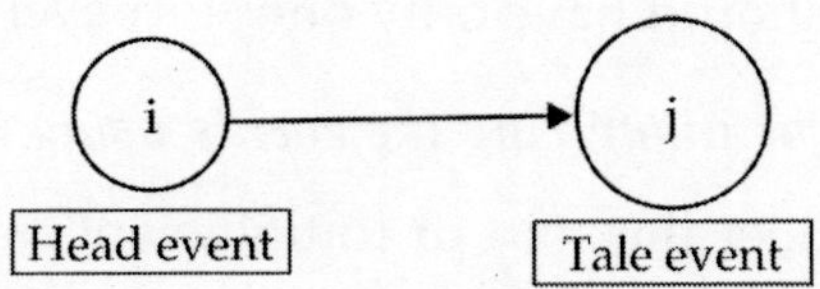

Fig. 6.3B Event

Merge and Burst Events

Fig. 6.3 Shows one or more activities can start and end simultaneously at an event

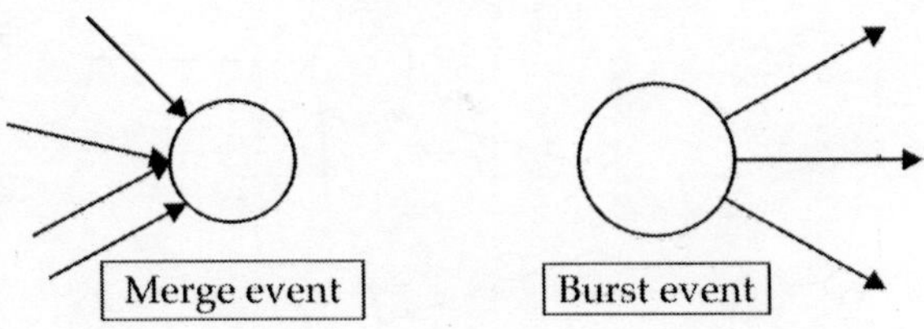

Fig. 6.3: C, D Merge and Burst Event

Preceding and Succeeding Activities

Activities performed before given events are known as preceding activities and activities performed after a given event are known as succeeding activities.

6.4.3.1 Rules in constructing a network

- No single activity can be represented more than once in a network. The length of an arrow has no significance.
- The event numbered 1 is the start event and an event with highest number is the end event. Before an activity can be undertaken, all activities preceding it must be completed. That is, the activities must follow a logical sequence (or – interrelationship) between activities.
- In assigning numbers to events, there should not be any duplication of event numbers in a network.
- Dummy activities must be used only if it is necessary to reduce the complexity of a network.
- A network should have only one start event and one end event.

6.4.3.2 Procedure for numbering the events using Fulkerson's rule

- *Step 1*: Number the start or initial event as 1.
- *Step 2*: From event 1, strike off all outgoing activities. This would have made one or more events as initial events (event which do not have incoming activities). Number hat event as 2.
- *Step 3*: Repeat step 2 for event 2, event 3 and till the end event. The end event must have the highest number

6.4.3.3 Errors in networking

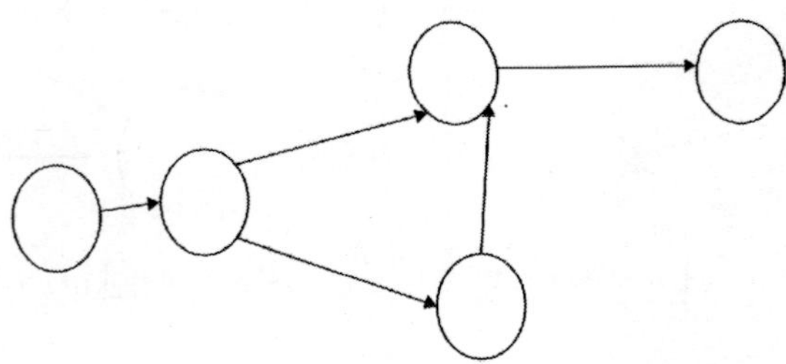

Fig. 6.4A: Formation of loop

Fig. 6.4 Shows formation of loop where. No reverse or back ward direction flow in networking. Looping error should not be formed in a network, as it represents performance of activities repeatedly in a cyclic manner.

Dangling: Fig. 6.4 B shows dangling of events. Whenever an activity is disconnected from the network it is called dangling error.No activity should end without being joined to the end event. So dummy activity must be introduced in between C to F to maintain continuity in the system.

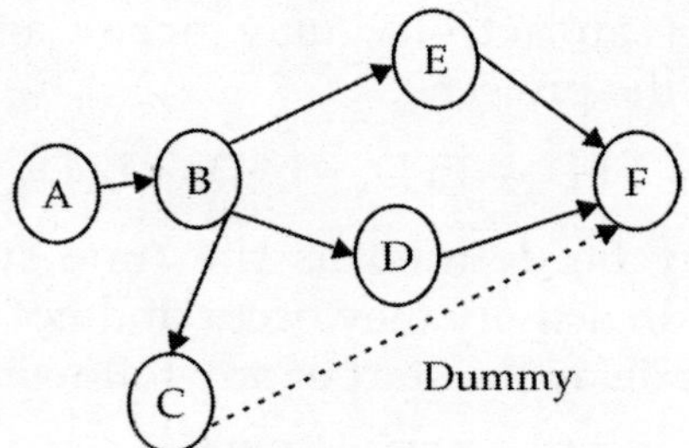

Fig. 6.4B: Dangling

Redundancy: Fig.6.4 shows that If the dummy activity is the only activity emanating from an event, it can be eliminated as the dummy activity is redundant. It is a method for ensuring network availability in case of a network device or path failure and unavailability. As such, it provides a means of network failover. Network redundancy is achieved through the addition of alternate network paths, which are implemented through redundant standby routers and switches. When the primary path is unavailable, the alternate path can be instantly deployed to ensure minimal downtime and continuity of network services.

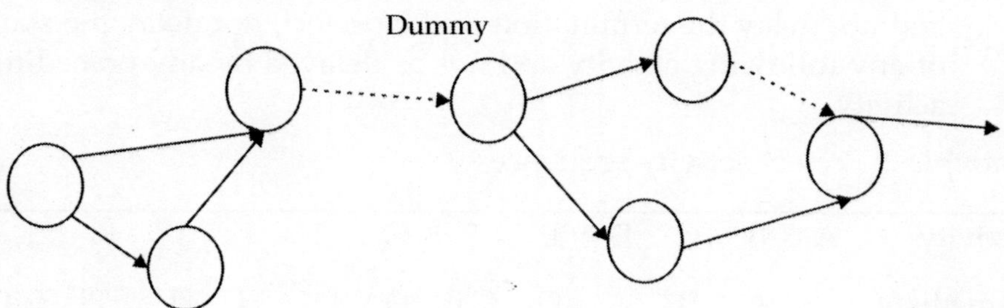

Fig. 6.4C: Redundancy

6.4.3.4 Critical Path

After determining the earliest and the latest scheduled times for various activities, the minimum time required to complete the project is calculated. In a network, among various paths, the longest path which determines the total time duration of the project is called the critical path. The following conditions must be satisfied in locating the critical path of a network.

- Total float may be defined as that time span in which the completion of an activity may occur and not delay the termination of the project.

  $$TF_{ij} = LFD_{ij} - EFD_{ij} = LSD_{ij} - ESD_{ij}$$

- Free float may be defined as the time span in which the completion of an activity may occur and not delay the finish of the project nor delay the start of any following activity.

  $$FF_{ij} = ESD_{jk} - EFD_{ij}$$

- That part of the total float which remains after free float has been deducted is the interfering float. It may be defined as: The time span in which the completion of an activity may occur and not delay the termination of the project but within which completion will delay the start of some other following activity.

  $$INTF_{ij} = TF_{ij} - FF_{i}$$

- Independent float, is the amount of scheduling leeway of an activity that is independent of the early starts and late finishes of any other activity. It may be formally defined as:

  The time span in which the completion of an activity may occur and not delay the termination of the project, not delay the start of any following activity and not be delayed by any preceding activity.

Example 2: Project activity sequence

Activity	A	B	C	D	E	F	G	H	I	J	K	L
Immediate predecessor	-	A	B	A	D	C,E	D	D	H	H	F,H	G,J

Ans.

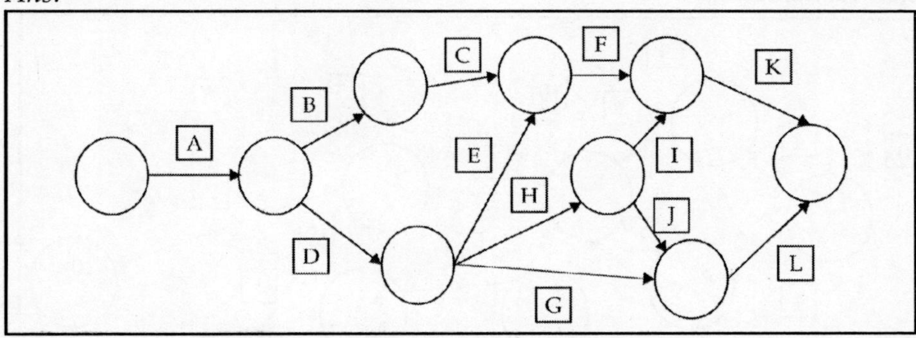

Fig. 6.5: Activity sequence of AOA network

Example 3: A composite project has the following schedule, construct PERT network. Compute TE and TL for each activity. Find the critical path.

Project schedule

Activity	*Name*	*Time*	*Activity*	*Name*	*Time*
1-2	A	4	5-6	G	4
1-3	B	1	5-7	H	8
2-4	C	1	6-8	I	1
3-4	D	1	7-8	J	2
3-5	E	6	8-10	K	5
4-9	F	5	9-10	L	7

Forward calculation

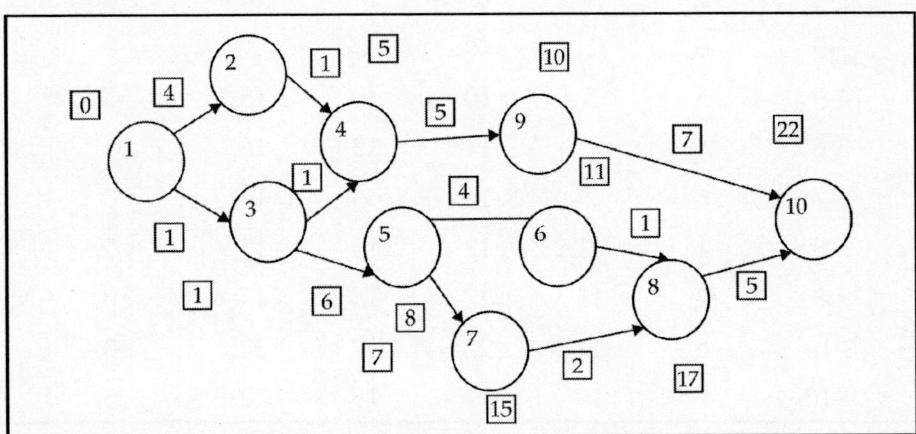

Backwardcalculation 1

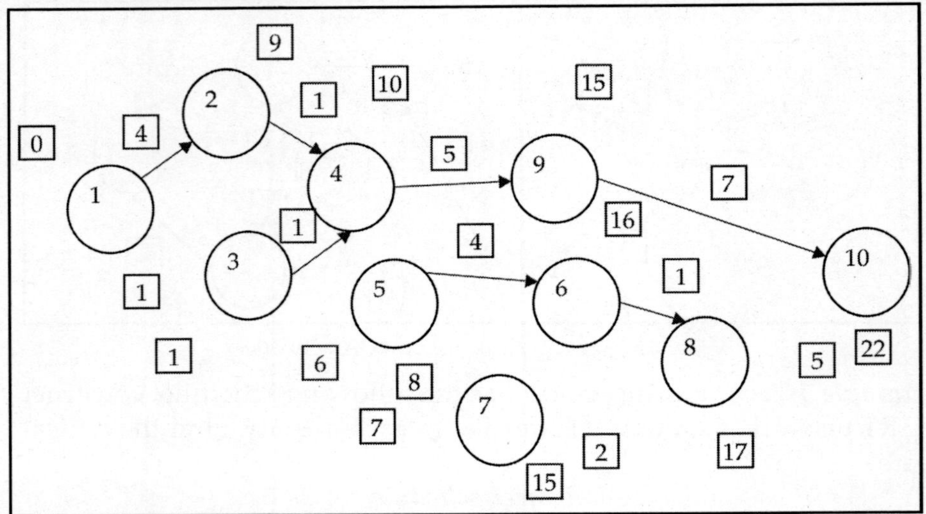

Critical path: 1-3-5-7-8-10

The calculations of LST and LFT are as follows:

Activity	*Time*	*EST*	*Eft*	*LST*	*LFT*	*Total float=*
1-2	4	0	4	5	9	5
1-3	1	0	1	0	1	0
2-4	1	4	5	9	10	5
3-4	1	1	2	9	10	8
3-5	6	1	7	1	7	0
4-9	5	5	10	10	15	5
5-6	4	7	11	12	16	5
5-7	8	7	15	7	15	0
6-8	1	11	12	16	17	5
7-8	2	15	17	15	17	0
8-10	5	17	22	17	22	0
9-10	7	10	17	15	22	5

Example 4: Three estmates of all activities of a composite project are given below.

Activity	*a*	*m*	*b*
1-2	0.8	1.0	1.2
2-3	3.7	5.6	9.9
2-4	6.2	6.6	15.4
3-4	2.1	2.7	6.1
4-5	0.8	3.4	3.6
5-6	0.9	1.0	1.1

Find the expected duration and standard deviation of each activity. Determine the critical path. What is the probability that the project will be completed two-months later than expected. What due date has about 90% chance of being met.

Ans.

Activity	*a*	*m*	*b*	T_e=*a*+4*m*+*b*/6	$\sigma^2=(b-a/6)^2$
1-2	0.8	1.0	1.2	1	0.067
2-3	3.7	5.6	9.9	6	1.03
2-4	6.2	6.6	15.4	8	1.53
3-4	2.1	2.7	6.1	3	0.5
4-5	0.8	3.4	3.6	3	0.47
5-6	0.9	1.0	1.1	1	0.033

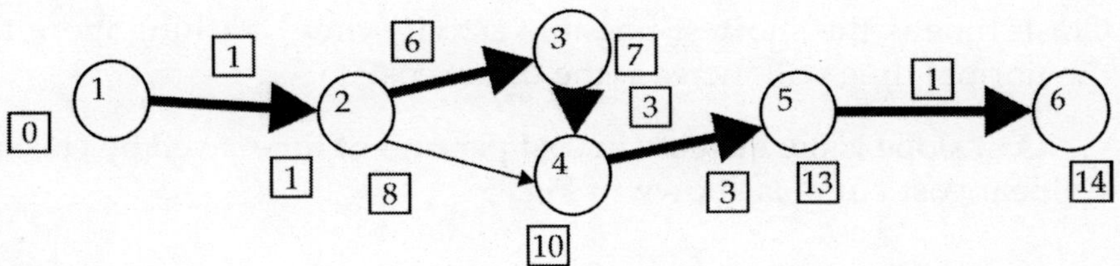

Critical path = 1-2-3-4-5-6 = 14 months

1-2-3-4-5-6 = $\sqrt{0.067^2 + 1.03^2 + 0.5^2 + 0.47^2 + 0.033^2}$

$= \sqrt{1.5374} = 1.2399$

Ts = 14 + 2 = 16 month

z = 16 – 14/σ1-2-3-4-5-6 = 1.61

Probability = 94.63%

z = 90% probability = 1.28 = Ts – 14/1.2399 = 15.59 months *Ans.*

6.5 CRASHING

Fig. 6.6 shows cost trade off in crashing. where the two important components of any activity are the cost and time. Cost is directly proportional to time and *vice versa.*

For example, in constructing a shopping complex, the expected time of completion can be calculated using the time estimates of various activities. But if the construction has to be finished earlier, it requires additional cost to complete the project. We need to arrive at a time/ cost trade-off between total cost of project and total time required to complete it.

Normal time

Normal time is the time required to complete the activity at normal conditions and cost.

Crash time

Crash time is the shortest possible activity time; crashing more than the normal time will increase the direct cost.

Cost slope is the increase in cost per unit of time saved by crashing. A linear cost curve is shown in Fig.

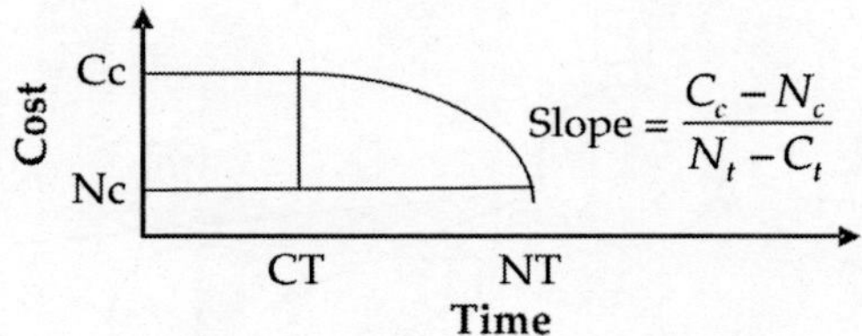

Fig. 6.6: Cost trade off in crashing

Steps of crashing

- Network is done
- Critical path is calculated and cost slope is calculated
- Including critical path other paths are also calculated
- Crashing must be done only for activities on the critical path
- Ist of all the activity is selected whose cost slope is lowest
- Crashing need to check whether non-critical activities are becoming critical or not.
- Then indirect cost saving *versus* increase in direct cost is always watched
- At last total cost is calculated when total cost is found more than previous total cost/no changes in total cost is found it means thatr is the final total cost.

Example 5: An Industrial ergonomic design of chair project has a list of tasks to be performed whose time estimates and costs are given in the Table, as follows. Draw the project network. If indirect cost is 70 Rs., find total minimum cost.

Activity	*Normal time*	*Normal cost*	*Crashing time*	*Crashing cost*
1-2	8	100	6	200
1-3	4	150	2	350
2-4	2	50	1	90
2-5	10	100	5	400
3-4	5	100	1	200
4-5	3	80	1	100

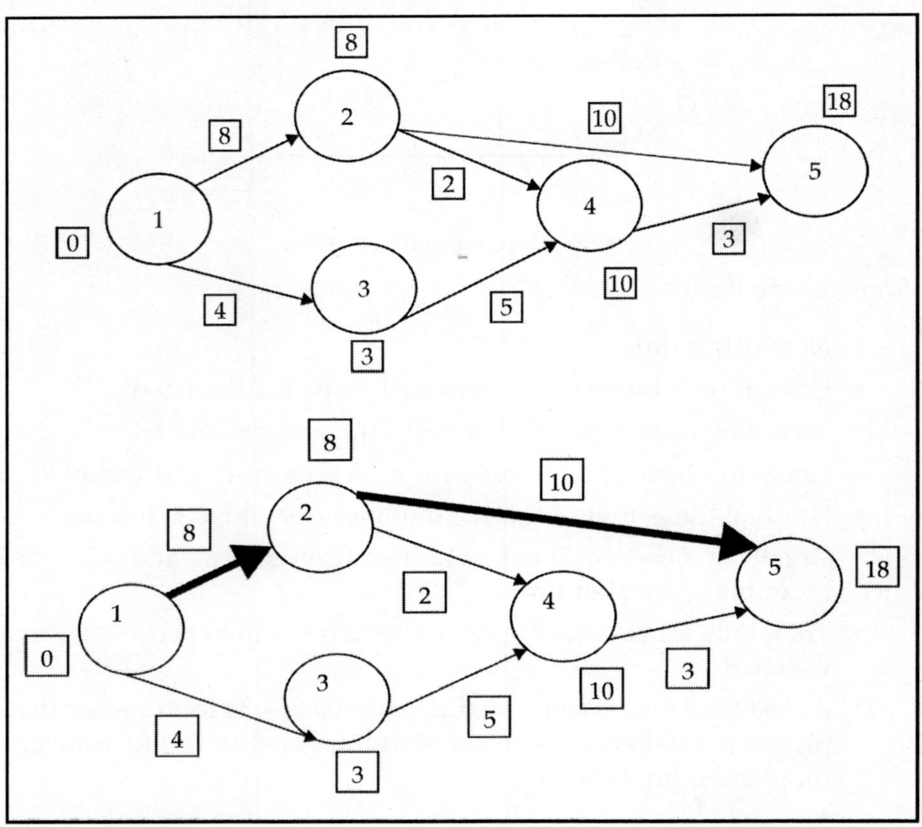

Ans. 1-1-2-5 critical path = 18 days

1-2-4-5 = 13 days

1-3-4-5 = 12 days

Activity	*Slope*
1-2	50 (2)
1-3	100 (2)
2-4	40 (1)
2-5	60 (5)
3-4	25 (4)
4-5	10 (2)

Normal time	*Crashing activity*	*Crash cost*	*Indirect cost*	*Total cost*
18	-	-	18*70=1260	1260+580=1840
17	1-2(1)	50	17*70=1190	1190+580+50=1820
16	1-2(2)	100	16*70=120	1120+580+100=1800
15	2-5(1)	160=100+60*1	1050	1790
14	2-5(2)	220	980	1780
13	2-5(3)	280	910	1770
12	2-5(4)	340	840	1760
11	2-5(1-2-5) and 4-5(1-3-4-5)	340+60+10 =410	770	1760

So minimum total cost Rs.1760/-.

Key notes

1. A project is an interrelated set of activities that has a definite starting and ending point and results in the accomplishment of a unique, often major outcome. "Project management" is, therefore, the planning and control of events that, together, comprise the project. Project management aims to ensure the effective use of resources and delivery of the project objectives on time and within cost constraints.
2. An activity or task is the smallest unit of work effort within the project and consumes both time and resources which are under the control of the project manager. A project is a sequence of activities that has a definite start and finish, an identifiable goal and an integrated system of complex but interdependent relationships.
3. A schedule allocates resources to accomplish the activities within a timeframe. The schedule sets priorities, start times and finish times.
4. A gantt chart is a simple technique that can be used to attach a time scale and sequence to a project. A gantt chart is a form of

horizontal bar chart and horizontal bars are drawn against a time scale for each project activity, the length of which represents the time taken to complete. To construct a gantt chart the following steps are necessary:

- Use the horizontal axis to represent time
- Use the vertical axis to represent activities
- Represent each activity by a horizontal bar of appropriate length
- Take activity procedures into account by starting each activity bar to an appropriate point along the time axis after its preceding activities. Normally the start point for an activity is the earliest time that it could start after its preceding activities had finished.

EXERCISE PROBLEM: 6.1

1. A project has the following activities, precedence relationships and activity durations:

Activity	*Immediate predecessors*	*Activity duration (weeks)*
A	-	3
B	-	4
C	-	3
D	C	12
E	B	5
F	A	7
G	E, F	3

a. Draw a Gantt chart for the project.

b. Construct a CPM network for the project.

c. Identify those activities comprising the critical path.

d. What is the project's estimated duration?

e. Construct a table showing for each activity, its activity duration, earliest start time, latest start time, earliest finish time, latest finish time, and the activity slack.

Ans.

c. C, D

d. 15 weeks

2. A project designed to refurbish a hospital operating theatre consists of the following activities, with estimated times and precedence relationships shown. Using this information draw a network diagram, determine the expected time and variance for each activity, and estimate the probability of completing the project within twenty days. If the probability of completion of project 0.8 find the expected project complition.

Ans. 17 weeks, 0.9382, 19 weeks

Activity	*Immediate predecessors*	*Optimistic time*	*Most likely time*	*Pessimistic time*
A	-	1	2	3
B	-	2	2	8
C	A	6	7	8
D	B	1	2	3
E	A	1	4	7
F	C,D	1	5	9
G	C,D,E	1	2	3
H	F	1	2	9

3. The project detailed below has the both normal costs and "crash" costs shown. The crash time is the shortest possible activity time given that extra resources are allocated to that activity.

Activity	*Normal time*	*Normal time cost*	*Crash time*	*Crash time cost*
1-2	13	700	9	900
1-3	5	400	4	46 0
1-4	7	600	4	810
2-5	12	800	11	865
3-2	6	900	4	1130
3-4	5	1000	3	1180
4-5	9	1500	6	1800

Assuming that the cost per day for shortening each activity is the difference between crash costs and normal costs, divided by the time saved, determine by how much each activity should be shortened so as to complete the project within twenty-six days and at the minimum extra cost. Indirect cost per week is Rs 250.

Ans. 1-3-2-5, 20 weeks, total cost = Rs 5340.

4. A project comprises the following activities:

Activity	*Immediate predecessors*	*Activity time (days)*
A	-	12
B	-	6
C	A	13
D	A, B	12
E	C, D	11
F	D	13
G	E, F	11

a. Construct a gantt chart which will provide an overview of the planned project.

5. A project has the following activity details:

Activity	*Immediate predecessors*	*Activity time (weeks)*
A	-	3
B	-	4
C	-	3
D	C	12
E	B	5
F	A	7
G	E, F	3

Draw a gannt chart to represent the project;

6. The following information is available on a management project:

Activity	*Immediate predecessors*	*Duration (Days)*	*Staff required (per day)*
A	-	3	6
B	-	5	3
C	B	2	4
D	A	1	4
E	A	6	5
F	D	3	6
G	D, E	3	3

At present you have nine staff available. Temporary staff can be hired at a rate of £100 per day.

a. Draw a gantt chart to show the shortest time it will take to complete the project.

7. Draw the network

Activity	*Description*	*Predecessors*
A	Select site for classes	
B	Define curriculum	
C	Plan courses	B
D	Order hardware/software	A, C
E	Install hardware/software	D
F	Determine personnel requirements	C
G	Hire adjuncts	F
H	Modify teaching assignments	F
I	Select students	B

8. Draw the network

Activity	*Description*	*Predecessors*
A	Select site for classes	
B	Define curriculum	
C	Plan courses	B
D	Order hardware/software	A, C
E	Install hardware/software	D
F	Determine personnel requirements	C
G	Hire adjuncts	F
H	Modify teaching assignments	F
I	Select students	B
J	Prepare classes	E, G, H

9. Draw the network

Activity	*Description*	*Predecessors*
A	Select site for classes	
B	Define curriculum	
C	Plan courses	B
D	Order hardware/software	A, C
E	Install hardware/software	D
F	Determine personnel requirements	C
G	Hire adjuncts	F
H	Modify teaching assignments	F
I	Select students	B
J	Prepare classes	H, E, G

10. a.) What is the soonest that classes could start? In 23 weeks.
    b) What is the start and completion date for each activity? See network and/or spreadsheet.
    c) What activities are critical to meeting the project deadline? B, C, D, E, J

d) If an activity is non-critical, how much delay can be incurred?
A, 5 weeks; F, 6 weeks; G, 6 weeks; H, 8 weeks; I, 13 weeks.

Activity	*Description*	*Predecessors*	*Time (weeks)*
A	Select site for classes		3
B	Define curriculum		5
C	Plan courses	B	3
D	Order hardware/software	A, C	4
E	Install hardware/software	D	8
F	Determine personnel requirements	C	2
G	Hire adjuncts	F	4
H	Modify teaching assignments	F	2
I	Select students	B	5
J	Prepare classes	H, E, G	3

11. Find Critical path by drawing network.

Ans. 38 days

Activity	*Description*	*Optimistic*	*Most likely*	*Pessimistic*
A	Select site for classes	2	3	5
B	Define curriculum	3	5	7
C	Plan courses	2	3	5
D	Order hardware/software	3	4	9
E	Install hardware/software	4	8	14
F	Determine personnel requirements	1	2	3
G	Hire adjuncts	2	4	8
H	Modify teaching assignments	1	2	4
I	Select students	3	5	6
J	Prepare classes	2	3	5

MULTIPLE CHOICE QUESTION AND ANSWER 6.1

1. **What enables us to determine the earliest and the latest times for each of the events and activities and thereby helps in the identification of the critical path?**
   a) Program evaluation
   b) Review technique (PERT)
   c) Both A and B
   d) Deployment of resources
   Ans. c
2. **In a PERT/CPM network, computing the critical path requires**
   a) Determining the total project duration
   b) Assigning the earliest finish time for an activity as the earliest start time for the next
   c) That the latest finishing time for an activity not delay the overall project beyond initial expectation
   d) A sophisticated and complex computer program
   Ans. a
3. **At the completion of the forward and backward passes, the slack for an activity is given by the**
   a) Difference between early start and early finish
   b) Difference between early start and latest finish
   c) Difference between latest start and early finish
   d) Amount of idle labor on the critical path
   Ans. a
4. **In a CPM/PERT network a dummy activity is necessary when**
   a) Two activities have the same starting node
   b) Two activities have the same ending node
   c) A node does not actually connect to another node
   d) When two activities share the same starting and ending node
   e) none of the above
   Ans: d

5. **Shared slack in an activity network is defined as**
   a) The amount of time an activity can be delayed without delaying the entire project.
   b) The amount of slack that an activity has in common with another activity.
   c) The amount of unused resources for an activity.
   d) The amount by which a time estimate can be in error without affecting the critical path computations.

   Ans: b

6. **The objective of project crashing is to**
   a) Teduce the project duration
   b) Revise the network critical path and completion times when the schedule falls hopelessly behind
   c) Minimize the cost of crashing
   d) Reduce indirect costs such a interest on investments
   e) More than one statement above is true

   Ans: e

7. **If an activity has zero activity slack it**
   a) Means that the project is expected to be delayed.
   b) Must be a dummy activity.
   c) Is on the critical path.
   d) All of the above
   e) None of the above

   Ans: c

8. **Assume that activity G has the following times:**

   Early start time = 7 days
   Early finish time = 13 days
   Late start time = 15 days
   Late finish time = 21 days

   Which of the following statements is true about activity G?
   a) Activity G takes 9 days to complete
   b) Activity G has a slack time of 8 days.

c) Activity G is on the critical path.

d) Activity G takes 8 days to complete

Ans: b

9. Assuming a beta distribution is being used, if the most likely time for an activity increases by 1 week, what will happen to the expected time for that activity?

a) It will increase by 4 weeks.

b) It will increase by 1 week.

c) It will remain the same.

d) It would increase by 2/3.

Ans: d

10. Using the network above, which of the following statements is true?

a) The critical path is 1-3, 3-5, 5-7

b) The earliest start data for activity 5-7 is 10

c) The latest start date for activity 2-5 is 11

d) The project completion time is 15 weeks

Ans: a

11. Using the data above to calculate the expected time and variance for each activity, which of the following statements is true?

a) The expected time for activity 1-3 is 12.67

b) The variance for activity 3-5 is 3.36

c) The largest expected time occurs for activity 1-4

d) The largest variance is for activity 1-3

e) More than one statement above is true

Ans: e

12. There is usually more pressure, real and perceived, associated with project management than in a normal management position.

a) True

b) False

Ans: a

13. In the PERT approach, using the project mean time and standard deviation to perform probabilistic analysis should be done with

caution unless the number of activities is large enough to support the assumptions of the central limit theorem.

a) True

b) False

Ans: a

14. As activities are crashed, the critical path may actually change.

a) True

b) False

Ans: a

15. Once the individual activity times have been determined, the computations to find the critical path in PERT are the same as in CPM.

a) True

b) False

Ans: a

16. Slack is something a project manager wishes to avoid if possible because it means the activity time estimates were inaccurate.

a) True

b) False

Ans: b

Subject Index